JAPAN IN DECLINE
FACT OR FICTION?

JAPAN IN DECLINE
FACT OR FICTION?

Edited by

Purnendra Jain
UNIVERSITY OF ADELAIDE

and

Brad Williams
CITY UNIVERSITY OF HONG KONG

GLOBAL
ORIENTAL

JAPAN IN DECLINE
FACT OR FICTION?

Edited by Purnendra Jain and Brad Williams

First published 2011 by
GLOBAL ORIENTAL
PO Box 219
Folkestone
Kent CT20 2WP
UK

Global Oriental is an imprint of Koninklijke Brill NV, Leiden, The Netherlands.
Koninklijke Brill NV incorporates the imprints BRILL, Global Oriental,
Hotei Publishing, IDC Publishers, Martinus Nijhoff Publishers, and VSP.

www.brill.nl/globaloriental

ISBN 978-1-906876-36-4 [Case]
978-1-906876-37-1 [Paper]

Set in Stone Serif 9.0 on 10.5 by Dataworks, Chenai, India
Printed in The Netherlands

Contents

Preface *vii*

List of Contributors *ix*

Introduction:
Japan: Descending Asian Giant? *xii*
BRAD WILLIAMS and FURNENDRA JAIN

Part 1: Economics and Politics 1

1 Financial System Reform: Recovery or Retrogression? 3
JENNY CORBETT

2 Political Earthquake in Japan: How Much of a Difference Will it Make? 18
J.A.A. STOCKWIN

Part 2: Foreign Policy and Security 35

3 Japan's ODA as Soft Power 37
MARIE SÖDERBERG

4 Japan in Global Governance: War and Peace 55
GO ITO

5 Japan's Politics of Environment and Climate Change: From NIMBY to Global Networks 74
LAM PENG ER

6 National Security in Japan's Space Policy 92
SAADIA M. PEKKANEN and PAUL KALLENDER-UMEZU

7 Japan's Regional Engagement: Network Diplomacy 110
PURNENDRA JAIN and ALEX STEPHENS

8 Can Japan Engage Northeast Asia? Overcoming Perceptual and Strategic Deficits 129
JONG KUN CHOI

Part 3: Social Challenges 145

9 Japan's Education System: Problems and Prospects in the Post-Industrial Age 147
BRAD WILLIAMS and SHOKO YONEYAMA

10 The Impact of Changing Age Structure on Demographic Dividends and Intergenerational Transfers in Japan 166
NAOHIRO OGAWA

11 Have Jobs and Hope Gone Forever in Japan? From Family and Firms to a New Social Network 187
YUJI GENDA

12 The Culture of Migration Politics in Japan 205
GABRIELE VOGT

Index *225*

Preface

Through the early post-war decades Japan forged ahead impressively as Asia's 'new giant', its economy surging from strength to strength. Today, two decades after the 1980s and the so-called bursting of Japan's economic bubble, how does Japan sit in its regional and global contexts? Many commentaries inside and outside Japan give the impression that Japan has declined not just economically through the 'Lost Decade' of the nineties and beyond, but is also in decline socially and politically. Signs of domestic malaise are sharpened by signs of external resurgence, especially in neighbouring China. Even Japan's long-standing superiority in fields such as technology has been seriously challenged by emerging economies like India, and in the IT field Japan's pre-eminence has been overtaken. Many observers have attributed this apparent national downturn to the turmoil in Japanese politics, some pointing in particular to a lack of visionary leadership.

Whatever the state of the nation, Japan remains in a strategically important location within Asia Pacific at a time of unmistakable transition in this region. It matters, then, what is the state of the nation: is Japan really in decline? To explore this far-reaching question, I organized a workshop at the University of Adelaide in November 2009 on the theme 'Japan: Descending Asian Giant?'. The question mark was deliberate, to inspire critical rethinking of the assumptions, speculation and axioms informing contemporary assessments and to raise new questions that feed a deeper understanding of where Japan is currently at. A number of Japan scholars from around the world, with diverse fields of expertise, were invited to consider whether Japan is indeed on a trajectory of descent. These scholars presented their perspectives on topics stretching from politics, finance, international affairs and technology, to demography, environment, education and youth. Their contributions presented a broad national canvas from which links and disjunctures were identified and overall assessments were made.

This volume brings together most of the workshop papers, revised, updated and refined in light of workshop discussion and the authors' further considerations. As readers will find in the pages that follow, the verdict on Japan's decline is mixed. This 'report card' identifies strengths as well as weaknesses, and explains why they matter.

Japan is certainly no longer 'Number One' in Asia or the world at large, as portrayed at an earlier historical moment. But at the same time Japan cannot be scratched off the list of powerful nations. In 2010 Japan is one of several Asian giants, with pockets of strength that should not be dismissed lightly. This fluidity shifts the question of decline from 'if' to 'how', provoking further questions about how smartly and efficiently Japan can play to its strengths and address weaknesses, to best position the nation in these liminal times when so much that has been taken for granted globally is passing. Some analysts here are more sanguine than others. Overall, however, the assessment points to policy stagnation and political quagmire, which has dogged Japan for quite some time and needs serious redress to orient the nation towards political, economic and socio-cultural recovery.

The Adelaide Workshop was funded by the Australia Research Council Asia Pacific Futures Research Network project. A number of early-career researchers in Japan studies were also invited to the workshop to participate in the discussion that followed each presentation and consider the full picture on conclusion. A brief mentoring session followed the workshop, facilitated by Professor Arthur Stockwin of Oxford University, Dr Judith Snodgrass of the University of Western Sydney and Dr Brad Williams of the National University of Singapore.

I want to thank the many people who have contributed generously to the production of this book. I very much appreciate the efforts of all the authors whose work appears in this volume. Participants in the workshop generally provided insightful feedback and comments on the papers, and some later offered constructive comments on revised drafts that authors found useful in finalizing their chapters. It has been a great pleasure to work with Brad Williams then of the National University of Singapore (now at the City University of Hong Kong) in co-editing this volume and bringing the workshop project to completion. Maureen Todhunter, Gerry Groot and Felix Patrikeeff provided intellectual and editorial input and their cooperation has helped this project to progress in timely fashion. Shoo Lin Siah contributed generously in organizing the workshop and liaising with participants. I thank Paul Norbury of Global Oriental for his interest in our project and his support at every stage of preparing this publication. Last but not least, I thank my unfailingly patient and supportive family.

PURNENDRA JAIN
Centre for Asian Studies
The University of Adelaide
August 2010

List of Contributors

Jong Kun **Choi** is an Assistant Professor in the Department of Political Science and International Studies at Yonsei University. He specializes in International Relations theories, Northeast Asian security, political psychology and public opinion on national identity and foreign policy attitudes. His articles have appeared in journals including *International Security, Global Asia, Asian Perspective, Journal of International Peace* and *International Relations of the Asia-Pacific*.

Jenny **Corbett** is Professor of Economics and Executive Director of the Australia-Japan Research Centre at the Australian National University. Her major research focus is on the Japanese economy, particularly banking, macro-economic policy and corporate governance, banking and financial crisis.

Yuji **Genda** is Professor in the Institute of Social Science at the University of Tokyo. His recent publications in English include *A Nagging Sense of Job Insecurity: The New Reality Facing Japanese Youth* (2005), 'Long-term Effects of a Recession at Labor Market Entry in Japan and the United States', with Souichi Ohta and Ayako Kondo, *Journal of Human Resources*, Winter 2010; and 'Hope and Society in Japan', in *Hope and the Economy*, in Hirokazu Miyazaki and Richard Swedberg (eds), forthcoming.

Go **Ito** is a Professor of international relations at Meiji University in Tokyo. Most recently, he has published 'Japan's Contribution to International Peacekeeping Operations', in Mike Mochizuki et al. (eds), *Japan in International Politics: Foreign Policy of an Adaptive State* (Boulder: Lynne Rienner, 2008) and 'Japan's Domestic Governance and its Foreign Policy', in Ka Ho Mok and Ray Forrest (eds), *Changing Governance and Public Policy in East Asia* (London: Routledge, 2008).

Purnendra **Jain** is Professor of Japanese Studies in the Centre for Asian Studies at Australia's University of Adelaide. Author and editor of ten books and numerous scholarly articles, his book *Japan's Subnational Governments in International Affairs* (Routledge, 2006) was translated in Japanese under the title *Nihon no jichitai gaiko* (Tokyo: Keibundo 2009).

Paul **Kallender-Umezu** is Japan Correspondent for Space News, and has published widely in Japanese and domestic international media. With an MS from Columbia University's Journalism School, Kallender-Umezu won the Horgan Prize for Excellence in Science Writing in 2000.

He is also the co-author of a book entitled *In Defense of Japan: From the Market to the Military in Space Policy* (Stanford University Press, August 2010).

Lam Peng Er is a Senior Research Fellow at the East Asian Institute at the National University of Singapore. He obtained his PhD from Columbia University. His latest book is *Japan's Peace-building Diplomacy in Asia: Seeking a More Active Political Role* (2009).

Naohiro **Ogawa** is Director of the Population Research Institute and holds professorial positions in the Advanced Research Institute for the Sciences and Humanities and the College of Economics at Nihon University, Tokyo. His books include *Human Resources in Development along the Asia-Pacific Rim* (1993), *The Family, the Market, and the State in Ageing Societies* (1994), and *Population Aging, Intergenerational Transfers and the Macroeconomy* (2007).

Saadia **Pekkanen** is the Job and Gertrud Tamaki Professor at the Jackson School of International Studies and Adjunct Professor in the School of Law at the University of Washington, Seattle. Her most recent book publications include *Japan's Aggressive Legalism: Law and Foreign Trade Politics Beyond the WTO* (Stanford University Press, 2008), a co-edited volume entitled *Japan and China in the World Political Economy* (Routledge, 2005), and a co-authored book entitled *In Defense of Japan: From the Market to the Military in Space Policy* (Stanford University Press, August 2010).

Marie **Söderberg** is Director of the European Institute of Japanese Studies at Stockholm School of Economics and is also Professor of Japanese Studies at Stockholm University. She serves as Chair of the Board of the Centre for East and Southeast Asian Studies at Lund University. Her recent publications include 'Foreign Aid as a Tool for Peacebuilding: Is the Goal Security or Poverty Reduction?' in Marie Söderberg and Patricia A. Nelson (eds) *Japan's Politics and Economy*, (Routledge 2010); 'Can Japanese Aid to North Korea Create Peace and Stability?' in Marie Söderberg and Linus Hagström (eds.), The Other Binary: Why Japan-North Korea Relations Matter, *Pacific Affairs* (Special Issue).

Alex **Stephens** is a visiting fellow at the Flinders University School of Political and International Studies and an Adjunct Professor of International Relations at Pannasastra University of Cambodia. His research is focused on the international political economy of the Asia Pacific, with Australian and Japanese trade policy, and capacity building in Third World states as primary interests.

J. A. A. **Stockwin** was Nissan Professor of Modern Japanese Studies and Director of the Nissan Institute of Japanese Studies at the University of Oxford (1982–2003) and is now also an Emeritus Fellow of St. Antony's College. Recipient of the 2009 Japan Foundation Prize, his most recent publications include *Dictionary of the Modern Politics of Japan* (2003), *Collected Writings of J.A.A. Stockwin: The Politics and Political Environment* *of Japan* (2004), *Governing Japan: Divided Politics in a Resurgent Economy* (4th revised edition, 2008).

Gabriele **Vogt** is the Professor for State and Society of Japan in the Asien-Afrika-Institut at the University of Hamburg. Her most recent publications are *The Demographic Change: A Handbook about Japan* (co-eds Coulmas, Florian; Conrad, Harald; Schad-Seifert, Annette) (2008) and 'Talking Politics: Demographic Variables and Policy Measures in Japan' in Herstatt and Kohlbacher (eds) *The Silver Market Phenomenon: Business Opportunities in an Era of Demographic Change* (2008).

Brad **Williams** was formerly a visiting fellow in the Department of Political Science, National University of Singapore. He currently has a teaching position at the City University of Hong Kong. Brad's research interests include comparative politics and international relations, with a geographical focus on Northeast Asia. He is the co-editor of *Japan, Australia and Asia-Pacific Security* (Routledge 2006), the author of *Resolving the Russo-Japanese Territorial Dispute: Hokkaido-Sakhalin Relations* (Routledge 2007), and has also published in several internationally refereed journals.

Shoko **Yoneyama** is a senior lecturer in Asian Studies at the University of Adelaide. Her fields of research are the sociology of education and Japanese studies. She is the author of *The Japanese High School: Silence and Resistance* (Routledge, 1999 and 2006) and has published widely on educational issues.

Introduction
Japan: Descending Asian Giant?

BRAD WILLIAMS AND PURNENDRA JAIN

During the 1960s, 1970s and 1980s, the world witnessed the swift ascent of post-war Japan as Asia's new giant. The nation broke record after record to become Asia's number one economy and the world's number two. Japan's economic leap inspired a so-called *tsunami* of interest in Japan and its language. Two decades later, regional and global geopolitical landscapes are in transition to a differently configured world order. Where is Japan placed in this transition? After the first decade of the twenty-first century, and fifty years after it began its economic ascent, is Japan still an Asian giant?

At the end of 2009, Japan remained the world's number two economy in terms of GDP (at market exchange rates). Japanese firms are still renowned for their innovation and cutting-edge technology and are prominent in global markets for automobiles, consumer electronics and computers. Japanese banks and financial institutions remain robust, despite the problems and crises they faced in the 1990s. Japanese popular culture enjoys enormous popularity throughout the world. Japan is a significant player in regional and global affairs and is increasingly active in areas beyond economics, such as peacekeeping and climate change issues. Yet its presence on the regional and global stage seems to be hardly noted in the international media and public commentaries, and the scholarly gaze of many has 'moved on'. Why is this the case?

SURVEYING JAPAN'S SOCIOECONOMIC MALAISE

Economic performance has been an important factor in Japan's perceived decline, just as it was intrinsic to Japan's post-war ascendance. Japan maintains its position as a major world economy, but has been in the economic doldrums for almost two decades following the bursting of the stock market and property bubbles in the early 1990s. The indicators of Japan's economic deterioration are numerous. During the so-called 'Lost Decade' of the 1990s, the national economy groaned under the weight of non-performing bank loans, which conservative estimates placed at seven per cent of GDP and others placed much higher.[1] In the same period, commercial property prices dropped by an average of 84 per cent in Japan's six biggest cities. Share prices also went into freefall, with the Nikkei 225 share price index contracting by three-quarters since it peaked in 1989. Corporate bankruptcies and, subsequently, unemployment reached post-war highs. The annual growth rate of the national economy averaged less than one per cent, compared to the four per cent achieved during the 1980s. The government's structural budget deficit also climbed – as did the national debt, the latter reaching over 130 per cent of GDP. These figures led one highly influential weekly to claim, 'Japan has suffered the deepest slump in any developed economy since the Great Depression.'[2]

The economy rebounded somewhat between 2003 and 2007, partly attributable to a surge in exports, encouraged by an undervalued yen and banking reforms. Many gains achieved during this brief period, however, have been wiped out by the current global financial crisis, which has hit Japan especially hard. According to the OECD, Japan's GDP contracted by just over five per cent in 2009.[3] Even a seemingly invincible Japanese company like Toyota has experienced financial difficulty, with the automaker posting an operating loss for the first time in its seventy year history. The Japanese automaker is also currently embroiled in a scandal in the US over several accidents caused by faulty parts for acceleration and braking. For many observers, Toyota's current woes are symbolic of Japan's decline. As a result of nearly two decades of virtual stagnation, Japan lost its status as the world's second largest economy – understandably the source of great national pride when achieved in the early 1970s.

Of course, it is not just that Japan's economic performance has declined. During this period the economic performance of China, Japan's neighbour on the Asian mainland, has been the virtual inverse of Japan. China's apparently peaceful economic resurgence has not only pulled the international spotlight from Japan but has displaced Japan from its number two status.

The decline in fortunes represents a dramatic shift from the 1980s when Japan's economy was expanding so rapidly and Japanese firms were investing and buying up prime real estate across the world. Japan's seemingly relentless economic march, coupled with remarkable social stability, led to a surge in 'success literature' – best exemplified by Ezra Vogel's *Japan as Number One* – which sought to unlock the secrets to the Japanese juggernaut. Some held up Japan's industrial and trade policies and system of industrial relations as models to be emulated. Japanese language education and studies enjoyed a *tsunami* of student enrolments internationally and funding bodies in Japan, both private and public, offered generous financial support to facilitate this growing global interest. Others meanwhile saw Japan's rising trade surpluses (with the US in particular) during this period as the product of an impenetrable developmental state that did not play by the rules of the international trading game and thereby threatened western interests.[5]

Japan's economic difficulties have contributed to enormous domestic social problems. Rising unemployment has been a factor in the upsurge in homelessness, divorce rates, suicide and crime. While crime rates, especially for violent crimes, are low by international standards, Japan's reputation for social order and peace has suffered somewhat. In a nation where the overwhelming majority of people identify themselves as middle class, socioeconomic disparities and inequalities are expanding. Centre–periphery differences are particularly evident as large parts of rural Japan are suffering under the weight of an ageing and declining population, shrinking tax revenues, few or no competitive industries and mountains of debt. Symptomatic of the rural socioeconomic malaise, one small city in Hokkaido made headlines when it was declared effectively bankrupt. Many other locales are also teetering on the brink of financial collapse. Japan's ageing population, which is by no means merely a rural phenomenon, is placing further strain on the nation's underdeveloped social security net – a net that was severely compromised after a bureaucratic bungle resulted in the loss of pension records in 2007.

Japanese schools, lauded for their ability to produce students who achieve exceptionally high academic standards, have also experienced their share of troubles. Problems such as school bullying, truancy and classroom breakdown (*gakkyū hōkai*) have come to characterize many schools as the young seem less willing to continue the discipline and self-sacrifice of their elders.[6] The regimentation of school life and the intense pressure to perform in entrance exams in order to secure a promising future are seen as factors now contributing to growing youth delinquency. As Williams and Yoneyama (Chapter 9) note, school education in Japan is now increasingly seen in an international light as less positive than before, much like the nation's generally indolent universities. The Japanese education system as a whole, with its continuing emphasis on rote learning and memorization rather than critical thinking skills, is in decline and is linked to the nation's broader socioeconomic malaise. Genda (Chapter 11) argues that stable employment opportunities for the young are declining and many are either forced or simply choose to work part-time. The educational pressures and bleak employment prospects are also partly to blame for a phenomenon known as *hikikomori* (social withdrawal) in which a large number of mostly young Japanese men remain holed up in their bedrooms, refusing to venture outside for months or years at a time. The prevalence of schoolgirls engaging in sex with older males in return for money and material reward (known as 'compensated dating' or *enjo kōsai*) also suggests at least differing, if not declining, moral standards among Japan's youth.[7]

POLITICAL SCLEROSIS

To further compound the situation for Japan, politics and policy mechanisms are hamstrung by a lack of leadership and long-term vision. The early 1990s offered the prospect of meaningful political change in Japan when an eight-party (seven plus one group in the House of Councillors) coalition government under the enormously popular Hosokawa Morihiro was inaugurated in August 1993. The Liberal Democratic Party (LDP) found itself out of government for the first time in thirty-eight years. Hosokawa's government embarked upon an ambitious programme of structural and policy reform. The most significant of these reforms was to the electoral system. The former system of single non-transferable votes in medium-sized electoral districts was perceived to be an important contributing factor to a style of politics that favoured personalities over policy and ideology and which consequently led to the salience of money politics. Reformers hoped that a new regime of single member districts (SMD) would lead to a two-party system in which campaigns would be policy-oriented, party-controlled and inexpensive and, therefore, less susceptible to corrupt practices. After difficult negotiations between the new government and opposition, a compromise was reached on a mixed system of SMD and proportional representation in early 1994. Hosokawa resigned shortly after, ostensibly for his involvement in a minor (by Japanese standards) funding scandal, and was replaced as prime minister by Hata Tsutomu who headed a minority government after efforts to maintain coalition harmony failed. Unsurprisingly, the Hata government was short-lived and the LDP was soon back in power but in a move that shocked the Japanese political world the party entered into the ultimate 'marriage of convenience' by joining its erstwhile foe, the socialists, in a coalition government under the formal leadership of Japan Socialist Party (JSP) Chairman, Murayama Tomiichi. The remainder of the decade (and beyond) saw a series of coalition governments and when the LDP regained its majority in late 1997 it seemed like 'politics as usual' had returned to Japan.[8]

The bureaucracy, which had worked closely with the LDP and whose foresight and planning was considered by many to be instrumental in Japan's post-war economic miracle (especially the then Ministry of International Trade and Industry [MITI] and the Ministry of Finance [MOF]), has come under the spotlight. Indeed, since the early 1990s, the reputation of Japan's once-exalted bureaucrats has been tarnished considerably in the wake of a seemingly constant stream of scandals. Revelations of negligence, greed and inability to help engineer a sustainable economic recovery added further impetus to longstanding calls to cut the size of the civil service. A major restructuring of the government bureaucracy was carried out in January 2001, reducing the number of ministries from twenty-three to thirteen. Although the authority of the Prime Minister was increased substantially, a perception remained in

Japan, especially among the opposition parties, that the bureaucracy still wielded too much power.

Following the unpopular Obuchi and Mori administrations (1998–2001), the LDP sought to avoid potential disaster in upcoming House of Councillors elections, selecting the reformist Koizumi Junichirō as party President and hence Prime Minister in April 2001. Koizumi promised 'reform without sanctuaries' and vowed to destroy both the clientelistic foundations upon which LDP rule was based and the intra-party forces that opposed his policies. A key component of his neo-liberal reform agenda was privatization of the Post Office system – a nationwide institution whose enormous financial reserves helped to fund LDP governments' pork barrel practices. This proposal subsequently threatened vested interests within the party. Image was an important tool in Koizumi's leadership kit and it was used with great effect to raise his popularity among the public and to promote his radical reform measures. The highpoint in his premiership was arguably the September 2005 Lower House election. Koizumi was able to transform the election essentially into a referendum on postal privatization and after ruthlessly removing anti-privatization rebels from the party, he led it to a spectacular victory. The LDP's 296 seats (out of 480), when combined with those of its coalition partner, New Komeitō, gave the alliance a controlling majority in the Lower House, enabling it to override legislation blocked in the Upper House. This power would soon prove vital for the LDP–Komeitō coalition after it lost its majority in the House of Councillors following elections in July 2007.

By this time, the Japanese government was under the stewardship of Abe Shinzō – the first Japanese prime minister born post-war – after Koizumi stepped down from office in September 2006. This marked the beginning of a period in which Japan went through three prime ministers in three years, all political bluebloods and none able to claim a direct mandate from the people. Abe's cabinet was beset by a series of scandals and Abe himself seemed more interested in engaging in nationalist politics than pursuing policies to restore the nation's economic health. Amid declining popularity, and citing poor health, Abe resigned a year into the post. Abe was followed as prime minister by the moderate Fukuda Yasuo who, frustrated by the opposition's obstructionist tactics in the Upper House, also resigned unexpectedly after only a year in office. The last of the revolving-door prime ministers was Asō Tarō, who, like Abe, was a right-wing revisionist and shared with his predecessor a low public approval rating. Asō's policy backflips (most notably on postal privatization) and verbal gaffes in particular enraged many Japanese and his inability to formulate policies to cure the nation's economic and social woes served to create a groundswell of public sentiment against the LDP. This was not the first time that the LDP had been under pressure before a general election. However, unlike much of the past, the ruling party was now faced with a credible opposition, as well as defections of traditional supporters. These factors fostered a pervasive mood in Japan emphasizing a need for change and a preparedness among voters to give the opposition Democratic Party of Japan (DPJ) a chance to govern.

POLITICAL CHANGE AND CHALLENGES

Change is indeed what voters in the Lower House election of September 2009 brought to Japan as the DPJ achieved a resounding victory. The DPJ's stunning electoral success through winning 308 of the 480 seats (64 per cent) surpassed the purportedly grand victory of Koizumi's LDP four years earlier and assigned the perennial ruling party to opposition for just the second time in its fifty-five year history. Stockwin (Chapter 2) calls it an electoral and political earthquake. Some have called it a third revolution after the Meiji Restoration of 1868 and the Occupation period (1945–52). However, Stockwin remains cautiously optimistic, noting that 'Whether the third revolution can fulfil the ambitious expectations vested in it remains unanswered.'

With the prospect of being out of office and subsequently unable to access government coffers to distribute pork to supporters over the short to medium term, the LDP remains vulnerable to significant shakeup that will render further political realignment to the party landscape. The DPJ has secured a large mandate to enact change, but it also faces great expectations from the Japanese people. Enormous challenges also lie ahead for the new government. The most pressing issue, of course, is fixing the economy. Predictably, the new government has sought a departure from previous LDP policies but will surely face difficulties in charting a new course. Domestically, the DPJ has pledged to enact social welfare policies, although how these policies will be funded without adding to the nation's already burgeoning debt remains unclear. The DPJ has vowed to curb bureaucratic influence and pursue a 'people-oriented politics' but Kasumigaseki[9] will surely remind the party that the bureaucracy's cooperation is indispensible for implementing the reforms that the party intends. The new government's announcement that it aims to cut Japan's greenhouse gas emissions by 25 per cent from the 1990 level by 2020 is likely to meet resistance from the business community fearing the financial burden, as in most countries pursuing emissions cuts.

Foreign policy also presents challenges. While relations with the US will remain the cornerstone of Japan's foreign policy, bilateral ties have been tested – most notably by the previous Hatoyama government's attempts to revise existing accords concerning the realignment of US forces in Japan and the Status of Forces Agreement, and by its decision to end the Maritime Self Defence Forces (MSDF) refuelling mission in the Indian Ocean. Following the debacle surrounding Japan's tortured response to the First Gulf War (1990–91) and the 'alliance drift' of the early 1990s, it could be argued that a closer relationship with the US – recent Okinawa military base-related tensions notwithstanding – has been one of Japan's few diplomatic success stories in the region.

Despite growing trade and investment linkages and enhanced people-to-people contacts, Japan's relations with China and South Korea reached a nadir during the Koizumi administration, primarily over the Yasukuni Shrine visits and history textbook issues. Relations with China are further complicated by that country's remarkable economic, strategic and military resurgence, contrasting starkly with Japan's socioeconomic malaise, and by the incipient great power rivalry this resurgence has engendered. Japan has been on much better terms with its Northeast Asian neighbours in recent times but ties are still fragile and seem only a history-related scandal away from renewed tension.

Friction and hostility seem to be enduring features of Japan's relationship with North Korea. Tokyo sees Pyongyang as the quintessential rogue state – a regime that represents a traditional, if over-exaggerated, military threat and, when one considers the abductions issue, a non-conventional menace as well. Choi (Chapter 8) argues that Tokyo's uncompromising stance on the abductions and the history issues has caused Japan to suffer from perceptual and strategic 'deficits', which have limited its influence when dealing with its Northeast Asian neighbours. Others have also argued the importance of Japan overcoming these obstacles on the basis that its leadership is vital in forging a successful multilateral body in East Asia in the context of a rising China and declining US hegemon.[10]

JAPAN: ALL DOOM AND GLOOM?

From the preceding analysis, it is easy to be pessimistic about Japan's prospects. The notion of a 'Lost Decade' during the 1990s and the suggestion Japan could be on the verge of 'losing another decade'[11] encourage the impression of a nation in complete and multifaceted stagnation. This is certainly not the case. Focusing solely on negative issues such as the troubled economy and demographic decline blinds us to important political and socioeconomic changes during this period.

Politically, the birth of Japan's first non-LDP government in 1993 initially raised the prospects of a policy-oriented, alternating-party system, less susceptible to pork barrel politics and corruption, taking root in Japan. Instead, with the LDP's swift return to office we witnessed the demise of the parliamentary Left and a subsequent shift further to the right along the political spectrum, reflected in a series of LDP-led domestic, foreign and security policy initiatives. The DPJ's electoral success in September 2009 once again raises the hopes of those seeking the development of a vibrant two-party system in Japan. Much depends on the success of the new government in addressing the myriad of challenges facing the nation, and on the capacity of the LDP as the erstwhile ruling party to adapt to the role of a responsible opposition in the short to medium term.

By mid-2010, however, many optimistic observers will be disappointed by the state of Japanese politics. The Hatoyama government's approval rating slumped with news of its LDP-like mismanagement of political funds and its inept handling of the relocation of the US base at Futenma in Okinawa. Hatoyama proved to be far from the decisive leader required to resolve Japan's enormous economic, political and social problems and, continuing the trend of his three LDP predecessors, resigned after a relatively brief time in office. The DPJ elected Kan Naoto as party president and prime minister in a bid to arrest the government's declining popularity ahead of important upper house elections in July 2010. A populist and former citizens' movement activist, Kan has declared he will accept Hatoyama's tortuous decision to abide by an agreement to relocate US marines to Henoko in Okinawa, thereby removing a thorn in relations with Washington. He has also reaffirmed the importance of healthy relations with China and South Korea. The new leader will subsequently focus his attentions domestically, in particular on the economy, as well as the potential challenge from Ozawa forces within the DPJ.[12] The LDP, weakened by a series of defections and also suffering from leadership problems, has been unable to take advantage of the DPJ government's sagging fortunes.[13]

Socially and politically, a positive development has been the growth of civil society, the spur for which came from a natural disaster. The 1995 Great Hanshin-Awaji Earthquake devastated the city of Kobe and caused over 6,000 deaths. The scale of the destruction and the government's inadequate disaster relief operations seemed symptomatic of the broader socioeconomic malaise and lack of political leadership. While many were quick to highlight the government's inept response, the disaster was also notable for the thousands of volunteers who descended upon the devastated areas to assist with relief operations. As one commentator noted, 'this surge in volunteerism' demonstrated 'that a sense of community is alive and well in Japan'.[14] The contrast between the government's and the public's response to the disaster created momentum for the 1998 Non-Profit Organization (NPO) Law, which has contributed to an explosion in the number of civil society organizations in Japan.[15] This upsurge in Japanese associational activity is a progressive development in terms of promoting social capital and improving both governance and the quality of democracy.[16]

The spirit of humanitarian goodwill also extends to the foreign policy arena. Japan has adopted a more robust security posture in recent years in response to rising regional uncertainties, the domestic political shift outlined above and US encouragement, and the shift has attracted growing international attention. Less noticed, however, is Japan's increasingly active role in international humanitarian relief operations, peace-building diplomacy and human security – a topic taken up in detail by Ito (Chapter 4). A prominent feature of Japanese ODA and international peace cooperation activities is public–private sector cooperation. A myriad of non-state actors such as NGOs, NPOs, business entities and individual citizens regularly work in collaboration with the relevant organs of the central government and with subnational governments, which have gradually become more cognisant of the advantages derived from utilizing the special skills and knowledge within these groups.[17]

Culturally, evidence of positive development is clear in international responses. Japan's culture and entertainment industries, as producers of *anime*, fashion, films, *manga*, pop music and video games to name a few, are enormously popular abroad, especially in Asia. In a creative and oft-cited expression, foreign journalist Douglas McGray argued that these products contribute to a 'Gross National Cool', giving Japan the appearance of a cultural superpower and providing it with a kind of 'soft power' that might be used to influence foreign consumers in a manner conducive to Japanese interests.[18] But while Japanese popular culture is influential outside Japan, some observers argue that it does not enjoy the hegemony in Asia that some might think, facing increasing challenge from local variants, most notably the Korean Wave phenomenon (*hallyu*). Leheny suggests that appeals to 'soft power' play a role in helping Japanese to 'cope emotionally and intellectually with national decline' through the belief that national virtues 'are validated overseas'.[19] And while McGray acknowledged Japan's cultural power, he also recognized that the fungibility of culture is less than clear and that deep-rooted insularity has prevented Japan from effectively utilizing this form of power.

Japanese insularity manifests itself most prominently in the lack of both government and public support for immigration, which many foreign observers see as an obvious panacea for the demographic problems from population decline. Vogt (Chapter 12) discusses this issue with case studies of new temporary workers who were invited to Japan to use their nursing skills, which are in short supply, with the prospect of possible migration. Her conclusion is pessimistic about Japan's insularity, observing that despite Japan's clear needs for international labour migration, it appears the nation's policies are still informed by the historical notion of *sakoku* (closed country). For Ogawa (Chapter 10), however, Japan's ageing population is not necessarily a cause for alarm. He argues that while in contemporary Japan the elderly are generally considered as 'debts', in fact Japanese elderly people may become powerful 'assets' to keep the country on a steady growth path in the years to come. His findings suggest that elderly Japanese are still playing a vital role, particularly in providing financial support for their offspring when the latter encounter economic difficulties.

Overall, then, we need to be careful not to make assumptions on the basis of selective evidence. The reality and the prospects of Japan's decline may be less intense than the economic and social data suggest. Even Japan's economic situation may not be as desperate as critics suggest. China has overtaken Japan to become the world's second largest economy but that has simply shifted Japan to number three – a position that most national governments would think extremely admirable, and one that Japan is likely to hold for a while to come. Japan's per capita GDP is several times greater than China's and economic despair is not plainly evident on the streets of most of the nation's glitzy, cosmopolitan cities. Japanese companies are still global leaders in technological innovation and their products are the item of choice for many consumers around the world. Difficulties now facing the troubled automaker Toyota could present its Japanese competitors, who have also earned reputations for manufacturing excellence, with an opportunity to increase their own domestic and international market shares.[20] Toyota's crisis, perhaps at least in the short-term, may not be as severe as some critics believe; amid the impending lawsuits and recalls, Toyota actually reported a significant increase in sales in the US in March 2010, stimulated by credit incentives and the 'huge reservoir of goodwill' it has accumulated with the American public.[21]

Furthermore, Japanese generally enjoy a comfortable standard of living – not to mention significantly greater civil and political liberties than many of their neighbours on the Asian mainland. Genda's 'hope' studies paint an optimistic picture of Japanese society, rejecting the common view that an ageing society is short on attractiveness and heavy on burdens. He sees the elderly virtuously, with valuable experience of setback and achievement that they can pass on to younger members of society. In his view, this passage of experience and wisdom will prepare younger people to deal effectively with growing uncertainty and risk, and will generate a brand new culture that will drive a new economy in Japan as a matured society.

Japan's role in the Asian region is valuable and is acknowledged as such by most players in the region, even while this role is changing. Jain and Stephens (Chapter 7) argue that with powerful players such as China and India challenging Japan for regional influence, Japan pursues a new international strategy of regional networks to try to prevent and forestall its decline in power. Through financial and politico-strategic networks, Japan mutualizes the interests of regional players in outcomes and priorities consistent with those of Japan on a wide range of concerns, seeking to maximize chances for cooperation with Japan's position. Japan is also an important trade and investment partner for many countries, especially in the Asia-Pacific region. As Lam notes (Chapter 5), with its own experience of overcoming severe environmental degradation and with considerable green technological capabilities and resources, Japan has emerged as a valuable provider of ODA for environmental protection to China and other developing countries and remains a leading player in key global environmental policy areas, especially climate change.

Importantly, Japan still retains strengths in science and technology. One clear manifestation, though not widely recognized, is Japan's rise as an advanced military space power, as Pekkanen and Kallender-Umezu explain in their study of Japan's space policy (Chapter 6). Unlike most of the post-war period, in recent years the passage of law and the new space plan of 2009 explicitly and paradigmatically shift the interests of Japan's space policy away from narrow commerce and further towards national security. This shift will affect not only the course of commercial players in the space industry but also Japan's foreign security relations at a broader level. Even Japan's financial system, as Corbett (Chapter 1) argues, 'is no longer one that should be considered in decline'. She further notes that following painful reforms, aspects of Japan's banking and financial regulations now appear to be more advanced than most OECD countries.

Overall, the chapters in this volume demonstrate that 'Japan' is not a monolithic entity. Pessimistic observers of Japan, domestically and abroad, point to the stagnant economy, ageing population and rising social instability as indicators of the nation's inexorable decline. The economic, political and social institutions credited with creating the 'Japanese miracle' from the ashes of wartime defeat and with transforming Japan into a regional power now seem incapable of dealing with the challenges of a globalizing post-industrial age. To be sure, as some of the chapters in this volume indicate, there is much to be discouraged about today when compared with Japan's economic spectacle several decades back. This is true in many nations around the world.

However, looking beyond the oft-cited socioeconomic problems also reveals cause for optimism about Japan. It is still a technological giant whose companies are at the forefront of innovation and have earned global reputations for producing high quality items. Japanese popular culture is admired around the world. Politically, Japan has a new non-LDP government and the growth of civil society augurs well for further democratic development. Criticized in the past for being a reactive and 'free riding' trading state, Japan now engages more actively in international affairs and contributes to the maintenance of global public goods. At the regional level, Tokyo is a major player in regional institutions. Japan of necessity is adjusting its role in a transforming strategic environment with the rapid rise of China, the steady emergence of India and apparent decline of the US, but in no way can its course in the region be regarded as descent.

As the chapters of this book make clear, Japan is in the midst of what Kingston refers to as a 'quiet transformation'.[22] While the direction and results of current socioeconomic and political changes are unclear, Japan's modern history demonstrates strong national capacity to achieve successful renewal. With an eye to the past and to the present course of history, it is premature and unwise to write Japan's obituary yet.

NOTES

[1] The data in this paragraph are from *The Economist*, 363(8269), 20 April 2002, p. 3 and 364(8292), 28 September 2002, p. 21.

[2] Ibid, 364(8292), 28 September 2002, p. 21.

[3] The OECD forecasts that output growth in Japan will rise to 3 percent in 2010 on a year average basis. OECD, *OECD Economic Outlook No. 87 – Japan*, May 2010.

[4] World Bank, 'Gross Domestic Product 2008, PPP', *World Development Indicators Database*, 1 July 2009.

[5] See for instance, J. Fallows, 'Containing Japan', *Atlantic*, May 1990, pp. 40–54.

[6] J. Kingston, *Japan's Quiet Transformation: Social Change and Civil Society in the Twenty-first Century*, Abingdon and New York: RoutledgeCurzon, 2004, p. 272.

[7] Some of these issues are analysed in M. Zielenziger, *Shutting out the Sun: How Japan Created its own Lost Generation*, New York: Vintage Books, 2006.

[8] On the political change in 1993 and subsequent electoral reforms, see P. Jain, 'A New Political Era in Japan', *Asian Survey* November 1993; 'Electoral Reform in Japan: Its Process and Implications for Party Politics', *Journal of East Asian Affairs*, Summer/Fall 1995, pp. 202–27.

[9] The district in Tokyo where offices of the national bureaucracy are concentrated.

[10] See P. Van Ness, 'Japan, the Indispensible Power in Northeast Asia', *Global Asia*, 4(4), Winter 2010.

[11] *The Economist*, vol. 391, iss. 8625, 4 April 2009, p. 75.

[12] See P.E. Lam, 'Japanese Prime Minister Kan Naoto: A Rocky Road Ahead?' *EAI Background Brief No. 533*, East Asian Institute, National University of Singapore, 9 June 2010; P. Jain, 'Kan Naoto's Parliamentary Debut in 1980', *East Asia Forum*, 11 June 2010, http://www.eastasiaforum.org/2010/06/11/kan-naotos-parliamentary-debut-in-1980/, accessed 16 June 2010.

[13] Early polling suggests Kan's appointment has been relatively well received by the Japanese public.

[14] Kingston, *Japan's Quiet Transformation*, p. 16.

[15] See R. Pekkanen, *Japan's Dual Civil Society: Members without Advocates*, Stanford: Stanford University Press, 2006.

[16] See R. Putnam, R. Leonardi and R. Nanetti, *Making Democracy Work: Civic Traditions in Modern Italy*, Princeton, N.J.: Princeton University Press, 1993; R. Putnam, *Bowling Alone: The Collapse and Revival of American Community*, New York: Simon and Schuster, 2000.

[17] See K. Hirata, *Civil Society in Japan: The Growing Role of NGOs in Tokyo's Aid and Development Policy*, New York: Palgrave Macmillan, 2008; P. Jain, *Japan's Subnational Governments in International Affairs*, Routledge, 2005.

[18] D. McGray, 'Japan's Gross National Cool', *Foreign Policy*, May/June 2002.

[19] D. Leheny, 'A Narrow Place to Cross Swords: Soft Power and the Politics of Japanese Popular Culture in East Asia', in P. Katzenstein and T. Shiraishi (eds) *Beyond Japan: The Dynamics of East Asian Regionalism*, Ithaca and London: Cornell University Press, 2006, pp. 211–33.

[20] P.E. Lam, 'Toyota's Stumble is Not a Metaphor for Japan Inc.', *YaleGlobal*, 26 March 2010, http:/yaleglobal.yale.edu/content/Toyotas-stumble-not-metaphor, accessed 29 March 2010.

[21] J. Kell, 'Toyota Outsells Ford as US Car Sales for March Leap by 37pc,' *The Australian*, 2 April 2010, http://www.theaustralian.com.au/business/news/toyota-outsells-ford-as-us-car-sales-for-march-leap-by-37pc/story-e6frg90o-1225848832273, accessed 3 April 2010.

[22] Kingston, *Japan's Quiet Transformation*.

PART 1

Economics and Politics

1

Financial System Reform: Recovery or Retrogression?

JENNY CORBETT

INTRODUCTION

The Japanese finance system has attracted a stream of international attention in the last decade, from Krugman likening Japan to the return of the depression economics of the 1930s, to Citrin and Wolfson heralding the return of Japan to respectable growth.[1] More recently several observers draw lessons from Japan's experience for the current crisis, drawing on the parallels between Japan's 'Lost Decade' and the Great Depression of the 1930s.[2] This suggests that after a long period of 'Japan passing', Japan's experience is in no longer being overlooked by international commentators. But what lessons are being taken from it?

Most discussions of Japan's experience during the 1990s suggested the lessons to be learnt for the international community were largely negative. Commentary focused particularly on bad policy in the banking crisis. The policy of 'forbearance', where both regulators and bankers try to wait out problems and do not take action against underperforming banks (in the case of regulators) or borrowers (in the case of banks), prolonged problems and ultimately resulted in real, not just financial, economic distress. Attention to these lessons often concluded with 'don't do what Japan did'. Additionally, it was argued that Japan's fiscal expansion during the 1990s showed the failure of Keynesian stimulus policy both because it had no effect and because it led to a build up of government debt.

The reality, as demonstrated in the economic data was, however, more complex. By 2006 Japan had its longest period of economic expansion since the Second World War and was amongst the strongest growing OECD countries. Bank health had been restored, corporate profitability recovered and unemployment, and government deficits, were reducing. The growth was based not only on exports but also on domestic consumption.[3] Wolf, drawing on Koo, concluded that Japan demonstrated a quite different set of lessons.[4] In the face of a potentially devastating financial crisis what is needed is immediate recapitalization of banks and really large fiscal injections of demand by the government. The mistake Japan made was to take too long to do this but the direction of the policies, when eventually implemented, was right and necessary. This was, in fact, the path followed by most countries hit by the global financial crisis of 2008–9.

This chapter will argue another element of an alternative view to the commentary on Japan's financial 'mess'. While forbearance was a mistake in Japan's circumstances, it was understandable in the initial phase and in different circumstances could have been the right policy. More importantly, the eventual policy design for 'micro prudential' management (i.e. the supervision and regulation of banks) could now be a model for the world (though macroeconomic management remains poor). This chapter first examines the financial elements of Japan's 'Lost Decade' and how the recapitalization and reform of banks shaped the slow and stumbling path to a solution. Through the change in the regulatory structure that followed, not only was a technical change seen, but the political economy of banking regulation was also changed. With the Takenaka Plan in 2002, Japan was at last seen to be 'banging heads together' and implementing steps for substantial change. Part of this process involved some far reaching reforms of the system for managing poorly performing banks, which have given Japan a leading-edge policy framework with lessons for other countries.

BACKGROUND TO CRISIS

A prominent feature of Japan's poor economic performance and banking crisis of the 1990s was the long, slow build up that preceded the worst years. During this time, from the initial drop in growth in 1990–1 to the mid-1990s, there was a belief that asset prices would recover and that banks' unrealized capital gains (that is, the value of the corporate shares they held which were valued at their initial purchase price rather than the market price) would support their balance sheet recovery. Coupled with the denial of the emerging scale of bad loans (since reliable data were not available at the time), there was an attempt to preserve the so-called 'convoy system' in which the Japanese Ministry of Finance (MOF) would keep all banks afloat and keep the whole 'convoy', the set of all banks, moving at the pace of the slowest. The method to do this involved MOF-orchestrated agreements for the rescue of weaker banks by stronger ones, which were neither public nor transparent. With the mishandling of the politics of the *jūsen* crisis, when housing loan associations backed by the banks lost money and a rescue scheme to restore the banks' lost capital was proposed, MOF's reputation was damaged and public antipathy to rescue packages for banks rose. Both factors contributed to the slow response by the authorities to the gathering storm. Early warning signs could have been seen in the failures of Tōhō Sōgo in 1991 (absorbed by another mutual institution with assistance from the Deposit Insurance Corporation of Japan (DICJ)); of Tōyō Shinkin (absorbed by Sanwa Bank with assistance from DICJ, Industrial Bank of Japan (IBJ), and Zenshinren) in 1992; of Cosmo and Kizu credit unions in 1995, and of Hyogo Bank (reorganized as Midori Bank with assistance from city banks, the Bank of Japan (BOJ), and DICJ). The foreign financial markets certainly saw these as a warning and began to charge Japanese banks a premium over the standard rate of interest at which banks lend to each other in the international market, the so-called 'Japan premium', because they perceived Japanese banks to be in a fragile state and, therefore, not good credit risks.

Despite these alarm bells, the slow build up of the crisis continued as the situation deteriorated with several bank failures in 1996. By April 1997, the MOF and BOJ had to lead a rescue, with financial assistance from other banks and insurance companies, for the Nippon Credit Bank, a large, specialist institution making long-term loans to big customers for physical investments in factories, construction and infrastructure. In autumn 1997 several large credit unions received assistance from DICJ to merge. The real crisis came in November 1997 with the failures of Sanyo Securities, Hokkaido Takushoku Bank and Yamaichi Securities and, at this point, the Japan premium rose sharply so that Japanese banks were paying nearly a full one percent more than the standard lending rate to borrow in international markets.

RESCUE THEN REFORM

Against this background the government arranged a series of packages to inject capital into banks and to guarantee deposits. The Prompt Recapitalization Act (October 1998) set aside ¥25 trillion for capital injection, in addition to the ¥17 trillion for deposit protection and ¥18 trillion for nationalization. ¥7.5 trillion was directed at fifteen major banks in March 1999, with varying terms, although the first attempts at recapitalization put money into all banks whether they needed it or not in an attempt to protect the reputation of the weaker ones. A further ¥0.5 trillion was directed to twelve regional banks by March 2001 when the act expired.

These developments have been described in many other places, so the details need not be repeated here, but the consensus view on the recapitalization plans is well-represented by Hoshi and Kashyap.[5] They argue that the recapitalization attempts in 1998 and 1999 did not have sustained impacts. Furthermore, the authorities were either uninformed or unwilling to face further public criticism so their recapitalization attempts were muted until much later. From late 2001 to early 2002, the Financial Supervisory Agency conducted 'special inspections' but announced that all banks were well capitalized and did not need further capital injections, though, in fact, as Fukao has argued, the banks were still financially weak at that time.[6] Hoshi and Kashyap conclude that what eventually restored the banks was the combined effect of the Takenaka plan and macroeconomic recovery. The eventual effect of reform and recovery can be seen in Chart 1, showing the amount of non-performing loans which continued to rise until the end of 2001 but began to decline rapidly and significantly after that. Subsequent recapitalization plans in the 2000s were more effective because they were targeted at weak banks, rather than the blanket approach used in the earlier attempts of the 1990s, and they had stronger conditions attached. The Act for Strengthening Financial Functions (ASFF) was passed in June 2004. That law allowed the government to inject public capital into banks without justifying their systemic importance. In 2006, ¥40.5 billion was injected into two regional banks under this law. When the law expired at the end of March 2008 it was revived in December 2008 so that the government could continue to inject capital into the banking sector when deemed necessary. In March 2009, ¥121.0 billion was provided to three regional banks. The Japan premium in international markets spiked briefly in 2001–2, though at much lower levels than previously, and then settled at a level barely above the international norm, suggesting that the market regarded the whole package of support for Japanese banks to have removed counterparty risk.[7]

While attention was focused on these large sums of money, several other elements of the reform programs for banks and their regulation

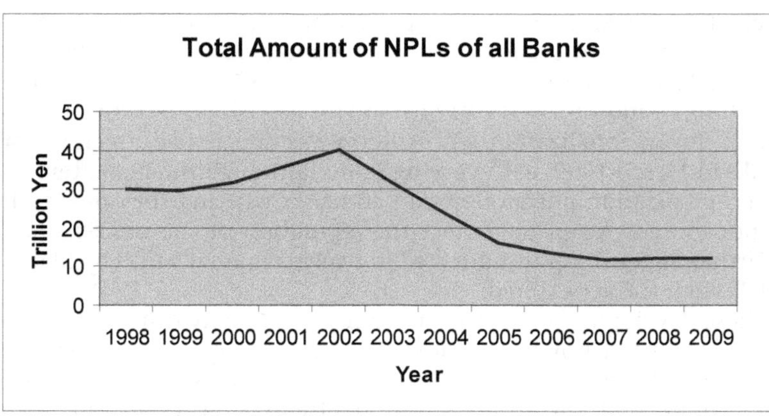

Chart 1 Source: Financial Services Agency, 'Status of Non-Performing Loans', http://www.fsa.go.jp/en/regulated/npl/index.html.

were arguably more radical though less well known. A classification by Hoshi and Kashyap of Japan's policy response into four key elements is useful.[8] One element, the recapitalization programme, has been described above. Another element was the Takenaka plan of 2002. Takenaka Heizō became the Minister of Financial Services and announced the 'Programme for Financial Revival' in October 2002. The key elements of the Takenaka Plan were to require banks to make a more rigorous evaluation of assets using discounted expected cash flows or market prices of non-performing loans. The plan also proposed to cross-check consistency between different banks in classifying loans to large debtors. Any discrepancy between the banks' self evaluations and the FSA's evaluations were to be made public to discourage banks from hiding problems. A key reform was to prohibit banks from declaring unrealistically large deferred tax assets (a technical element on balance sheets which many observers believed was allowing banks to appear to be in profit when they were not) and, importantly, to impose business improvement orders for banks that substantially underachieved the revitalization plans. The Takenaka plan therefore put much tougher conditions on banks both before and after they received public capital injections. The result was the turnaround in the non-performing loans ratio of the major banks, as shown above, to about half by March 2005. Crucially, Takenaka also wanted a *prior commitment* that the government would be prepared to inject public funds if necessary rather than relying on the piecemeal response to crisis of the past. This plank of the reform was directly related to other forward-looking features described below.

Two other elements of the reform plan, largely unnoticed outside Japan but in fact quite remarkable by international standards, were the creation and use of asset management companies and the resolution mechanisms for failed banks introduced by the Financial Revitalization Act of 1998. These two features heralded the shift away from the old 'convoy system' and the use of what might be called a 'modern' approach to banking reform. What the change achieved was a public commitment to the idea that banks could be closed or nationalized and that even big banks could fail. Together with the Takenaka conditions, these created a near comprehensive set of conditions that spell out what will happen to individual banks in distress and what the government will do in the event of a systemic crisis.

The process involved several elements. Responsibility for bank supervision was removed in stages from the MOF and eventually the Financial Supervisory Agency (FSA) replaced the MOF role entirely, using a rules-based regulatory approach. The rules-based approach was designed to remove the problem of discretion and forbearance by regulators, so that if inspection revealed any problems, rules dictated the 'prompt corrective action' to be taken. While this was originally an American idea, backed by the IMF as best-practice, its use in Japan coincided with its abandonment in the UK and, to some extent, in the US itself, in favour of the so-called 'principles-based' approach which handed responsibility for compliance to the banks themselves and which has been blamed for some of the conditions that led to the global financial crisis at the end of the first decade of the twenty-first century.

This process of establishing a new supervisory agency began with the Financial Revitalization Act of 1998 that established the Financial Reconstruction Commission (FRC). A key power of the FRC was the authority to decide whether a failed bank should be nationalized or put under receivership. Weak banks were allowed to apply for nationalization and the most prominent example was the Long-Term Credit Bank (LTCB) which applied to be nationalized in October 1998. The FRC also forced the nationalization of Nippon Credit Bank in December 1998 while several other failed regional banks were put under receivership between 1999 and 2001. The FRC was aggressive under its first chair, Yanagisawa Hakuo, but less so after he was replaced in October 1999. When the Prompt Recapitalization Act expired, the FRC was subsumed into the FSA in January 2001. Though initially there was concern about the resources and expertise of the new regulatory body,[9] it is now large and well-resourced.

At the same time, various methods for removing bad assets from banks' balance sheets were tried. This process of experimentation with asset management mechanisms (as the methods for taking toxic assets off banks' balance sheets are known) was part of the eventual development of a well-developed process for handling failing banks. Despite the initial disorder surrounding the change in regulatory structure of this period, key decisions were made that led to a largely unheralded 'micro prudential' reform. Though the formulation process took some time, Japan's structures are now quite remarkable.

Japan's response to the growth of bad loans in the banking system at the beginning of the 1990s began with allowing banks to set up their own asset management companies, many of which simply turned into warehouses of non-performing loans. The result was rather similar to the problem of the structured investment vehicles (SIVs) used by US banks to remove bad assets from the regulated institution (the bank itself) to an unregulated institution, without addressing the problem loans themselves. However, the intended purpose of removing bad assets from banks' balance sheets from the policy maker's viewpoint, is to enable banks to make new loans, unconstrained by the need to provision or to hold capital against loans that will never be repaid.

There is no agreement on the best way to manage banks' bad loans in a crisis. An influential study at the World Bank notes:

> The two alternatives for asset management strategies include setting up a government agency with the full responsibility for

acquiring, restructuring, and selling of the assets (the centralized approach) or letting banks and other creditors manage their own non-performing assets (the decentralized approach).[10]

However, in practice the distinction between centralized and decentralized is not completely straightforward. Decentralized methods of restructuring debtors have been located both inside banks (keeping the loans on the books, with the bank taking an active role in reorganizing the defaulter) or outside the bank via an off-balance-sheet vehicle or 'bad bank' which takes all the non-performing assets and works exclusively on those. The advantage of the 'bad bank' approach, as Klingebiel points out, is to 'maximize the recovery rate through active restructuring reducing drains on managerial capacity and improving overall incentives'.[11] Lindgren and Balino et al. show that within Asia, the private solutions (i.e. not centralized) frequently included the creation of private asset management companies (i.e. 'bad banks') and, in the best examples, resulted in the development of a private asset management industry where one had not existed previously.[12]

Centralized asset management mechanisms also come in different varieties, with centralized, publicly-funded AMCs set up either to help corporate restructuring or merely to acquire bad loans from banks and to dispose of the assets. Klingebiel's study of seven cases indicates that most did neither job very well and concludes '[centralized] AMCs are rarely good tools to expedite corporate restructuring'.[13]

As it struggled to build a policy framework to cope with the growing bad debts of the 1990s, Japan established first the privately-financed Cooperative Credit Purchase Company (1993) to allow banks to transfer loans off their books and claim tax deductions, then, with a major amendment to the Deposit Insurance Law in 1996, the Housing Loan Administration Corporation (HLAC) to resolve the *jūsen* housing loan crisis and the Resolution Collection Bank (RCB) to receive the assets of failed credit cooperatives (both nominally under the control of the DICJ). As more financial institutions failed during 1997 and 1998, there were further amendments to the DICJ Law, and the HLAC and RCB were merged to form the Resolution and Collection Corporation (RCC) and the Bridge Bank of Japan in April 1999 and March 2002, respectively. The RCC had the combined functions of recovering loans from the former *jūsen* companies, the purchase and collection of non-performing loans from failed financial institutions, the purchase and collection of non-performing loans from sound financial institutions and subscribing shares to enhance capital adequacy of financial institutions. It was also charged with the pursuit of civil and criminal liabilities of former executives and debtors of failed financial institutions. Thus the DICJ, through its subsidiaries, acquired multiple functions relating to deposit insurance, to the disposal of non-performing loans and to the management and recapitalization of ailing financial institutions. What the

DICJ was not required to do was to take on the restructuring or 'revitalizing' of ailing corporate borrowers which was left to the private banks to achieve.

Despite these multiple institutional developments, criticism of slow reform in the financial sector grew. As a result, the countermeasures deflation package of February 2002 called on existing institutions (FSA, DIC and RCC) to become more aggressive in their purchase of NPLs. The responsibility for corporate restructuring still lay with the banks which were encouraged to set up corporate reconstruction funds ('deleveraging funds') with help from the Development Bank of Japan.[14] Even under the Takenaka plan there was no shifting of responsibility for corporate restructuring away from the banks to a central or government organization. But as the view that the private sector was making unacceptably slow progress on corporate restructuring grew, the government established a new public institution to take the lead. A Strategic Headquarters for Industrial Revival and Employment, headed by the Prime Minister, was put in place late in 2002, and subsequent bills established the Industrial Revitalization Corporation of Japan (IRCJ) to purchase loans of companies that could be rehabilitated and to supervise the restructuring. The IRCJ thus took on the role of buying bad loans from borrowers that could be expected to be rehabilitated within three years of the purchase of the loan. The structure is illustrated in Figure 1.

This moved Japan from a model of an asset-disposal type AMC to a restructuring one with an active role in corporate workouts. The IRCJ was successful in winding up a small number of large borrower

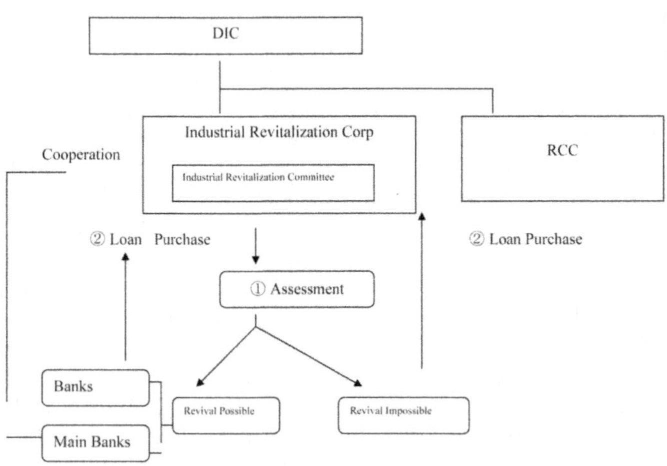

Figure 1: Industrial Revitalization Process by IRCJ. Source: *Nihon Keizai Shimbun*, 20 December 2002.

companies where banks had been unable to do the task themselves but, more importantly, its role was in due course superseded by the development of an active private market in corporate restructuring.

The other element of the new approach was the significant strengthening of the DICJ, giving it a clear mandate to close failed banks in addition to its role in managing impaired assets. The legislation of October 1998 made this clear by creating the mechanism to close down large banks, resulting in the nationalization of the LTCB and NCB (Nov 1998). Established in 1971, DIC Japan had been small, underfunded and known to have inadequate capital to cover insured deposits even when these were limited to the 10 million yen per deposit limit that applied before the blanket insurance. With the introduction of a blanket, hundred percent protection for all time and demand deposits, there was a big increase in the funding for DICJ, which rose steadily to 2003 when the model finally changed to stable, long-term funding. The DICJ is now supervised by MOF and FSA but the Governor and Deputy are appointed by the Prime Minister so that it has a significant degree of independence. The main function of the DICJ is now the winding up of failed and failing banks.

The process now in place is illustrated in Figure 2.

LEARNING LESSONS FROM JAPAN

With these reforms, Japan's system moved from a haphazard and non-transparent process of MOF-orchestrated, private workouts for failing banks to a system with clear intervention procedures. The failures of 1997–99 demonstrated how procedures would operate for both large and small banks and, significantly, showed that banks could be closed. Although the 2003 rescue of Resona Bank when it was known to be failing and was not obviously systemically important, set back the credibility of the system, Japan's system is arguably, now, a state-of-the-art procedure for dealing with failing banks. Surprisingly this cannot be said about many other countries including the UK and Australia.

Despite an active academic literature on the need for, and best design of, procedures to close banks when they fail, the 1998 comment by Aghion et al. remains distressingly applicable:

> In most recent banking crises bank regulators have been caught off their guard and have been forced to respond to the crisis in a hurry without the support of an institutional or legal framework designed to deal with bank failures. Unfortunately most bank regulations ... are concerned with the ex-ante problem of how to avoid bank failures and few rules have been devised on how to deal with bank failures when they occur.[15]

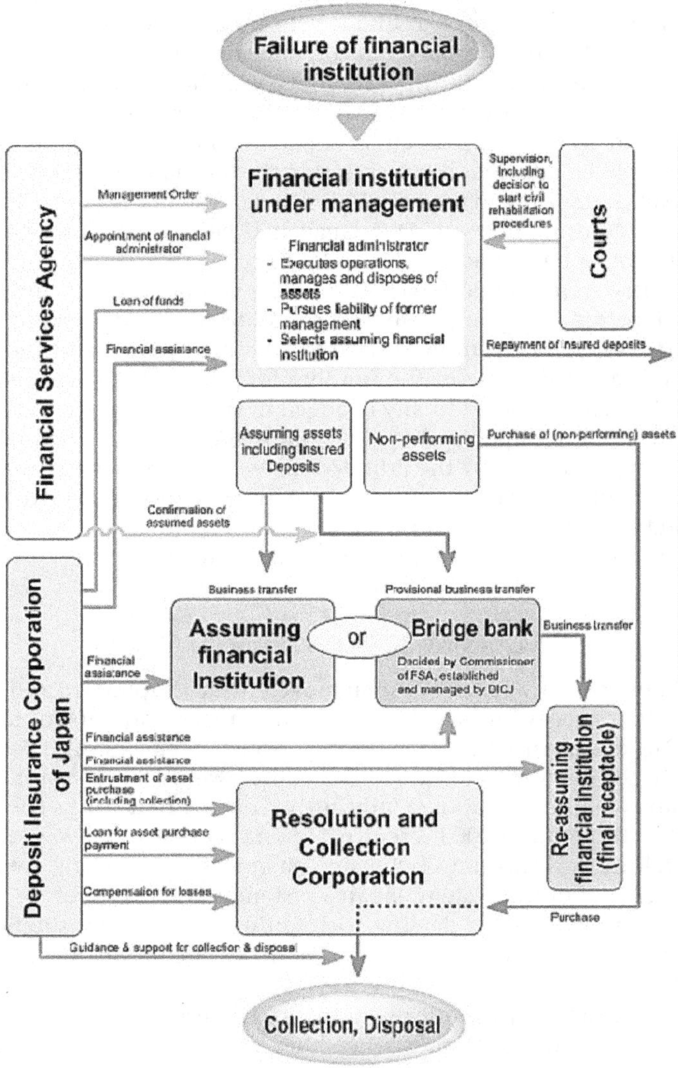

Figure 2: The Winding-up process. Source: Deposit Insurance Corporation of Japan, Annual Report, 2007.

Recent studies of those countries that do have resolution procedures show that, while here is variation in the institutional structure of bank failure resolution policies in different countries, those 'where the deposit insurer has the responsibility of intervening in failed banks and the power to revoke membership in the deposit insurance scheme are more stable and less likely to become insolvent'.[16] Thus, while Japan

Table 1 Policy Frameworks for Bank Failure Resolution

	Separate Bank Insolvency Law	Temporary Government control	Special Resolution Regime	Toxic Assets	Specific body for winding up banks?
Australia	No	Not clear	Not clear	Not clear	No
US	No	Bridge bank option. FDIC has control as receiver. Only occasionally used.	FDICA for deposit banks. System risk exemption. Compulsory receivership when below 2% leverage ratio within 90 days.	No prior arrangement existed. Troubled Asset Relief Program (TARP) introduced in response to 2008 crisis.	Yes, Federal Deposit Insurance Corporation (FDIC) under FDICIA.[1]
UK	Yes	Bridge bank and nationalization options. BoE has control as administrator or through exercise of stabilization powers. Nationalization used twice, bridge bank once, but government now major share owner in several banks after 2008.	Banking Act 2009 for banks and building societies. Stabilization powers.	No previous arrangement. Asset Protection Scheme now introduced.	Yes, BoE may wind up bank with green light from the FSA, under the Banking Act 2009.[2]

[1] Mayes, p 10.
[2] Mayes, p 20.

(continued)

	Separate Bank Insolvency Law	Temporary Government control	Special Resolution Regime	Toxic Assets	Specific body for winding up banks?
NZ	Yes	Use of public funds avoided through liquidation or Bank Creditor Recapitalization. Some public guarantee of a resolved bank. RBNZ has control through process of statutory management.	Statutory management.	None	No, statutory manager appointed.[3]
Japan	No	Bridge bank, nationalization and capital injection options. FSA appoints administrator (generally the DICJ). Three banks nationalized, capital injection totalling JPY 12 trillion.	Financial Crisis Management Council decides if 'systemic risk' exception applies. If so, blanket guarantee of deposits by DICJ is applied. Nationalization and capital injection options become available.	Collected and disposed of by the RCC, financed by the DICJ.	Yes, DICJ.[4]

Source: Adapted from Mayes, D.2009. "Banking Crisis Resolution Policy – Lessons from Recent Experience". CESifo Working Paper 2823 with additional information from World Bank. 2007. "Bank Regulation and Supervision", database of banking regulation, http://econ.worldbank.org/.

3 Mayes, p 28.

4 DICJ, 2008, Overview of Japan Deposit System, mimeo, p14.

may have taken some time to arrive at a best-practice design for bank bailout policy, it now has one, while several OECD countries still do not. As Table 1 shows, in comparison with US, UK, NZ and Australia, Japan has more of the pillars of a transparent crisis response policy.

Hoshi and Kashyap draw parallels between the crisis in Japan's financial system in the 1990s and the 2008 crisis in the US.[17] They set out eight lessons that can be learnt from Japan, all concerning what *not* to do. In the list are comments about Japan's approach to managing troubled assets based on the system as it was at the beginning of its crisis. There is no comment on how far Japan has travelled in the design of its system for handling a crisis should one arise now. Mayes reinforces the message of Aghion et al. a decade earlier, in lamenting how few countries had put in place the structures needed even when they could see a looming crisis, as in the example of Iceland.[18] Against that background it may now be time to start looking to Japan for some positive lessons, chief amongst them being not to wait until a bank crisis sets in before designing a strategy for managing it. Mayes also notes how few have a bankruptcy plan for banks. Many countries' experience, Japan's included, show that it is much harder to design a bankruptcy plan in the middle of a crisis because bank rescues are politically unpopular. On the other hand, disorderly closures are also very damaging. Without a systematic method for closing non-systemically-important banks, there is a danger of rescuing more banks than is necessary. Carefully considering the design of Japan's system could assist in the creation of such bankruptcy plans for banks.

CONCLUSION

It appears that Japan's financial system is no longer one that should be considered in decline. Furthermore, aspects of Japan's banking and financial regulation appear to be at the leading edge of OECD countries. The test of these systems of course only comes when the next crisis occurs, and Japan's current system has not yet been tested. In addition, political commitment to following the rules that have been set up remains a critical element of how well a regulatory system will function. The current government in Japan (the DPJ government elected in 2009) has not focused on banking policy in its first year in office and has shown some signs of a willingness to roll back the disciplines that have been put in place by previous reforms. It is not possible to conclude that Japan would easily weather another financial crisis but it is clear that policy structures in place are as good as they can be on paper.

NOTES

1 P. Krugman, 'The Return of Depression Economics', *Journal of Foreign Affairs*, 78, 1999; P. Krugman, K. Dominquez and K. Rogoff, 'It's Baaack:

Japan's Slump and the Return of the Liquidity Trap', *Brookings Papers on Economic Activity*, 1998(2), 1998, pp. 137–205; D. Citrin and A. Wolfson, 'Japan's Back!', *Finance and Development*, 43(2), 2006.

2 E. Rosengren, 'Addressing the Credit Crisis and Restructuring the Financial Regulatory System: Lessons from Japan', Speech given at the Institute of International Bankers Annual Washington Conference, Washington, D.C., 2 March 2009, http://www.bos.frb.org/news/speeches/rosengren/2009/030209.htm; M. Wolf, 'Japan's Lessons for a World of Balance-sheet Deflation', *Economist*, http://blogs.ft.com/economistsforum/2009/02/japan%E2%80%99s-lessons-for-a-world-of-balance-sheet-deflation/ 2009; B. Bernanke, and J. Rotemberg, 'The Japanese Banking Crisis: Where Did it Come From and How Will it End?', *NBER Macroeconomics Annual 1999*, 14(1), 1999, pp. 129–212.

3 Citrin and Wolfson, 'Japan's Back!'

4 Wolf, 'Japan's Lessons for a World of Balance-sheet Deflation', *Economist*, http://blogs.ft.com/economistsforum/2009/02/japan-lessons-for-a-world-of-balance-sheet-deflation/2009; R. C. Koo, *The Holy Grail of Macroeconomics*, Singapore: John Wiley & Sons, 2008.

5 T. Hoshi and A. K. Kashyap, 'Japan's Financial Crisis and Economic Stagnation', *Journal of Economic Perspectives*, 18(1) 2004, pp. 3–26.

6 M. Fukao, 'Japan's Lost Decade and Weaknesses in Its Corporate Governance Structure', Paper presented at a conference on *Analytical Issues in the Trade, Foreign Direct Investment and Macro/Financial Relations of the United States and Japan*, Keio University, May 2001.

7 For a different interpretation, see T. Ito and K. Harada, 'Bank Fragility in Japan', in M. Hutchison and F Westermann (eds) *Japan's Great Stagnation: Financial and Monetary Policy Lessons for Advanced Economies*, Cambridge, Mass.; London: MIT Press, 2006, pp. 33 - 61.

8 T. Hoshi and A. K. Kashyap, 'Will the U.S. Bank Recapitalization Succeed? Eight Lessons from Japan', *NBER Working Papers 14401*, National Bureau of Economic Research, 2008.

9 'FSA Lacks Manpower to Carry Out Increased Powers,' *Nikkei Financial Daily*, 2003.

10 M. Dado and D. Klingebiel, 'Decentralized Creditor-led Corporate Restructuring: Cross Country Experience', *World Bank Policy Research Working Paper 2901*, Washington: World Bank, 2002.

11 D. Klingebiel, 'The Use of Asset Management Companies in the Resolution of Banking Crises: Cross-Country Experience', *Policy Research Working Paper 2284*, World Bank, 2000, p. 4.

12 C-J, Lindgren and T. Balino et al., 'Financial Sector Crisis and Restructuring: Lessons from Asia', *Occasional Paper 188*, Washington: IMF, 1999.

13 Klingebiel, 'The Use of Asset Management Companies', p. 21.

14 'The FSA has requested major banks to take the following actions; expeditious resolution of problem enterprises by...establishment of reconstruction plans...through legal procedures... [and] accelerated disposal of NPLs ... to RCC ... and active utilization of corporate

reconstruction funds (deleveraging funds).' Financial Services Agency, 'Prompt Countermeasures to Deflation', Tokyo, 2002.

[15] P. Aghion, P. Bolton and S. Fries, 'Optimal Design of Bank Bailouts: The Case of Transition Economies', European Bank for Reconstruction and Development, *Working Paper 32*, 1998, p. 1.

[16] T. Beck, and L. Laeven, 'Resolution of Failed Banks by Deposit Insurers: Cross-country Evidence', *Policy Research Working Papers 3920*, Washington, D.C.: World Bank, 2006.

[17] Hoshi and Kasyap, 'Will the U.S. Bank Recapitalization Succeed?'.

[18] D. Mayes, 'Banking Crisis Resolution Policy – Lessons from Recent Experience', *CESIfo Working Paper No 2823*, 2009.

2

Political Earthquake in Japan: How Much of a Difference Will it Make?

J.A.A. STOCKWIN

INTRODUCTION: CONCERNING EARTHQUAKES

Earthquakes are part of the normal fabric of Japanese life, even part of the culture of Japan. Anyone who has stayed in Japan for some time will have experienced buildings shaking, often noisily. Most earthquakes do little damage, but occasionally they are deadly. 'Ordinary' earthquakes are so much part of the fabric of life that some Japanese spending a year or more abroad will confess to their bemused hosts that they feel 'nostalgic for earthquakes'.

It therefore might seem paradoxical that until 30 August 2009 Japan had been without a real political 'earthquake' for well over half a century. For year after year, the same self-perpetuating coterie of politicians, attached to the ever dominant Liberal Democratic Party (LDP), and linked in a complex web of iron triangles with powerful interest groups and even more powerful government ministries and agencies, were able to persuade a satisfied, apathetic or frustrated electorate that 'there is no alternative'[1] to voting for the only party they had ever known in government. To continue the geological analogy, when a tectonic plate tries to move under another plate, but for years is blocked and cannot do so, the accumulation of frustrated energy becomes so great that you have a super-earthquake that re-formulates the ground under your feet. In 2009 it is eighty-six years since the Great Kantō Earthquake that destroyed much of Tokyo and Yokohama, and experts warn that the next 'big one' is overdue (therefore extremely big) – as they have been warning for some decades.

What happened on 30 August 2009 was an electoral 'super-earthquake', though how far it is likely to prove a political displacement of equal magnitude remains an open question. Let us start with the figures: In the House of Representatives elections held on 11 September 2005 the Liberal Democrats won 296 seats (out of 480), and the Democratic Party (DPJ) 113. In the 2009 elections the DPJ won 308 seats and the LDP 119. The Kōmeitō, which had been the coalition partner of the LDP for over a decade, was reduced from 31 seats to 21. Admittedly, the 2005 lower house elections had been an exceptionally good result for the LDP, and had been a severe setback for the DPJ, which previously had been adding to its seat total from election to election. Koizumi Junichirō, Prime Minister from April 2001 to September 2006, had just expelled the privatization rebels from the LDP and run alternative individuals (the 'assassins', or 'Koizumi's children') as candidates in their stead. This won over many votes to the LDP, a party that Koizumi, ironically, had once said he wished to smash (*bukkowasu*). The previous elections, held in November 2003, represent a more typical pattern,[2] and the 2005 elections in retrospect might be seen as the 'last fling' of the LDP.

THE SIGNIFICANCE OF 30 AUGUST

The argument of this chapter is that what happened on 30 August 2009 does indeed represent a political, as well as an electoral, earthquake. The new Government faces huge challenges, in particular the legacy of nearly two decades of economic stagnation and what was an increasingly dysfunctional politico-economic system. In some ways, the composition of the DPJ, and the views to be found within it, are not entirely different from those of the LDP, though in broad terms, the balance within it is somewhat more to the left. The future cohesion of the DPJ remains an issue. Nevertheless, it appears most plausible that a crucial political shift is occurring

There are four basic reasons for this belief.

The first derives from a brief analysis of LDP electoral dominance since it was founded in November 1955. In the almost fifty-four years to September 2009 the LDP governed alone for approximately thirty-five years, the LDP was the largest party in coalition governments for eighteen years, and it was out of office entirely for just eleven months (August 1993 to June 1994). As the price of returning to power after the non-LDP coalition governments of 1993–4, it had to offer the post of prime minister to a Socialist, Murayama Tomiichi, and the legislative achievements of the coalition governments in power between August 1973 and January 1976 should not be underestimated.[3] After a year and a half the LDP resumed its firm dominance of the House of Representatives, even though it still needed coalition partners, lacking from 1989 a clear House of Councillors majority. The upper house was able to veto legislation following Opposition victory in the upper house elections of July 2007 – in retrospect the harbinger of the

2009 lower house result – which led to the *nejire kokkai*, or 'twisted Diet'.[4]

Even so, the LDP has been exceptionally dominant, by any comparison of democracies with free and fair elections, over Japanese electoral politics. The change of government in 2009 is a unique event in postwar political history, with the possible exception of the lower house general elections of January 1949.

It is worth comparing this record with other systems based on the Westminster model. Australia since 1945 has seen six complete changes of government from the Australian Labor Party (ALP) to the coalition of Liberal and National (formerly Country) Parties, and vice versa. The longest period without a change of government was the 23 years between 1949, when the Chifley Labour Government fell, to 1972, when the Whitlam Labour Government was elected. The main reason why the ALP was out of power so long was that it split in the late 1950s and the breakaway Democratic Labour Party (DLP) was able to use the preferential system of voting to block a return to power by the ALP. That, however, was an exceptional period.

In the United Kingdom, things have been remarkably similar: since the Labour Party victory in 1945 bringing the formation of the Attlee Government which lasted until 1951, government has moved from the Labour Party to the Conservative Party, or from the Conservative Party to the Labour Party, on six separate occasions. The longest continuous period in office was by the Conservative Party for eighteen years between 1979 and 1997. Here again, Labour was in difficulties because it split in 1981 with the formation of the Social Democratic Party. But the important point is that both major parties have governed for substantial periods. In the sixty-four years since 1945 the Conservative Party has held office for approximately thirty-five years and the Labour Party for about twenty-nine years. There have been no coalition governments.

Thus both the Australian and British electorates have recurrent experience of removing a government from office and replacing it by its alternative. Neither system is wholly based on 'alternation in power', but when one party takes over from another, this is seen as part of the normal political process. In Britain, a general election must be held in the first half of 2010, when the Conservatives may well replace Labour in government. But if this happens, it will hardly be seen as a political earthquake, since on many issues their policies appear similar,[5] and because the electorate is used to experiencing changes of government.

The second reason for emphasizing the crucial importance of the 2009 shift is that finally the ever-patient Japanese electorate has spoken. Over the past two decades or so of economic under-performance, it has not been uncommon to hear observers of the Japanese political scene[6] complain that the electorate is far too complacent about economic failures, loss of industrial capital and rising unemployment, demographic decline, social pathologies such as *hikikomori* (social withdrawal), high levels of suicide, *freeters* (young people working at casual dead-end jobs) and NEETs (those not in employment, education or training), as well as policy mistakes and ideological bigotry, widespread corruption and declining Japanese international prestige in the face of the rise of China.[7]

A third reason lies simply in the severe economic problems facing Japan, and the pressing need for structural reform of decision making processes to be able to tackle such problems. The decisive majority won by the DPJ gives it a clear mandate to introduce innovative policies and to confront vested interests. Japan faces a serious problem of excessive government debt, built up over years of government stimulus packages and wasteful expenditure.[8] The new Government's efforts are helped by a sustained recovery in industrial output, beginning in April 2009, after a collapse in late 2008 and early 2009.

The fourth reason is the fact that the Hatoyama Government is moving to concentrate power in its own hands, through a structural reform of the processes of decision making that would relegate the government bureaucracy to the position of adviser and servant of the elected representatives of the people, rather than as policy-maker.

CONVERGENCE WITH, THEN DIVERGENCE FROM, THE WESTMINSTER MODEL

Structurally, the Japanese political system that emerged from the Occupation between 1945 and 1952 has more in common with the Westminster model than with the political system of the United States.[9] Whereas the US separates powers between the Executive (the President and his officials), elected separately from the Legislature (the two houses of Congress), in Britain and Australia a general election for the lower house of Parliament is in effect an election for both the Legislature and the Executive – both Parliament and Government. In this crucial respect, the Japanese system cleaves to the Westminster, not the Washington, model. Thus in Australia, the UK and Japan, the electorate elects members of Parliament, almost all these members belong to parties, the majority party or parties form a government (Prime Minister and Cabinet), which forms the executive together with the non-elected government bureaucracy.

General MacArthur understood that the system that had developed under the Meiji Constitution of 1889 lacked clear lines of authority, given that the Emperor, even before 1945, for the most part did not exercise real power. This had allowed the armed forces to usurp power in the 1930s, since the Constitution provided no effective obstacle to their doing so. A cabinet government system based on the Westminster model, would concentrate power sufficiently to frustrate this kind of development. Of course, in pre-war Japan there had been a prime minister, a cabinet and a parliament, but these had been far weaker than in the British system of the same period.[10]

The political system that emerged from the Occupation melded the old and the new, but the essential principles of the Westminster model were fixed in place. The accompanying extension of personal freedoms was ambitious, in particular the freedom to participate in politics and to speak and write freely about political matters. Most of the apparatus of control from the pre-war system was removed.

Beginning in the 1950s, however, the political system of Japan came to diverge in certain important respects from the Westminster model.

The first divergence, already mentioned, is the long-term electoral and political dominance of a single party, the LDP. There may be advantages in having one party continuously in power over a very long period. It may create stability and facilitate long-term planning, in the confident knowledge that policy priorities are not likely to change suddenly with a change of party in power. But there are also strong contrary arguments. Whenever one party is in power for a long time, corruption tends to emerge, with entrenched interests linked to the ruling party disproportionately asserting their influence. Moreover, when a party has been in power for many years, the party comes to find it difficult to examine its own policy record critically, or to take radical new initiatives that might imply criticism of that record. The most effective way of changing course is to bring in a new team. It is also much easier to have a proper debate about the merits of different policy choices if changes of party in power mean that different policies have actually been tried.

A second point of divergence from the practice of the Westminster model relates to opposition parties. When a party or coalition of parties win an election, the party or parties in opposition will have lost. But when opposition parties lose election after election, then most likely, either the electoral system is rigged against them, or the opposition as a whole is dysfunctional. It is true that there has been over-representation of rural electorates and under-representation of big city electorates in the Japanese case.[11] Yet, this seems to be a much less important reason for Japan's single party dominance than the failure of opposition parties, until the formation and development of the DPJ, to provide effective opposition or to sell themselves as a potential future government. This was particularly true of the former Japan Socialist Party (JSP), now Social Democratic Party (SDP), the largest party of opposition up to the mid-1990s. For many years it gave the impression that it was content with opposition status and was rather scared of having to govern the country. Other opposition parties up to the 1990s were mostly sectional, religious or ideological groups, incapable of mobilizing those outside their particular limited sphere of influence. Starting, however, in the chaotic party political atmosphere of the 1990s, plans were initiated to form a genuinely competitive party of opposition, determined to replace the ruling party as the government of Japan. The first attempt, the *Shinshintō* (New Frontier Party, or literally 'New Progress Party), proved abortive and was disbanded in December 1997. But the Democratic Party, founded in 1996 and then re-founded with an expanded base in 1998, proved much more successful. The August 2009 electoral result confirms just how far the party could come in thirteen years.

A third way in which Japan has diverged from the Westminster model (though it never really adhered to it) is in the degree of political influence and power in the hands of government ministries and their officials. In Australia and Britain senior government officials exercise influence, but the principle that civil servants advise ministers and implement ministers' decisions, whereas ministers (who are all politicians) make policy decisions, is taken very seriously and for the most part followed. In Japan, many decisions have been made by government officials and endorsed by ministers. For many years weekly cabinet meetings were preceded by meetings of the permanent heads (*jimu jikan*) of the principal ministries, which took decisions that were simply endorsed by cabinet. The Hatoyama Government has now abolished this practice. Bureaucratic influence was extended into a range of public and private institutions through *amakudari*, or 'descent from heaven' by retired public servants, though the new Government is seeking to abolish it. It is also forbidding government officials from giving press conferences without political authorization. In sum, the new Government is pledged to reduce the power of the government bureaucracy and assert the dominance of elected politicians over policy making. How far they will succeed in this, given their political inexperience and consequent need for advice from officials remains to be seen.

A fourth divergence relates to the effective power of the prime minister. Australia, in the sixty-four years from 1945 to 2009, from Chifley to Rudd, has had eleven prime ministers. The UK, from Attlee to Brown, has had twelve. By contrast Japan, from Higashikuni to Hatoyama, has enjoyed the services of no less than thirty-one. This is symptomatic of a broader problem, namely that many political leaders (ministers as well as prime ministers) were in power for too short a time to impose their influence on policy. There were exceptions (Koizumi, for instance), but it is worth noting that the previous three prime ministers lasted a year each, with September as the month when you suddenly find a new prime minister in office. This shift happened in September of 2006, 2007, 2008, and for the first time with a change of party in office, in 2009. Connected with this was the great influence exercised by internal LDP committees over policy making, further reducing the policy making autonomy of the prime minister and cabinet.

A fifth divergence concerns the very Japanese institution known as *habatsu* and usually translated as 'faction'. Parties in Australia and the UK often contain factions, but for the most part factions are loosely structured groups professing a particular ideology or set of policy preferences. Power-oriented factions are also not unknown, and may overlap with the previous type. But in Japan, and most particularly within the LDP, *habatsu* have been an integral – if unofficial – part of the way a party operates. They have offices, elect their leaders, produce in-house publications, raise political funds and bargain to get their members cabinet and party positions. Under the pre-1994 lower house electoral system (*chūsenkyokusei*, or 'medium-sized district system'), the fact that the LDP could expect to elect two, three or even four members in many multi-member electoral districts meant that LDP candidates were fighting each other as well as fighting candidates from other parties, and in consequence each LDP candidate in the same district would derive support from a different faction. Under the current lower house electoral system, which is a mixture of single-member districts and proportional representation (PR) blocs, the electoral rationale for *habatsu* has somewhat declined, but they still exist in the LDP, and are identifiable in the DPJ as well, where they are more loosely structured.

A sixth divergence from the practice of the Westminster model is the Japanese phenomenon of 'dynastic' politicians, or political families. Different members of the same family going into politics are not unknown in Australia or the UK, but in both countries it is extremely rare for a politician to 'inherit' a seat from a relative.[12] In Japan, by contrast, this is a remarkably widespread pattern, most especially in the LDP, where as many as 35–40 per cent of sitting members of the House of Representatives have been relatives of previous members who had represented the same districts. In the LDP especially, there has been a structural reason for political dynasties. With the crucial electoral importance of personal political machines (*kōenkai*)[13] in electoral districts, the easiest way to enter Parliament under the LDP banner is to 'inherit' a *kōenkai*. It is much more difficult to build one up from scratch. Indeed, the secretary of a Diet member may well 'inherit' that member's *kōenkai* and be elected in the same district after the member retires or dies. The secretary may be considered part of the 'extended family' of the former member. The new Prime Minister, Hatoyama Yukio, is a member of a famous political family, since his grandfather was Prime Minister in the 1950s and his father was Foreign Minister in the 1960s, while his brother is an LDP Diet member and nephew an aspiring politician. On the other hand his Cabinet contains only two dynastic politicians, whereas that of his immediate LDP predecessor, Asō Tarō, included ten.

There is a seventh, and final, way in which the patterns of the Japanese political system have diverged from the practice of the Westminster model. At general elections in both Australia and the UK, voters generally vote for a party rather than for a candidate, and on issues of national policy rather than local policy, though there are of course exceptions. It is rare in the politics of Australia or the UK for a candidate unaffiliated with any party to be elected to Parliament. By contrast, Japanese voters have had (in the past at least) a strong tendency to vote for a candidate rather than for a party, and on local rather than on national issues.

To sum up these seven elements of divergence from the Westminster model, the politics of Japan came to be based in practice on an extensive network of 'iron triangles', whereby a group of political operators in the LDP, in government departments and from private interests, worked together over a long period to maintain policies that were in line with the views and interests of those groups. Iron triangles are highly conservative institutions, deeply entrenched and difficult to shift, potentially or actually corrupt, and largely excluding interests that are outside the power system that has been constructed in this particular policy area. Put simply, the iron triangles are undemocratic. The new Government seems determined to tackle head-on such undemocratic institutions and practices. A day or two after the Government's formation, the newly appointed Transport and Construction Minister, Maehara Seiji, halted building of the contentious Yanba dam project in Gunma and the Kawabegawa dam project in Kumamoto. He suspended for re-assessment a total of 143 dam constructions works, some in the planning stage and some already under construction, so that a proper cost-benefit analysis could be made, and local interests consulted.[14] The extent of the challenges facing the Government in trying to curb unproductive expenditure is shown by the subsequent uproar in Gunma, where the cessation of work on the Yanba dam project was expected to increase local unemployment and disrupt various local interests.

POLITICAL EVOLUTION, 1990s TO 2009

The new Government that came into office on 16 September 2009, following the elections of 30 August, did not have to deal with a wholly unreformed system. Significant changes had taken place, though in a process of stops and starts, since the LDP briefly lost power in 1993–4. There had been important evolution in five principal areas.

First, the one substantial achievement of the 1993–4 coalition governments was a major revision of the lower house electoral system. The former system, dating back to the 1920s, was based on multi-member districts and a single non-transferable vote. It was replaced by a new system, in which 300 seats are elected from single-member districts (again, with no vote transfer), and 180 (at first 200) seats are elected by proportional representation from eleven regional blocs. The original purpose of the reform was to make voters think more in terms of party and less in terms of the merits of a particular candidate, and to orient politics more towards national policy issues and less towards issues that are merely local. The interests of smaller parties and new candidates were to be protected through the 180 PR seats. The reform was also designed to facilitate the emergence of a viable opposition party, capable of aggregating diverse interests, and eventually capable of taking over the reins of government.

This last aim has finally been realized, fifteen years after the reform was originally introduced. Reaching this point required a journey through the chaotic politics of the mid-to-late 1990s, the Koizumi period of the early-to-mid 2000s, and finally the period of annual prime ministers from September 2006 to September 2009. The Democratic Party pioneered the issuing of an election 'manifesto', setting out the aims of party policy – a practice apparently borrowed from British parties. The focus of recent elections does appear to be on party rather than on candidate, and on national rather than local issues, revealing also unprecedented volatility in the voting behaviour of metropolitan electorates in particular. Voters in Tokyo and other big cities who heavily favoured Koizumi in 2005 shifted over in huge numbers to the DPJ in 2009. A possible common factor in electoral behaviour between the two elections was voters' desire to break away from 'politics as usual'.

Connected with this is an increase in the number of women elected to the House of Representatives. In the 2009 elections, out of the 480 members elected, fifty-four (of which forty from the DPJ) were women, representing 11.3 per cent of the total, the first time that the percentage of women in the lower house has risen to double figures.

A second aspect of the system that had already changed to some extent over the past few years was the importance and role of LDP *habatsu*. Under the old electoral system *habatsu* were sustained by contests between different LDP candidates fighting the same electoral districts. This rationale largely disappeared with the change to the new electoral system. A tightening of laws governing electoral funding put in place in the mid-1990s also made it more difficult for factions to exercise influence over parliamentary candidates and members through the provision of electoral funds. On constructing his first cabinet in 2001, Koizumi was able largely to ignore the demands of rival factions. Nevertheless, factions did not disappear, though the ideological differences between them became clearer. The appointment of Mori Yoshirō as Prime Minister in April 2000 signalled a shift from the conservative but rather pragmatic policy approaches of the faction founded by Tanaka Kakuei in the early 1970s, to the more ideologically right wing policy line of the faction founded by his great rival, Fukuda Takeo, also in the 1970s.

A third force for change from the 1990s onwards has been a gradual reduction in the prestige and effective influence of government ministries and of their officials. The practice of senior government officials answering questions in Parliament on behalf of ministers was largely abolished in the late 1990s. From January 2001, the number of ministries and agencies of government was substantially reduced by amalgamation and restructuring, in order to reduce the scope for interdepartmental rivalries. At the same time the power of prime minister and cabinet was enhanced by the formation of the Cabinet Office (*naikakufu*). This reform was a stroke of luck for Koizumi, who became Prime Minister three months later, and helped him assert control over key aspects of economic policy. From the 1990s, the reputation of some ministries had suffered from corruption charges, tarnishing the image of government officials as selfless and dedicated servants of the State. This was compounded when gross inefficiencies were found in some areas of administration, including the revelation that some fifty million pension records were inaccurate or lost, which has probably done more to harm bureaucratic reputations than any other issue in recent decades. Nevertheless, bureaucratic power remains strong in many areas of policy, and the iron triangles I mentioned earlier still exert an influence that is difficult to combat. The Democratic Party in its manifesto for the 2009 elections targeted excessive bureaucratic power, and once in office initiated measures to assert the primacy of the people's elected representatives over unelected government officials.

Fourth, Koizumi ensured his control of key aspects of economic policy by his control of the Council on Economic and Fiscal Policy (*keizai zaisei shimon kaigi*). He could thus bypass interference from LDP committees as well as from bureaucratic interests.

Fifth and finally, substantive reforms were undertaken under Koizumi (through the CEFP) to improve the economic situation by ridding the banks of their toxic debt that had accumulated after the collapse of the bubble economy at the beginning of the 1990s. Economic recovery seemed to be under way from about 2004, but was dealt a heavy blow by the onset of the global recession from October 2008. As we have seen, by the end of 2009 industrial output was steadily improving.

ELECTORAL EARTHQUAKE INTO POLITICAL REVOLUTION?

A key decision of the new government, formed on 16 September 2009, was to establish a National Strategy Bureau (*kokka senryaku kaigi*), headed by Kan Naoto and an Administrative Renovation Council (*gyōsei sasshin kaigi*), headed by Sengoku Yoshito. Both these bodies were geared towards budget making, and designed to centralize policy making in the Prime Minister and Cabinet. They are reminiscent of Koizumi's Council on Economic and Fiscal Policy.

The new Government is in fact a three-party coalition, including, apart from the DPJ with its 308 seats in the lower house, the small Social Democratic Party, with seven seats, and the even smaller People's New Party (PNP), with three. The two small parties were invited to join in order to boost the Government's numbers in the House of Councillors, which can block much of the legislation it receives from the House of Representatives.[15] As 'payment' for joining the Government, these two mini-parties were allocated one portfolio each. The leader of the SDP, Fukushima Mizuho, is in charge of policy towards consumers and policy to combat the low birth rate, continuing the tradition that the task of stemming population decline should go to a woman. With supreme irony, since he was the leader of the rebellion within the LDP in 2005 against the Koizumi project to privatize postal services, the PNP leader, Kamei Shizuka, has been put in charge of postal services reform. The new Government had insisted that it wished to modify radically the liberalization of postal services initiated four years previously by Koizumi. Many complaints had been received about a decline in the quality of service at local postal branches. Following intense pressure from the Government, the President of the Postal Services holding company, Nishikawa Yoshifumi, a liberalizing enthusiast, resigned on 19 October.[16] He was speedily replaced by Saitō Jirō, who had earlier been Administrative Vice-Minister of the Ministry of Finance. His appointment drew concerns that an ex-bureaucrat had been appointed to such a politically sensitive post, but the Prime Minister countered that he was the most qualified person for the position.[17]

This episode throws an interesting light on the character of the new Government, and on possible contradictions in its policy ambitions. On the one hand, it is actively tackling the budgeting process, slashing many budgets that had previously been untouchable because they constituted the territory of privileged interests. This involves cutting back on wasteful infrastructure projects that gave Japan the reputation of a 'Construction State'.[18] Undoubtedly, huge savings can be made by these endeavours. On the other hand, such savings are earmarked for welfare projects that include generous grants to mothers for child rearing and to families for education, including abolishing fees for senior high schools (students aged fifteen to eighteen). Plans to improve health care facilities include the long term aim of doubling the supply of doctors. In conditions of extreme budgetary constraint, it is difficult to see how these aims will be achieved without still further increasing the national debt.

A particular example of where different policies appear to contradict each other relates to motorway charges and policies to improve the environment. The Government proposed to reduce, and ultimately abolish, motorway (*kōsoku dōro*) tolls, but also aimed for ambitious reductions in carbon emissions by 2020. But it was unclear how a policy that must surely increase motorway traffic can avoid augmenting carbon emissions, at least in the short term before cleaner engines are perfected. Once in power, the new Government has moved to introduce a more nuanced system that would advantage micro-cars with small engines, as well as long distance trucks, but penalize larger passenger cars.[19]

In these areas, the DPJ was appealing to a disillusioned electorate, badly affected by the recession and inadequate facilities for personal and family welfare. It also understood that a decline in local postal services entailed by Koizumi's drive for privatization caused widespread resentment. Now that it is running the country, it has to face these potential contradictions. Nevertheless, the new Government is pursuing a radical approach with undiminished enthusiasm. This is logical from an electoral point of view, because the DPJ needs a convincing win in the House of Councillors elections of July 2010 in order to establish a majority for its coalition in the upper house. It is well aware how fickle the electorate may be currently, and how great is the risk of electoral defeat if the Government is seen to be backsliding from its manifesto commitments.

On foreign policy, at the time of the elections it appeared that the new government might begin to disengage from its military-strategic relationship with the United States. In an article in the Japanese-language journal *Voice*, Hatoyama Yukio appeared to suggest that his government would seek to roll back the convergence in Japan-US relations that had occurred over the past decade.[20] An abbreviated version of the article was later translated in the *New York Times*, and caused anxiety in US government circles.

While stating that the Japan-US security relationship was 'obviously an important pillar of Japanese foreign policy', he argued that 'we must not forget our identity as a State located in Asia'. Speaking of Asia as economically dynamic and increasingly integrated, he suggested that the US dollar's hegemony might not last for ever, that with failure in Iraq and the US financial crisis, American-led globalization was ending and the world was moving from American dominance to multi-polarity. He qualified this by writing that no currency could easily replace the US dollar, nor was it clear what the new global architecture would look like. American influence might be declining, but for the next two or three years the US would remain the leading world power. China would soon overtake Japan economically, and Japan would be sandwiched between the United States, fighting to remain the global hegemon, and China, battling to become the hegemon. His conclusion was cautious and pessimistic about Japan's foreign policy dilemmas, rather than signalling radical changes in orientation.[21]

It is too soon to say that Japanese relations with the United States will be transformed by the change of government in Tokyo, though the atmosphere is evolving. US bases on Okinawa remain a contentious issue, and Hatoyama (to US annoyance) has postponed until mid-2010 a decision whether to transfer the Futenma base elsewhere on the island, remove it to Guam, or put it elsewhere in Japan. A shift in emphasis towards closer involvement in regional organizations in East and South-East Asia is likely. Relations between Japan and China had already improved after Koizumi – disliked by the Chinese Government – had stepped down, and the relationship may be further consolidated. Japanese relations with the two Koreas appear unlikely to change fundamentally, barring a collapse of the North Korean regime (something that should not be ruled out of consideration, but carefully prepared for). The territorial dispute over the southern Kurile islands (Chishima shotō) between Japan and Russia may possibly come onto the active agenda of the new Government. It was Hatoyama Ichirō, grandfather of the present Prime Minister, who negotiated an agreement with the former Soviet Union in 1956, and it is possible that the Hatoyama name might open doors in Moscow. But the Russian position on the territorial issue shows scant signs of softening. A theoretical possibility is that Russia, in trouble economically and demographically, might at some stage seek to use Japan as a counterweight to China and thus make concessions on the southern Kuriles.

The DPJ in its manifesto, and the new Government since it was formed, have targeted a range of social issues. A broad but increasingly pressing problem – evident from the 1970s – is demographic decline. The Japanese population has peaked at around 127 million, and if current trends continue, it may soon start to decline rapidly, falling perhaps to 100 million by mid-century. The key phrase is 'if current trends continue', and government policy could perhaps bring about changes in behaviour, and thus in population trends. The ambitious plans of the new Government to increase child benefit, and to improve child-minding facilities, go far beyond anything contemplated by governments led by the LDP. A more radical policy would be to ease restrictions on immigration. The numbers of immigrants needed to maintain the population at its present level over the long term would be entirely unacceptable politically, but there is considerable scope for easing bottlenecks in areas such as health and welfare. Immigration has tended to be a taboo subject for politicians who think that to accept more immigrants would offend a public wary of diluting Japanese cultural norms. Those of Japanese descent (*nikkeijin*) from Brazil and elsewhere in Latin America find it relatively easy to enter and work in Japan. They look Japanese, but they think in Portuguese (or Spanish) and their mind-set is essentially Latin American, rejoicing in the carnavalesque aspects of life. They lend colour to Japanese society (and are well accepted for that) just as immigrants from other Asian countries or elsewhere would do if immigration restrictions were gradually relaxed.

Some other social areas could invite reform, should the new Government decide to give them priority. Police procedure in criminal cases, with its reliance on the extraction of confessions from suspects, sometimes with physical and mental coercion, and a harsh regime in prisons, may perhaps have reduced the crime rate, but at the cost of widespread infringements of internationally accepted human rights. Even though much of the population favours retention of the death penalty, there are excellent arguments against it which have led to its abolition throughout Europe over the past forty years. If these arguments were to be vigorously expressed in an education campaign by the Hatoyama Government, coupled with a suspension of executions, to provoke a national debate, then perhaps total abolition might eventually become possible. Previous governments have wisely maintained extremely tight gun control, and it is to be hoped that this policy will be fully preserved and strengthened.

A much contested issue since the 1950s is constitutional revision. The Koizumi and Abe Governments (2001–7) tried hard to promote a process leading to revision. As a result, a law was passed providing for a constitutional referendum, to come into force in May 2010. But with Fukuda replacing Abe as Prime Minister in 2007, the steam went out of the revision project, and it receded to the back of the agenda. There are constitutional revisionists in the DPJ, but there is little sign that the new Government, with an over-full agenda and internal divisions on the Constitution, will be keen to walk across this uncomfortable carpet of nails.

What are the prospects for political stability and cohesion in the new Government? The DPJ, like the LDP, contains a wide range of political opinion, and the views of the two parties overlap. DPJ politicians come from a variety of backgrounds, from the former Japan Socialist Party to the LDP itself. Some worry that the party might not remain together for long as a cohesive whole. But most of the younger members of the new parliamentary intake have only ever belonged to the DPJ, which is the only party they have known. There is also concern that strife may break out between the Prime Minister and his predecessor as party leader, Ozawa Ichirō, whose roots are in the former Tanaka faction of the LDP. For the time being, they have devised a division of labour between them, with Hatoyama working on general policy and Ozawa preparing the party for the next House of Councillors elections in July 2010.[22] The Hatoyama-Ozawa relationship raises the question of DPJ interference in policy making by government, reminiscent of a similar problem under the LDP. Both, moreover, are under investigation over political expenses.[23]

A final important question relates to the LDP and its future. For healthy politics, any government needs an opposition capable of examining and criticizing its policies. The LDP has to reform itself to become an effective opposition – a role it is not used to playing. The party has appointed a moderate, Tanigaki Sadakazu, to succeed Asō Tarō as its leader. It may take him and his team several years to modernize the party, but it is extremely important that this should happen. Without it, an LDP, starved of the oxygen of power, could wither away, like the Italian *Democristiana* in the early 1990s, and Japan once again will be without an effective party of opposition.

CONCLUSIONS

The new Government has presented an ambitious programme of reform, whose implementation presents enormous challenges. It is attempting bold and radical measures to restore the economy to health after two decades of lacklustre economic performance. The Government perceives that the root of the problem lies in the privileged status of special interest networks, and that public expenditure unduly favouring such interests needs to be slashed. But it also realizes that large numbers of ordinary people have been hurt by failed or misdirected policies in the past, and that it needs to tackle pressing social issues. It is trying to divert funding away from projects favouring special interests towards the genuine interests of ordinary people struggling to make a living and bring up their families. But to make a real difference, it needs to redirect funds on a huge scale, and with State finances in great difficulty, the national debt may spiral further out of control. This is clearly not an easy time to increase public spending, even if extra resources become available through a radical exercise in cutting wasteful expenditure.

Visitors to Japan who travel down the country on the *Shinkansen*, or contemplate the splendour of Roppongi Hills in downtown Tokyo take away with them the reasonable impression that Japan is a supermodern society. But in fact, it is a society suffering from a raft of problems accentuated by a dysfunctional political system over many years. Serious political change, which seemed about to happen in the 1990s, dribbled away into the sand, no doubt because the runaway boom of the late 1980s was too recent a memory. The economic and other problems facing Japan remain daunting. The new Government apparently understands their seriousness, but whether its remedies will work remains moot.

What happened on 30 August 2009 was an electoral earthquake of staggering proportions. Eda Satsuki, Speaker of the House of Councillors since 2007, argues that Japan has had three revolutions: the Meiji Restoration of 1868 and its aftermath, the Occupation period and the period beginning in 2009, which might turn out to be the most important.[24] Whether the third revolution can fulfil the ambitious expectations vested in it remains unanswered, but the present writer remains very cautiously optimistic.

NOTES

1 A phrase used by Margaret Thatcher in the 1980s to characterize her policies. It was abbreviated to TINA.

2 In November 2003 the LDP won 237 seats and the DPJ 177.

3 Luke Nottage, 'The New DPJ Government in Japan: Implications for Law Reform', in Japanese Law and the Asia-Pacific: http//blogs.usyd.edu.au/japaneselaw/2009/09/the_new_dpj_government.html (copy received from author).

4 In the situation it faced between July 2007 and September 2009, the coalition Government of LDP and Kōmeitō could technically override an upper house veto over its legislative proposals, because it enjoyed the required two-thirds majority to do so. Politically, however, this was an extremely difficult exercise to bring off.

5 But not all, however: Conservative Party policies on relations with the European Union have diverged to a position far to the right of the main stream.

6 For instance Glen Fukushima, in a discussion at the Foreign Correspondents Club of Japan, 30 March 2009.

7 It is widely expected that the size of the Chinese economy will surpass that of Japan in 2010 or 2011, relegating Japan from second to third place after the US and China. Of course, China has more than ten times Japan's population, so China's standard of living remains much lower than that of Japan.

8 Japanese government debt as a percentage of GDP, forecast for 2009, was 187 per cent. The comparable figure for the United Kingdom was 67.8 per cent. *International Herald Tribune*, 21 October 2009, citing as sources the IMF, the Japanese Government and the US Congressional Budget Office. But the debt is mostly internal and households have much lower personal indebtedness than in Europe.

9 The best known example of the 'Westminster Model' is the political system of the United Kingdom, but the Australian system belongs to the same family of systems, with obvious differences such as federalism, preferential voting and an elective upper chamber with the power to block supply.

10 A further consideration was that with MacArthur determined to retain the Emperor, albeit stripped of all political power, it would have been hard to square that with a presidential system.

11 The Osaka High Court has now ruled that more than a 1:2 vote disparity between different districts is unconstitutional. *Asahi Shimbun*, 28 December 2009.

12 With the exception of the House of Lords, where, until the near-elimination of the hereditary principle in 1999, many members simply inherited their seats.

13 The classic work on *kōenkai* is Gerald Curtis, *Election Campaigning Japanese Style*, New York and London, Columbia University Press, 1971.

14 *Asahi Shimbun*, 18 September 2009.

15 Even with the addition of the two extra parties, the Government is very slightly short of an upper house majority.

16 *Asahi Shimbun*, 20 and 21 October 2009.

17 *Asahi Shimbun*, 22 October 2009. Saitō had drawn up a plan during the non-LDP Hosokawa Government in 1993 for a 'people's welfare tax', that had, however, proved abortive. Ibid.

18 Gavan McCormack, *The Emptiness of Japanese Affluence*. Armonk and London, M.E. Sharpe, 1996.

19 *Asahi Shimbun*, 28 December 2009.

20 *Voice*, September 2009, pp. 132–41.

21 Ibid.

22 Oka Takashi, private communication.

23 *Asahi Shimbun*, 26 December 2009.

24 Eda Satsuki, interview with the author, 7 October 2009.

PART 2

Foreign Policy and Security

3

Japan's ODA as Soft Power

MARIE SÖDERBERG

In this chapter I explore an important aspect of Japan's soft power. Developed by Harvard Professor Joseph Nye in his 2004 book, *Soft Power: The Means to Success in World Politics,*[1] soft power refers to the ability to obtain what you want through cooption and attraction. Japan is considered to possess considerable soft power. Japan's global cultural influence has grown constantly through the media of popular culture: cartoons and animated films, fashion, food, pop music and the game industry. Although the influence through these cultural flows does not translate into stronger state power as usually recognized in international affairs, these cultural flows have enabled Japan to become an important norm setter, particularly in Asia.

One area mostly overlooked when considering Japanese soft power is the field of official development assistance (ODA).[2] ODA is foreign aid as officially defined by the Development Assistance Committee (DAC) within the Organization for Economic Cooperation and Development (OECD). During the 1990s, Japan was the world's largest donor of ODA. In East and Southeast Asia the results of Japan's ODA are visible in the large number of roads, railways, power plants, harbours and airports constructed through infrastructure projects financed at least partly by Japanese aid money. Japan's ODA projects have been designed and implemented largely on the basis of Japan's own economic development model. These infrastructure projects cannot be seen as a sign of Japanese soft power *per se*, but since they result from the injection of Japanese development thinking as well as large amounts of Japanese capital, they hint at the soft power Japan has generated through its ODA projects. The Japanese development modelling that guided Japan's ODA projects is now also influencing the former recipients of Japan's ODA that are now themselves aid donors, drawing heavily from the Japanese ODA model they know well. Thus, by default and/or design, ODA now appears to attract and co-opt of itself – a source of soft power for Japan in the Asian region.

The Japanese model of development took off in the 1960s and inspired many countries in Southeast Asia to follow the same path. This often included a strong state, export-led economic growth and national development through industrialization. The Japanese model was initially very successful in generating economic growth and today some of the former recipients of Japanese ODA, such as China, South Korea and Thailand, have become donors themselves. Japan's long economic slowdown in the 1990s has tarnished Japan's reputation in the field of economic development and Japan is now rarely presented as a model for other countries.

In this chapter we consider whether influences from the development philosophy inherent in Japanese ODA actually carry soft power for Japan that is now transmitted through other Asian countries' development aid. We begin by analysing the concept of soft power and the debate surrounding it. We then venture into the foreign aid policy of Japan and then of South Korea, China and Thailand. On this basis, we explore traces of Japanese soft power in Asian development aid and economic development models.

THE CONCEPTS OF SOFT POWER

Joseph Nye developed the term 'soft power' to contrast with commanding or coercive power, to define the power of a country to achieve its goals by attracting others to want what it wants. Soft power might be called indirect or co-optive power; it can rest on the attraction of one's ideas or on the ability to set the political agenda. Nye introduced the concept in the study field of international relations. He argues that the soft power of a country primarily derives from three sources: its culture, its political values, and its foreign policies. Exercising soft power is not, however, restricted to states or international relations. Politicians in democratic societies rely constantly on their soft power of attraction to win office through elections. Similarly, commercial enterprises need more than good products; they rely on soft power through the attraction of their products to buyers. Soft power clearly applies to a much wider range of actors and context than international relations.

The original idea of soft power has been twisted in academic discourse so that now any non-military power can be constructed as soft. Yet this convolution loses sight of the distinction that Nye made between coercive and cooperative action. Military forces appear to be a defining resource for hard power, but even they can contribute to soft power as well. Dictators such as Hitler and Stalin created myths to attract people to their policies.[3] Economic resources can produce both hard and soft power behaviour and sometimes distinguishing between the two can be difficult. A successful economy is, as Japan has discovered, an important source of attraction but at the same time it can also provide hard power resources in the form of coercive sanctions.

In 1979 Prime Minister Ohira Masayoshi created the Study Group for Comprehensive National Security in his search for non-military security options, making clear then that Japan's view of national security reached beyond a strictly military understanding. This group considered secure supplies of food, natural resources and other essential needs as part of the 'comprehensive' policy package. It introduced the concept of strategic aid,[4] which was followed in the 1990s by introduction of the 'human security' concept.[5] Foreign aid was to play an important part in comprehensive security. Japanese national security planners have for quite some time recognized ODA as a 'power instrument'. It is seen as one of the few tools Japan can use to smooth relations with other countries since Japan's constitution denies it the legal capacity to dispatch military to assist in fighting abroad, although Japan's Self Defence Forces nowadays can be sent overseas for reconstruction work in conflict zones.

But can ODA as a 'power instrument' be considered soft power? Japan's stoppage of official aid to China and imposition of all kinds of sanctions in response to the incident at Tiananmen Square in 1989 cannot be considered the exercise of soft power but rather of hard power. In this chapter we consider ODA from a soft power perspective. We ask if Japanese ODA has had any effect on the policy of other Asian nations through its 'attractiveness' and in particular if it has influenced their foreign aid policies. Here we face numerous problems. First we have to make clear what the characteristics of Japanese ODA are, by comparing it with the ODA of other donors. There is not just one style of aid delivery within DAC but perhaps as many styles as there are DAC members. Another difficulty in this assessment concerns transparency. Whereas Japanese ODA is open and data on it are accessible rather easily, this is not the case with, for example, Chinese aid, where borderlines between foreign aid and commercial activities are often blurred and there is a mixture and entwining between the two. We therefore need to be mindful that it may not always be comparable entities that we are mapping here in examining for traces of Japanese soft power in other Asian donors' aid policies.

JAPANESE AID

Historical Context

Japan's contribution of US$50,000 to the Colombo Plan in 1954 and its war reparations agreements that were tied to procurement from Japanese companies are seen as the origins of Japan's foreign aid programme. In the 1960s Japan directed its foreign aid almost exclusively towards Asia, overwhelmingly to serve commercial purposes. This approach changed with the oil crisis of 1973, when Japan's aid programme took a strategic turn with a huge aid package for the Arab world to secure continued supply of oil to Japan. A stable supply of natural resources became another ingredient of Japanese aid policy. Japanese policy planners saw ODA as a necessary cost for achieving both a secure and peaceful world and Japan's own economic development. In Japan, aid has always been seen as part of the wider concept of economic cooperation (*keizai kyōryoku*), which also encompasses two other components: other official flows (OOF)[6] and private investment. Economic cooperation encompasses almost all activities considered helpful to economic development, without distinguishing between official and private, commercial and non-commercial funds.[7]

In 1977 came announcement of the first of Japan's aid-doubling plans, which eventually led Japan to become the world's leading aid donor. Aid was also a way of improving Japan's image in Asia, where Japanese businessmen had left far from favourable impressions of their country. This was the start of the gift-giving diplomacy (*omiage gaikō*) that Japanese prime ministers touring Asia have used extensively. After the end of the Cold War in 1992 an ODA Charter was adopted. This stipulated that environmental considerations and development be pursued in tandem, that ODA could not be used for military purposes, and that it could not be given to countries experimenting with production of weapons of mass destruction but should be used to promote democracy and introduce the principles of a market economy. The Charter did more than embody a commitment to certain values and goals in Japanese aid giving. It also signified a turn away from the aid model Japan had upheld until then – 'request-based', with no intervention in the internal affairs of the recipient nation – to a 'consultative' model where the Japanese government began to formulate country-specific strategies.

Structural Arrangement

During the 1970s and early 1980s, Japanese aid policy making was usually uncontroversial. ODA was mainly handled by bureaucrats, and the ODA budget was dealt with by the Diet annually without political debate or deliberation on its content. Until administrative reforms of the bureaucracy from the late 1990s, about twenty different government bodies were involved in administering the ODA programme. Three 'main' ministries and one agency held more responsibility than others: the Ministry of Finance (MOF), the Ministry of Foreign Affairs (MOFA), the Ministry of International Trade and Industry (MITI), and the Economic Planning Agency (EPA). For policy implementation, several government organizations were responsible. The Overseas Economic Cooperation Fund (OECF) dealt with loan aid, and the Japan International Cooperation Agency (JICA) handled grant aid and technical cooperation. Administrative reforms from the end of the 1990s shifted both the structural arrangement and policy formulation of ODA. In 1999 the OECF was merged with the Export–Import

Bank to form the Japan Bank of International Co-operation (JBIC), to deal with both aid loans and other official flows to developing countries and promote the interests of Japanese companies. In 2003 JICA was relaunched as an independent administrative institution. In 2008 the loan aid part of JBIC was merged with JICA to form the 'New JICA', which is responsible for implementing all three types of Japanese aid: loans, grants and technical cooperation.

Characteristics of Japan's ODA Programme

Perhaps the most distinctive feature of Japan's ODA programme is its huge size; for roughly a decade from the late 1980s, Japan was the world's number one aid donor. Yet although large in absolute terms – over US$7.6 billion in 2007 – in terms of percentage of gross national income (GNI) Japan's ODA is less impressive. In 2007 it amounted to 0.17 per cent of GNI as compared to the 0.31 average for the DAC countries.[8] Per capita ODA in Japan was US$98 in 2005–6 as compared to $119 on average for DAC members.[9] Another distinctive characteristic of Japanese bilateral ODA as compared with the ODA of many West European countries concerns its quality. During the 1980s and 1990s, Japan's ODA consisted largely of bilateral loans so that although quantitatively Japan's ODA was large, its quality (by share of grants, which are not re-paid, rather than loans, which are) was rather low. Here the stated justification was moral/ideological – help those who help themselves – with the stated rationale that when recipients know they must repay the money, they will use it more carefully. There were, however, other reasons as well for providing loans rather than grants. Japan did not want to increase ODA within the national budget while simultaneously cutting domestic expenditure items such as education, which would certainly have been unpopular with domestic public opinion.

Furthermore, the focus of Japanese aid was in Asia. In 1970, Japan gave 98 per cent of its ODA to Asian nations; in 1980 the figure was 70 per cent, and in 2000 it was 54.8 per cent. The Asian share has decreased with the rise in living standards of some Asian recipient nations to the extent that, no longer eligible to receive, they have 'graduated' from the ODA programme.[10] Japan's ODA to East Asian nations between 1970 and 2004 was approximately US$71.6 billion (in terms of net disbursement), which was 54.4 per cent of the total ODA to these nations from DAC members.[11] The number one recipient on a cumulative basis is Indonesia. China has a much shorter history of receiving Japanese aid (since 1979) but was the largest recipient during much of the 1990s. The Chinese share is much smaller today since Japan ended loan aid to China to coincide with the 2008 Olympics, explaining that China is itself experiencing strong economic growth and has its own resources to pursue economic development. The emphasis on Asia during the 1990s gave rise to another feature of Japan's ODA programme:

its largest share was to low middle-income countries rather than to the poorest countries.[12]

A final characteristic concerns the nature of Japan's ODA programme: what the ODA is spent on and through what channels. More than other DAC donors, Japan's ODA program has always heavily emphasized economic infrastructure: roads, railways, harbours, airports, power plants and other infrastructure necessary for economic development.[13] As to spending channels, while much is through bilateral aid, a relatively large share in percentage terms is distributed through multilateral channels. With the heavy focus on recipients in Asia, the Asian Development Bank (ADB) is a case in point. The ADB has sixty-seven members but because Japan is one of the Bank's largest shareholders (alongside the United States), the President has always been Japanese and the Bank has always been heavily influenced by Japanese development thinking.[14] The allocation of resources in the ADB is more influenced by donors' interests than is the case with the World Bank.[15]

Global environmental issues and the widening gap between rich and poor countries were part of the background to the United Nations' adoption in 2000 of the Millennium Development Goals (MDG) that aspire to halving the proportion of the world's population living in poverty by 2015. The terrorist attacks in the USA on 11 September 2001 raised awareness of the need to prevent terrorism and build peace, recognizing that poverty in developing countries can create a breeding ground for terrorism. In response Japan's ODA Charter was revised in 2003, making the object of ODA 'to contribute to the peace and development of the international community, and thereby to help ensure Japan's own security and prosperity'. However many of the characteristics of apanese ODA mentioned above remain unchanged.

As noted above, in this chapter we consider whether influences from Japan's ODA carry soft power for Japan transmitted through the development aid of Japan's ODA recipients. Let us turn, then, to consider three nations that are now themselves aid donors and received considerable Japanese ODA during their earlier years of strong economic development. We start with South Korea, followed by China and Thailand.

SOUTH KOREA'S AID EXPERIENCE: RECIPIENT AND DONOR

Historical Context

South Korea's involvement in modern aid programmes reaches back to the 1960s when, as an economically poor nation, it qualified as a recipient of ODA. In the early 1960s South Korea received trainees from developing countries with financial support initially from the United States Agency for International Development (USAID). But soon it also began to invite trainees itself and to both dispatch South Korean experts and offer project-type technical cooperation. Although

South Korea's gross national product (GNP) per capita in 1969 was only US$210 in current prices, the country already had in place a programme of technical cooperation. The reason was clearly political: South Korea sought desperately to gain an 'edge' over North Korea in a diplomatic competition.[16] Although the United Nations had recognized the South Korean government as the only legitimate government of Korea, the country had been denied UN membership through a veto in the Security Council by members that supported North Korea. In 1960 South Korea's economic development took off. In 1965 diplomatic relations were established with Japan and South Korea received from Japan an economic cooperation programme of considerable size.

The early 1970s were, however, a golden age for North Korean diplomacy. North Korea played a leading role in the Non-aligned Movement (NAM), which South Korea did not join as a full member. The Nixon Doctrine, the partial withdrawal of US troops from South Korea, the fall of South Vietnam and the rapprochement in Sino–US relations, increased South Korean awareness of its vulnerability and inspired a focus on improving relations with the non-aligned countries. Grant aid was one way of doing this.[17] In the 1980s the South Korean economy improved considerably whereas the North Korean economy deteriorated, reducing need to worry about rivalry with the North. Yet South Korea undertook its first significant aid programme with another motivation – economic benefit for South Korea through promoting South Korean companies' business on the global market. In the early 1990s, South Korea became a member of the UN and established relations with the governments in both Beijing and Moscow. Its economy had been booming and in 1996 it joined the OECD as the second Asian member to do so after Japan.

During the 1990s when South Korea began to look for a model for its own foreign aid program, it did not turn to the West European and American models and instead favoured the Japanese model, with which South Korea had most experience itself as recipient. Thus, as with its own economic development inspired by the Japanese model of strongly state-led, export-driven economic growth, South Korea would again turn to Japan as a role model for its foreign aid programme.

Structural Arrangement

Traces of Japan's ODA modelling and approach are evident throughout the South Korean ODA programme, conceptually, institutionally, and in various aspects of aid delivery. Conceptually, the broader notion of 'economic cooperation' is often used in South Korea as it is in Japan, referring to all outflows of financial resources to developing countries. In institutions, we find a number of parallels. In 1987 South Korea created the Economic Development Cooperation Fund (EDCF) to provide bilateral concessional loans. The EDCF was directly modelled on the Japanese OECF.[18] EDCF loans are extended through the South Korean

EXIM bank under the supervision of the Ministry of Finance (MOF). These loans are tied almost completely to procurement from South Korean firms and have mostly been offered with commercial considerations in mind, just as were Japan's ODA loans. In 2008, 98 per cent of South Korean bilateral aid was either fully or partially tied.[19] Since the ODA loans are tied, South Korean companies use them as an entrée to the commercial life of developing countries, and once there make their own private investments as well.[20]

In 1991 the Korean International Cooperation Agency (KOICA) was established to implement aid policy for the South Korean government. It was clearly modelled after the Japanese organization, JICA. KOICA deals with grant aid and technical cooperation and is under the supervision of the Ministry of Foreign Affairs and Trade (MOFAT). Other ministries are also involved in technical cooperation, including the Ministry of Education and the Ministry of Information and Communication, as are institutions such as the Korean Development Institute (KDI).

Characteristics of South Korea's Foreign Aid

Again, the parallels with the Japanese aid programme are striking. A large part of South Korea's bilateral aid consists of loan aid, which so far has been tied to procurement from Korean companies. During 2007, for the first time, one project financed by untied aid was run on a trial basis.[21] And just as Japan promoted the Japanese model of economic development in the 1980s, South Korea points to its own experience with economic and social development as a valuable asset that it is pleased to share with developing countries.[22] The priority sectors for KOICA in recent years have been social infrastructure (health and education), and economic infrastructure. These two sectors accounted for almost 80 per cent of KOICA's budget in 2007. And again like Japan, rather than less developed countries, South Korea mostly targets lower middle-income countries to receive its aid.[23]

South Korea's ODA Policy in the twenty-first Century

MOFAT's ODA reports explain South Korea's overall policy and need to expand ODA, revealing a rather passive attitude that recognizes ODA mainly as a tool for gaining diplomatic advantage. The amounts of money involved have remained small so ODA has played a minor role as a diplomatic tool in the nation's foreign policy. And similar to Japan's experience of the withdrawal of popular support for foreign aid since Japan's economic downturn began in the early 1990s, the financial crisis in South Korea in 1997 created economic insecurity that impacted negatively on the willingness of the nation's people to provide foreign aid.

Adoption of the UN Millennium Development Goals and the general consensus among developed countries that the level of development aid should be raised have encouraged South Korea to adopt a new strategy for ODA. In November 2005 the Council of Ministers approved the so-called ODA Reform Plan by which South Korea was to increase its ODA to 0.1 per cent of GNI by 2009 and to 0.25 per cent by 2015.[24] In 2007 South Korea's ODA was 0.07 per cent of GNI.[25] (The DAC average for 2007 was 0.28/GNI and the UN target for 2015 is 0.7 per cent of GNI.)

According to the new strategy in the ODA Reform Plan, South Korea should join the DAC in 2010, which it also did. The plan contains three main objectives for South Korea's ODA: (1) to assist in poverty reduction in developing countries; (2) to assist the sustainable development of developing countries; and (3) to improve conditions for the advancement of South Korean interests in foreign countries. Of these, the two first goals are in line with ODA norms while the third clearly represents pursuit of national interests.

In recent years KOICA has undergone major reorganization with new geographical departments put in place. It has trimmed the number of partner countries in accordance with the principle of 'focused and selective implementation'.[26] That a South Korean, Ban Ki-moon, is Secretary-General of the UN has stimulated interest in development and international issues in South Korea. Nevertheless, to most South Koreans, humanitarian issues in North Korea and a future reunification are still most important. The value of South Korea's aid to North Korea is almost the same as the value of South Korea's total ODA, but the former is not counted as foreign aid since North Korea is not considered a foreign nation. Only one ministry, the Ministry of Unification, is responsible for the aid to North Korea.

CHINA'S FOREIGN AID POLICY

Today China is both a recipient and a donor of foreign aid. As a developing country, China has accepted foreign aid from the DAC countries since beginning its policy of opening up in 1979. China has received large sums, and was for several years at the top of the list of recipients from the DAC countries (except for the period immediately after the 1989 Tiananmen Square incident, when western aid was stopped). Yet aid has never been a significant part of its economy and China was never an aid-dependent country. Among aid-dependent countries, the inflow of aid amounts to 20 per cent of gross domestic product (GDP), whereas the development aid China received in 2003 amounted to some 0.1 per cent of GDP.[27] Today the PRC is emerging as a significant aid donor.

Historical Context

China has a long record of providing aid to developing countries. After 1949, China quickly established diplomatic relations with many African states. This was as an ideological demonstration by President Mao Zedong to show his support for the fight against imperialism and colonialism.

It was also a way to counter the diplomatic recognition of Taiwan.[28] In 1956 China launched its first aid programme to Africa. A significant aim was to knit African and other developing countries into a third world alliance with China to counterbalance the superpowers and the developed North. During the Cultural Revolution, China expanded its aid to Africa. One of the most famous projects was the Tanzania–Zambia railway (1967–75), a turnkey project completed at the cost of US$600 million and with the effort of 15,000 Chinese workers. The project was conducted during a period of considerable domestic hardship in China itself. One direct payoff was the support of a large number of developing countries for the PRC's bid to join the UN, taking the permanent seat in the Security Council that Taiwan had held until 1971. After taking control of the country's politics, from the early 1980s Deng Xiaoping stressed China's own economic development and introduced new guidelines for dealing with aid. His policy was 'Let China be a recipient and a donor at the same time' (*you jin you chu*). Deng's policy was to 'give moderately and receive a lot'.

Structural Arrangement

The State Council, the highest executive organ above the ministerial level, takes decisions on Chinese overall policy and the Chinese leaders often announce cooperation agreements with countries in connection with state visits. There is no single main agency responsible for all foreign aid from China. The main body in both receiving and giving foreign aid is the Ministry of Commerce (MOFCOM), which has a special department for giving foreign aid. The department is responsible for compiling and executing annual foreign aid programmes and supervising the implementation of aid projects. This is done through the Economic and Commercial Counsellors' Offices of the Chinese embassies in the partner countries. MOFCOM is in charge of grant aid and government interest-free loans. The Ministry of Foreign Affairs takes part in policy formulation and the Ministry of Finance is in charge of the budget. Each year the two ministries negotiate an aid budget with MOFCOM. Other ministries also play a role. The Ministry of Health is involved in medical and health projects, the Ministry of Education in educational projects, the Ministry of Agriculture in rural development and so forth. The China Exim Bank is the lending bank for Chinese government concessional loans. It evaluates loan aid projects and has a special list of companies (roughly 150) that are allowed to participate in tenders. Most of the companies are state-owned. Besides the Exim Bank, a couple of other policy banks under the jurisdiction of the State Council play an increasing role in the provision of financing for Chinese companies as part of China's 'going out strategy'. One of those is the China Development Bank (CDB) with US$300 billion in assets, making it one of the largest financial institutions in the world.[29]

Characteristics of China's Foreign Aid

One of the difficulties in carrying out research into Chinese aid is that China has no standardized criteria for what is to be considered as aid, unlike the DAC member countries that adhere to DAC criteria for ODA. China does not use the language of donor and recipient. Aid is loosely defined and carried out within the framework of South–South cooperation which also encompasses other types of cooperation such as commercial or semi-commercial cooperation. Nor does China make public disclosure of the amount or value of aid, although the budget for individual projects is sometimes disclosed.

Most of China's foreign aid is bilateral. The Chinese government has demonstrated little inclination to become involved in multilateral development initiatives, which are often incompatible with the PRC's policy of non-intervention.[30] Aid has been closely linked to securing access abroad to major natural resources such as oil or precious metals. Oil in particular is vitally important for the continuation of China's economic growth. Aid to Angola is a case in point. For Angola, which has now emerged as China's biggest supplier of oil, China has announced two credit lines totalling US$4.4 billion for 'reconstruction and national development'. A significant portion of this is tied to the purchase of Chinese goods and services.[31] A high element of Chinese aid is tied, through provision of commodities and services as well as technical cooperation. Chinese products are provided and Chinese doctors and construction workers are sent abroad. China has long traditions in agriculture and in capacity building in the social sector, especially for science, health and education. A large number of African technicians are now receiving training in China.

Another characteristic of Chinese aid is its involvement in a number of publically visible projects in the form of high-profile buildings such as stadiums, state houses and parliament buildings. In 2006 President Hu Jintao pledged to build a conference centre for the African Union. Chinese aid is also characterized by an almost complete absence of political conditionality, with the exception that recipients must support the 'One China' principle. China's aid policy builds on the principle of 'non-interference in internal affairs', which gives it a very distinctive quality *vis-à-vis* the politically conditional aid of DAC members.

THAILAND'S FOREIGN AID

Thailand's economy has advanced very well particularly since the 1980s. In 2003 then Prime Minister Thaksin Shinawatra, in his speech 'Forward Engagement: The New Era of Thailand's Foreign Policy', announced that Thailand would take no more aid and instead would emerge as an aid donor. Today, Thailand, like China, is both a donor and a recipient of foreign aid.

Historical Context

By the 1990s, when the Thai economy had reached a certain standard of development and Thailand's GNP exceeded US$1,000 per capita annually, some nations such as Japan that had been ODA donors to Thailand terminated their grant aid. The country still received ODA loans, and did not have a general policy for becoming an aid donor itself. Thailand has, however, long been a supporter of South–South cooperation and has promoted partnership cooperation on a cost-sharing basis. Its oldest aid programme, the Thai International Cooperation Programme (TICP), was begun in the 1960s. After Thailand recovered from the Asian financial crisis in the late 1990s, the decision was taken that Thailand should become a donor nation. The then Prime Minister Thaksin announced a grand strategy aimed at making Thailand a key player in the region on the strength of its strategic geographical location, history, and the level of economic development it had achieved. The aid policy was part of this strategy.

Thailand's Forward Engagement policy has shaped its relations with its neighbours, in particular those in Indochina – Cambodia, Laos, Myanmar and Vietnam (CLMV). Announcing the policy, Thaksin spoke of Thailand as an emerging donor nation, cooperating with other donors such as Japan and western nations, and taking responsibility to assist less developed countries (LDCs) in the neighbourhood by providing economic assistance.[32] Thailand sees its role as a prime mover first within its surrounding region, helping its neighbours to reach a higher level of economic development. This can sometimes be a sensitive issue, with Laos and Cambodia in particular being very sensitive to too much Thai influence in the region.

Structural Arrangement

In 2004, the Thailand International Cooperation Agency (TICA) was established as a new organization under the Ministry of Foreign Affairs. TICA implements the national programme for international development cooperation. Its main responsibilities are to prepare, strategically plan and administer Thailand's international technical cooperation. TICA administers bilateral programmes, training programmes and various other contributions. But, as we have seen above with other national models for aid administration, depending on the type of project, other actors such as the Ministry of Education, the Ministry of Public Health, the Ministry of Finance and the Ministry of Transportation may also be involved. Infrastructure projects have been administered since 2005 through the Neighbouring Countries Economic Development Cooperation Agency (NEDA). Concessionary loans are dealt with by the Ministry of Finance or the Export–Import Bank of Thailand.

Characteristics

The vast bulk of Thailand's ODA goes to infrastructure in the form of road projects connecting Thailand to its neighbours. Thai contributions are coordinated with the ADB and with other development partners' investment in this area.[33] The new roads are not only to help neighbours' economic growth but also to strengthen Thailand's own leadership position in the area through increased trade. Better infrastructure in the region is needed for the extraction of energy resources. Thailand is heavily interested in development of hydropower and the electricity sector along the Mekong River delta. The Thai government has adopted the concept of 'mutual benefits' and the 'demand-driven' approach to development cooperation. Most of the aid it provides is tied to procurement of Thai goods and services. In earlier times, Thailand's bilateral programmes were directed mainly to its immediate neighbours. In recent years, however, the geographic reach of these programs has been expanded to other developing countries such as East Timor, Sri Lanka, and some African countries. The amounts involved are still very small and appear to have decreased with the global financial crisis in 2008–9. According to Thai government statistics, Thai economic cooperation programmes in 2008 amounted to roughly US$ 11.5 million (374,758,000 baht).[34]

The emergence of Thailand as a donor nation was a policy for which former Prime Minister Thaksin pushed hard. With Thaksin's fall due to a military coup in September 2006, a wait-and-see attitude has prevailed on foreign aid policy under his successor Abhisit Vejjajiva. Political instability has continued and it is not yet clear how the government will develop its aid policy.

JAPANESE SOFT POWER AND ASIAN DEVELOPMENT AID

As the discussion above reveals, there are some striking similarities between the Japanese aid programme and the aid programmes of South Korea, China and Thailand. All three have been recipients of Japanese aid and China and Thailand still receive Japanese aid. Having experienced Japanese aid (Japan was the main bilateral donor to all three), each has created their own aid system that is heavily influenced by the Japanese system. Whether intended by Japan as a donor nation or not, the Japanese aid program has served as a role model for the formation of Asian aid development and its soft power has left considerable traces. The three other Asian donor nations do not follow exactly the same pattern as Japan and the aid policy of each has been mediated by that nation's historical experiences and present circumstances. Still, their aid programmes share certain similarities that contrast with mainstream international aid. At the same time Japanese ODA, as described above, has been changed considerably over the years and is not the same today as it was when, for example, South Korea was a recipient in the 1970s and 1980s.

The concept of aid as such is different between the Asian and western donor nations. For the former group, the principle of mutual benefit – for donor as well as recipient – is strong. The Japanese concept of 'economic cooperation', which the other Asian donors' policies have incorporated, involves working together. The motivation for aid giving is not merely sympathy for others, as the Japanese Foreign Minister Asō Tarō said of development assistance in a speech in 2006.[35] By implication, this assistance is also to be linked to Japan's own stability and prosperity. South Korea's ODA loans are to help the recipient country and to improve South Korea's economic growth. In China, whose many state-owned companies operate abroad, the borderline between private investment, official flows and aid becomes even more blurred. China's aid vocabulary does not include 'donor' and 'recipient', preferring 'mutual benefit' and 'win–win relations'. In Thailand's economic cooperation programmes with Laos, the term 'aid' is said to have bad connotations and here too the language is 'cooperation'.[36]

Other common features of the four Asian aid programmes are not so common among the DAC members in general and seem to derive from the soft power of Japan's aid programme. In Japan and the other Asian donor nations there is support for a strong state, a weak role for NGOs in planning and distributing aid, and a relatively very small element of conditionality, especially by comparison with the World Bank's approach. Table 1 summarizes the characteristics of the four Asian countries' ODA policies and compares them with the approach of DAC members overall.

Inspired by Japan, the Asian donor nations favour heavy reliance on loan aid. Most aid loans are tied to purchase of the required goods and services from the donor nation, and so are intended to assist companies in the donor nation as well. The one exception here is Japan, which over time has somewhat reduced the share of its aid as loans, but still retains a high proportion by DAC standards. Japanese loans are now to a great extent untied.[37] Connected with loan aid is spending on recipient nations' economic infrastructure. The Asian donors recognize that economic infrastructure is needed to secure resources and energy and for trade and investment to facilitate economic growth and reduce poverty. The mutual benefit concept applies; trade, investment and natural resources are also necessary for economic growth in the donor countries. This was intrinsic to Japanese philosophy in its ODA to Southeast Asia during the 1980s. Now China has adopted this way of thinking. Not only does China seek to advance its own trade performance, it has an imperative to secure energy resources for its own economic growth. The importance of resources to China becomes clear in its choice of cooperation partners in Africa.

Japan is well known for using ODA to sponsor a number of showcase buildings such as a large culture centre in the Philippines during the 1980s. China is also following that path, as evident in grandiose government buildings and cultural centres it has sponsored in developing countries.

Table 1 Characteristics of Asian and DAC Development Assistance

Characteristics	Japan	South Korea	China	Thailand	DAC
Aid within the framework of economic cooperation	Yes	Yes	Yes	Yes	To less extent
Mutually beneficial	Yes	Yes	Yes	Yes	No
Heavy reliance on bilateral loan aid	32%	Yes	Yes	Yes	7.4%
Untied	96%	All tied	All tied	All tied	95%
For economic infrastructure	24.3%	23%	Large share	Large share	11.00%
Showcase projects	Sometimes	Not common	Sometimes	Not common	Not common
Aid to least developed countries	17%	24.8%	Very high	Very high	22%
Support of own companies	Yes	Yes	Yes	Yes	Not to a large extent
Bilateral versus multilateral	Both	Both	Mainly bilateral	Mainly bilateral	Both
Policy of non-intervention	No	Yes	Yes	Yes	No
Transparency	High	High	Low	Low	High
Use of NGOs	0.01%	Low	Low	Low	0.04% of GNI

Sources: OECD and DAC statistics, various years

Besides emphasis on commercial programmes fostering trade and investment, Japan's ODA includes agriculture programmes and institution building. Huge amounts of Japanese aid are directed to environmental issues, peace-building and peace preservation. Considerable aid supports education and health programmes. Japan also has a long track record in emergency assistance. China, South Korea and Thailand are now following along that path in terms of the types of programmes they support. Japan now has a policy of promoting NGOs in foreign aid, but this is a relatively new development. The same is true for the other Asian donors.

CONCLUSION

Over the past few decades Japan has given a huge amount of official foreign aid, most of it to countries in Asia. While it is likely that the complex mix of hardware and software provided through Japan's aid programmes has left some mark on recipient nations, here we have considered a less conspicuous source of influence. This chapter's examination of the aid programmes of three Asian nations that were recipients of substantial amounts of Japanese aid and are now themselves giving official aid to nations in Asia and elsewhere begins to reveal the nature and extent of Japanese influence on their aid policies. We see signs of Japan's way of giving in philosophy, concept and practice – in how, what and why these three other Asian nations give, as well as how they understand their giving.

If we accept Joseph Nye's explanation that 'soft power' can rest on the attraction of one's ideas, ODA policy is surely a source of soft power for Japan in Asia. It is not clear whether this outcome was part of Japan's intention or is a strategically convenient byproduct of Japan's ODA policy. The soft power that years of ODA now brings for Japan bequeaths the nation with valuable influence over the national aid models of neighbours in Asia but more strategically over the national economic development models that their aid projects guide. Japan's ODA has been and still is a trendsetter in Asian foreign aid and the soft power it generates for Japan does not seem to be declining. Precisely what longer-term power Japan can derive from influencing national aid models and importantly national economic development models through its aid model via other Asian donors remains to be seen. Meantime, by 'attracting others to want what it wants' in terms of economic development, ODA policy is a valuable source of soft power for Japan in Asia.

NOTES

1 Joseph S. Nye, *Soft Power: The Means to Success in World Politics*, New York: Public Affairs, 2004.

2 ODA is defined as grants, technical assistance and loans to countries or territories on the DAC list of ODA recipients. It includes bilateral assistance and that from multilateral agencies. It is aid provided by the official sector on concessional terms (i.e. with a grant element of at least 25 per cent) and its goal is promotion of the economic development and welfare of developing countries. Grants, loans and credits for military purposes are excluded.

3 Joseph Nye, 'Foreword', in Yasushi Watanabe and David L. McConnell (eds), *Soft Power Superpowers: Cultural and National Assets of Japan and the United States*, Armonk, N.Y.: M.E. Sharpe, 2008, p. xii.

4 Dennis T. Yasutomo, *The Manner of Giving: Strategic Aid and Japanese Foreign Policy*, Lexington, Mass.: Lexington Books, 1986, pp. 19–40.

5 For an overview of human security, see Bert Edström, *Japan and the Challenge of Human Security: The Founding of a New Policy 1995–2003*, Stockholm: Institute for Security and Development Studies, 2009.

6 These are a different kind of subsidized official flows on terms below market rate, but their conditions are not concessional enough for them to qualify as ODA.

7 Marie Söderberg, 'Japanese ODA: What Type, For Whom and Why', in Marie Söderberg (ed.), *The Business of Japanese Foreign Aid: Five Case Studies from Asia*, London and New York: Routledge, 1996, pp. 33–5.

8 OECD, *Development Cooperation Report 2009*, Vol. 10, No. 1, 2009, Table 1, p. 148.

9 OECD, *Development Cooperation Report 2007*, Vol. 9, No. 1, 2008, Table 7, p. 149.

10 Ministry of Foreign Affairs, *Japan's Official Development Assistance*, Tokyo, 2008, p. 172.

11 Ministry of Foreign Affairs, *Japan's Official Development Assistance*,Tokyo, 2006, pp. 19–20.

12 OECD, *Development Cooperation Report 2009*, Vol. 10, No. 1, 2009, p. 209.

13 Ibid., pp. 196–7.

14 Saito Tomoyo and Ishida Kyoko (Revised by Tanabe Yuki and Gupta Rupa), ADB and Japan (Philippines: NGO Forum on ADB), 2007. Online, http://www.jacses.org/en/sdap/agm/adbandjapan.pdf, accessed 5 October 2008, p. 15.

15 Christopher Kilby, 'Donor Influences in Multilateral Development Banks: The Case of the Asian Development Bank', *Vassar College Economic Working Paper*, No. 70, 2006, http://irving.vassar.edu/VCEWP/VCEWP70.pdf, accessed 5 October 2008, p. 26.

16 Kim San-Tae, *ODA Policy of the Republic of Korea: In the Context of its Evolving Diplomatic and Economic Policies*, KOICA Working Paper, T 2003–9–41, Korea: Dong Hwa Printing, 2003, p. 15.

17 Ibid., p. 18

18 The Korean name of this body is an exact translation of the name of its Japanese counterpart. The standard English translation has dropped 'overseas' from the name, most probably to avoid confusion with the Japanese organization.

19 OECD, *Development Cooperation Report 2009*, p. 137.

20 Kim, *ODA Policy of the Republic of Korea*, pp. 46–7.

21 Interview with Sung-yong Um, Senior Deputy Director at EDCF Planning Office, Seoul, April 2007.

22 EDCF, *Annual Report 2006*, Seoul: Ministry of Finance and Economy, Export–Import Bank of Korea, 2006, p. 39

23 EDCF, *Annual Report 2008*, Seoul: Ministry of Finance and Economy, Export–Import Bank of Korea, 2008.

24 EDCF, *Annual Report* 2006, p. 39.

25 OECD, *Development Cooperation Report 2009*, p. 137.

26 KOICA, *Cooperation for a Better World: Annual Report,* Seoul, 2005, p. 10.

27 Elling N. Tjonneland, Bjorn Brandtzaeg, Åshild Kolås and Garth Le Pere, *China in Africa: Implications for Norwegian Foreign and Development Policies*, Norway: CMI, 2006, p. 12.

[28] Centre for Chinese Studies, Stellenbosch University, *China's Engagement of Africa: Preliminary Scoping of African Case Studies*, a research report prepared for Rockefeller Foundation, 2007, p. 1.

[29] Penny Davies, *China and the End of Poverty in Africa: Towards Mutual Benefit?*, Sundbyberg, Sweden: Diakonia, 2007, p. 45.

[30] Centre for Chinese Studies, Stellenbosch University, 'China's Interest and Activities in Africa's Construction and Infrastructure Sector', a research report prepared for Department for International Development (DFID) China, 2007, pp. 78–9.

[31] Tjonneland et al., *China in Africa*, p. 13.

[32] See http://www.thaiembdc.org/pressctr/ststemnt/pm/sifa031203.html, accessed 13 April 2007.

[33] Ministry of Foreign Affairs of Thailand and UN Country Team, *Global Partnership for Development: Thailand's Contribution to the Millennium Development Goals*, Thailand, 2005, p. 16.

[34] http://www.tica.thaigov.net/tica/index.jsp?sid=1&id=65&pid=1, accessed 15 November 2009.

[35] Speech by the Minster of Foreign Affairs, http://www.mofa.go.jp/announce/fm/aso/speech0601-2.html, accessed 22 February 2010.

[36] JBIC, *Kaihatsu kinsoku kenkyū jōhō* (Journal of JBIC Institute), no. 35, October 2007, p. 44.

[37] The quantity of Japanese loan aid is still very large and to a certain extent the decrease is due to the methods of calculation whereby loans now being paid back are deducted from the amounts given.

4

Japan in Global Governance: War and Peace

GO ITO

JAPAN'S IDEAS FOR 'GLOBAL GOVERNANCE' IN INTERNATIONAL SECURITY

Defeated by the United States in the Pacific War, Japan started the post-war period as an occupied country. Japanese have subsequently never thought of the Self-Defence Force's (SDF) activities in the context of global governance. Those on the left argued that any military-related actions would again lead Japan on the path of militarism, while those on the right tended to think of the military only in the context of national security. The term 'international security' has been an awkward one for many Japanese because of the conventional wisdom that war is a product of elite machinations, while the general public desires peace.

The end of the Cold War has seen a weakening of the Japanese left. Politically, the Japan Socialist Party (since 1996, the Social Democratic Party) has suffered a decline in its public popularity. This is partly the result of the reduced appeal of pacifism, which has led those on the left to seek to regain their popularity by focusing attention on the general public in China, Korea and the other Asian countries that suffered at the hands of the Japanese military during war and occupation.

The Japanese left's efforts at regional reconciliation have encouraged some Asian governments to politicize the history issue. In Korea, some people demand that the Japanese remember the wartime past, while at the same time arguing that Japan needs to forget the history of the abductions of Japanese citizens by North Korea. If Japanese believe they can forget the history of their aggression towards the Asian countries during the Pacific War, while at the same time continue to criticize North Korea over the abductions issue, many in Asia will find it difficult to agree to Japanese foreign activities in the region. Thus, there is a need to keep a balance between the incessant claims of Asian countries and the way Japan's actions are perceived by others.

Although espousing a 'UN-centred diplomacy' since its entry into the United Nations in 1956, the Japanese government has not fully participated in the organization's activities. Although it bankrolled nearly a fifth of the total cost of the coalition forces' military operations during the Persian Gulf War, Japan was not included in the list of countries thanked by Kuwait for helping end the Iraqi occupation in *The Washington Post*. The Japanese government then began to adopt a more active stance regarding human contributions, mindful that the world expected Japan to play a more global role commensurate with its economic power. 'International contributions' in line with a 'UN-centred diplomacy' emerged as the most significant topic of debate regarding Japanese foreign policy for the first time.

Since then, the Japanese government has voiced a need for the country to make 'positive contributions' towards international peace and stability. A key element of these 'contributions' has been the participation of the SDF in international peacekeeping missions. For an avowedly pacifist Japan, which has desired to contribute substantially to world affairs through non-military means, the UN has provided an ideal forum in which to carry out its global responsibilities and enhance its status and prestige.[1] The nation's prestige has been damaged by seemingly intractable socioeconomic problems. Therefore, greater non-military contributions to global peace and security also provide an opportunity to demonstrate that Japan's decline is neither absolute nor is it necessarily reflected in this aspect of foreign and security policy making.

Since the Law Concerning Cooperation for United Nations Peacekeeping Operations and Other Operations (the Peacekeeping Law) was enacted in June 1992, the Japanese government has been eager to increase the number of SDF officers who can be deployed to troubled spots around the world. Despite official pronouncements to this effect, however, Japan's contributions to international peacekeeping activities have been much more constrained in terms of size and operations, compared with other advanced industrialized countries.[2] A large number of domestic regulations and principles have prevented Japan from taking part effectively in peacekeeping activities. In contrast to the number of dispatched peacekeepers from the other G8 countries, Japan's participation has been viewed as far from sufficient.

Given the shortage of Japan's 'international contributions' in the peacekeeping arena over the past decade, this chapter examines what has been at stake in overall discussions regarding this topic. At the same time, it documents recent cases involving Japanese peacekeepers and examines the regulations and principles which have stymied Japanese participation. The argument presented here will begin to shed light on the issues and agendas that have been discussed in the context of Japan's 'international contributions' in the past decade. The chapter also traces the history of Japan's PKO activities and humanitarian relief operations since the country entered the UN in 1956, documenting how the dispatch of SDF officers, civilian officials and NGOs has been debated by bureaucrats and politicians alike. Finally, it will seek to articulate the domestic principles that underlie Japan's dispatch of those with the mission to create and maintain international peace and stability, examining the relationship between constitutional constraints and Japanese foreign policy options.

IDEAS AND AGENDAS REGARDING 'INTERNATIONAL CONTRIBUTIONS'

Ever since it was criticized for failing to contribute militarily to the Gulf War, the Japanese government has tried to come up with alternate ways to contribute to international peace and security. As far as international development is concerned, Japan has become the world's top donor of official development assistance. Faced with international criticism, however, Japanese politicians and bureaucrats recognized that traditional economic diplomacy could not be a substitute for the pursuit of a security agenda. Foreign Ministry officials remember Japan's traumatic experience during the Gulf War, when it was excluded from UN Security Council deliberations on peacekeeping activities. UN Ambassador Yoshiro Hatano went so far as to say that Japan could have put together a package of proposals for action if it had a seat on the Security Council.[3]

The term 'international contributions' began to emerge as something that could reform Japan's traditional immobilism in foreign policy. From August 1990 through June 1992 when the Peacekeeping Law was passed, 'international contributions' became particularly focused on the following three areas.

First, 'human' contributions have become valued more than financial contributions. Although it contributed $13 billion to military operations during the Gulf War, Japan's financial contributions were condemned by the United States as 'too little, too late'. Judging from changes in Japan's security policy since the Gulf War, which include the 1992 passage of the Peacekeeping Law, the 1999 US-Japan Security Guidelines and the 2001 Anti-Terrorism Special Measures Law, it was clear that the Japanese government rushed to show its readiness to dispatch SDF personnel with the goal of doing more than what other countries had pejoratively labelled 'chequebook diplomacy' when criticizing Japan's role in the Gulf War.

Second, among the various issues pertaining to 'human contributions', the dispatch of SDF personnel overseas has become a focal point of discussion. For the last decade, the Japanese government has recognized the UN and the security relationship with the US government as the core institutions that enable the country to play a bigger role in international affairs. On the other hand, the fear among East Asian countries that Japan's increasing unilateral contribution would lead to Japan's remilitarization has dissuaded the government from dispatching SDF troops abroad.[4] Deliberations over Japan's security role for the decade in the Diet focused on whether and to what extent the Japanese government would be able to dispatch SDF personnel and still maintain the traditional 'pacifist' stance in upholding Article 9 of the Japanese Constitution.[5]

Finally, reflection of Japan's failure to conduct military contributions in the Gulf War has prompted a more general debate over whether Japan, with its military operations restrained by Article 9 of the Constitution, will ever become a 'normal state', with the capacity to conduct military operations as it sees necessary. Discussions over Japan's sending SDF personnel overseas have also expanded to include the need to establish new diplomatic norms and political values that will create a more positive image of 'Japan' with a role in international security that transcends its traditional 'pacifist' stance.[6]

During the 1990s, in fact, Japan's international role with respect to security expanded towards not only conducting UN-centred peacekeeping operations, but also working more closely with its chief ally, the United States. Such issues as collective self-defence rights and US-Japan Security Guidelines emerged as key issues in an updated US-Japan security relationship. In this sense, discussions regarding 'international contributions' have strived for something greater than merely funding UN-led activities.

The great breakthrough in Japan's 'international contributions' that occurred following the Gulf War related to drastic changes in the aforementioned three policy initiatives. How then has Japan handled its PKO policy since its entry into the UN? Next, this chapter examines the history and decision-making processes behind Japan's peacekeeping operations.

JAPAN'S EFFORTS FOR INTERNATIONAL PEACEKEEPING OPERATIONS

Initial Stage after Japan Joined the UN

The debate over Japan's participation in UN peacekeeping operations can be traced back to the late 1950s and early 1960s. Since entering the UN, the Japanese government has repeatedly emphasized the importance of the institution for ensuring international peace and stability. A 'UN-centred diplomacy' was announced by then Prime Minister Nobusuke Kishi as the focal point of a post-war foreign policy consisting of three pillars: 1. use of the UN as a major forum in which Japan should pursue its national goals; 2. close cooperation with 'free, democratic states', and 3. identification with Asia.

The announcement attracted a wide range of popular support and eventually resulted in a national consensus. It was hoped at the time that Japan could eventually rely on the UN to maintain its security and also guarantee world peace. As Robert Immerman once wrote:

> The only major tenet of post-war Japanese foreign policy that has received the support of all segments of the domestic political spectrum – from the conservatives...to the Socialist and Communist parties constituting the left opposition – has been the nation's commitment to an otherwise undefined 'UN-centred diplomacy'.[7]

Nevertheless, there has been no consensus concerning the definition of the term 'UN-centred diplomacy'. From today's perspective, it was not meant to make the UN the central focus or arena of Japanese foreign policy, but only to have Japan's diplomacy conform to the purposes and principles of the United Nations Charter. Moreover, for Prime Minister Kishi, whose foreign policy priority at the time was to modify the US-Japan Security Treaty, the emphasis on the UN provided a good excuse to attract civilian support and strike a balance between the idealistic 'identification with Asia' and the more realistic 'cooperation with free, democratic states'.[8] Within the Japanese government, there were no specific or realistic policy options regarding how international peace could be maintained within a collective security system.

During the early Cold War period, there were at least two occasions when the UN sought the assistance of Japanese SDF officers and other personnel. In 1958, UN Secretary-General Dag Hammarskjold requested that the Japanese government send SDF officers to Lebanon in order to monitor the weapons-collecting activities. During a debate in the Diet, Foreign Minister Fujiyama Aiichiro rejected the dispatch of the SDF, since the SDF Law had no provision for sending the units abroad. A few years later, Japan's UN Ambassador Matsudaira Koto criticized the government's immobility, saying 'it is not logical that the Japanese government emphasizes the importance of the UN, while at the same time it avoids participating in the UN Forces'.[9]

The second case happened two years later when Congo, a newly independent country, sought UN intervention when Belgium unilaterally sent forces into its former colony. Although there was no formal mandate from the UN regarding Japan's involvement, rumour held that the UN approached the Japanese government about possibly dispatching SDF personnel. In reality, rising tensions between the conflicting parties made it impossible even for normal UN missions to monitor the buffer zone, and the Japanese government eventually decided that it was too dangerous for SDF members to act within Japan's constitutional framework.[10]

Japan as a Rising Economic Power

After the initial period of Japan's 'UN-centred diplomacy', the UN increasingly came to be seen as a forum for third world or non-aligned states, and more powerful countries, frustrated with the situation, subsequently established other forums where they could exclusively discuss their own policy issues.[11]

From the 1970s until the mid-1980s, the international situation was such that the Japanese government could not be compelled to take the initiative on UN-related issues. As an international organization, the UN began to change and reflect the interests of third world countries. Moreover, the US-Japan relationship was threatened by the Nixon administration's abrupt announcements of an opening to China and a New Economic Policy. The 1973 Oil Crisis also resulted in Japan placing greater emphasis on relations with oil-rich countries. Faced with this situation, the Japanese government, mindful of its longstanding interest of securing access to natural resources, sought to act as a mediator between the developed and third world countries in the UN General Assembly.[12]

A major breakthrough came when Takeshita Noboru became prime minister in November 1987. Eager to expand Japan's involvement in international issues, Takeshita announced the International Cooperation Initiative in 1988. It included stepped-up contributions to the UN for activities aimed at preventing and resolving conflicts. In Takeshita's mind, Japan, which had achieved global economic prominence, should pursue its own global ambitions. He adopted several initiatives, playing a substantial agenda-setting role on humanitarian issues and UN reform. Dispatching Japanese peacekeepers for international missions became an urgent issue. The Foreign Ministry began preparing to send an official to Afghanistan and Pakistan (UNGOMAP), and another official to the border between Iran and Iraq (UNIIMOG). In 1989, thirty-one Japanese personnel were sent to Namibia (UNTAG) to monitor an election. Similar assignments followed in Nicaragua and Haiti.[13]

Despite the policy change in the Takeshita cabinet, the dispatch of Japanese UN peacekeepers was strictly limited to 'civilians'. The government still adhered to the SDF Law of the 1950s, which made no clear statement regarding the international deployment of Japan's SDF. The Foreign Affairs Establishment Law, which had been enacted after the US occupation, was still in force with respect to Japan's involvement in international UN peacekeeping efforts. It was not until the Diet passed the Peacekeeping Law that SDF officers could finally be sent to troubled regions.

The Gulf War as a Turning Point for Japan

The Gulf War changed Japan's inertia. US criticisms of Japan's 'chequebook diplomacy' prompted the government to finally alter its 'non-dispatch' principle. The passage of the Peacekeeping Law in 1992 enabled the Japanese government to send the SDF to areas in conflict. The Foreign Ministry's long-held hope of dispatching SDF troops abroad was finally realized.

The decision-making process during the passage of the Peacekeeping Law can be divided into two stages. The first was Prime Minister

Kaifu Toshiki's October 1990 submission of the Peacekeeping bill to the Diet, which failed to gain the approval of the opposition parties. The proposed bill stated that Japanese peacekeepers would be able to conduct 'substantive activities' such as monitoring ceasefire agreements and patrolling buffer zones. They would also be able to provide administrative assistance, transportation and participate in humanitarian relief operations. Moreover, the peacekeepers would be able to carry small arms, although they would not be able to use them unless they were threatened or fired upon.

In response to the cabinet's submission, the opposition parties began questioning the validity of the Peacekeeping bill mainly on the grounds that the dispatch of SDF officers would violate Article 9 of the Japanese Constitution. They also indicated that, already in 1980, the government had stated the unlawful nature of the SDF's participation in UN-led missions, if such missions included the use of weapons.[14] The government then sought to make a distinction between 'participation' and 'cooperation', arguing that Japan's involvement would not go beyond 'cooperation'. The statement, however, was taken as an excuse to justify the government's position. A lack of consensus between the LDP and other Diet members regarding the outline of the 'contributions' resulted in the failure to pass the bill.

The second attempt to enact a peacekeeping law was made when the Liberal Democratic Party (LDP) started to hammer out a consensus with moderate political parties, Komeitō and the Social Democratic Party (SDP). After the bill was rejected in its original form, the LDP reached an agreement, in November 1990, with Komeitō and the SDP to create a separate military unit that could take part in international relief operations in the future.

In addition, the LDP made several concessions when it submitted a new version of the bill. First, Komeitō strongly argued that Japan's contributions should be limited to logistical, rear-area support. The party was concerned that once engaged in UN missions, Japanese peacekeepers would conduct activities beyond the permissible boundaries of Article 9 of the Constitution. Furthermore, it suggested that the government could dispatch SDF officers abroad, although they should be considered as being on leave from active SDF duties. Second, the SDP contended that although SDF officers could directly become UN peacekeepers, the government would require Diet approval. It argued that while the distinction between 'substantive activities' and logistical support would not be required, the Diet should control the foreign dispatch of Japanese peacekeepers.

In order to create a consensus among the three parties, which would enable the House of Councillors to pass the peacekeeping bill, the LDP accepted both Komeitō's and the SDP's suggestions. It was decided that SDF participation in UN missions would not be limited to 'substantive activities' of peacekeeping and to logistical and rear-area support.

However, sending SDF personnel to hot spots around the world would require Diet approval. The opposition parties also demanded that SDF officers be immediately recalled from their assignments if they were exposed to excessive danger.[15] With these conditions imposed, the bill was finally passed in June 1992.

Several cases involving the dispatch of SDF peacekeepers should be documented. The first was United Nations Transitional Authority in Cambodia (UNTAC). Right after the Peacekeeping Law was passed, 8 SDF soldiers, 41 civilians (election monitors), 75 civilian policemen, and about 600 SDF engineers were sent to Cambodia. Their assignment generally went smoothly, however, the SDF soldiers were asked to do more than what was stipulated in their original assignment. For the Japanese government, which restricted the substantive activities of peacekeeping forces, the most critical issue was to maintain a balance between the international contributions that would satisfy the international community and the safety of its peacekeepers. The rigid implementation of the Peacekeeping Law in the field of operations, however, sometimes frustrated UN personnel and the Cambodians who needed the assistance. Given this dilemma, the Japanese members were reluctant to serve in unstable border areas.[16]

Unlike the glamorous image associated with UNTAC, the Mozambique operation (ONUMOZ) attracted little attention. In 1993, the UN Secretary-General Boutros Boutros-Ghali proposed that Japan should send SDF units to Mozambique. The Foreign Ministry and the International Peace Cooperation Headquarters (IPCHQ) already evaluated the safety of the region and urged the dispatch. The Miyazawa cabinet sent fifty-three SDF personnel to serve in liaison offices and provide transportation, and fifteen civilians to monitor the election. The operation went smoothly and lasted approximately eight months. However, the Japanese public was ignorant of the area and felt it had little relevance for Japan.

While the above two cases were UN peacekeeping operations, Prime Minister Murayama Tomiichi's decision to send missions to Rwanda qualified as a humanitarian relief operation. Thousands of refugees, which had already fled Rwanda to neighbouring countries, were suffering from a lack of food, water and sanitation. Based on the recommendation of Ogata Sadako, Director of the United Nations High Commissioner for Refugees (UNHCR), the Murayama cabinet, which incidentally marked the first coalition between the LDP and the Socialist Party, sent nearly 400 SDF officers and ministry officials for transportation and administrative liaison duties.[17]

Finally, Japan's dispatch to the Golan Heights (UNDOF) and East Timor (UNTAET, UNMISET) is still in operation. In the former case, the debate in the Diet focused on two issues: whether or not the transportation of ammunition and foreign combat troops by SDF units would violate the Peacekeeping Law, and whether it would be possible to ask Japanese officers to serve two-year assignments in accordance with UN regulations.

After more than a year of debate, forty-five SDF officers were sent to the area, of which two were assigned to administrative liaison offices. The dispatch has continued as of early 2010, and more than 1,000 SDF officials have been sent.

Concerning the latter, following 9/11, the Japanese government modified the Peacekeeping Law so that it could conduct 'substantive activities' for peacekeeping operations. Although reluctant to dispatch SDF officers in 1999, out of a desire not to damage relations with Indonesia, the Japanese government decided to send almost 700 SDF officers at this time, who are currently engaged in monitoring the cease-fire agreement and patrolling the buffer-zones. The dispatch of such a large number to UN operations has resulted in the sudden increase of Japanese peacekeepers in comparison with other G8 countries. The dispatch was the largest mission in the number of SDF officials sent, and such a big mission became possible with the revision of the Peacekeeping Law.

Aside from these cases, Japanese peacekeepers have also been sent to monitor elections in Angola and El Salvador, South Africa, Palestine and Romania. On the other hand, elections in Somalia, Yugoslavia and East Timor have been ignored. Compared with the initial period of Japan's nominal 'UN-centred diplomacy', the passage of the Peacekeeping Law enabled the government to send SDF units abroad. Considering that the law resulted from a compromise among three political parties, Japan's participation in peacekeeping operations has been influenced by unique principles. Next the chapter examines how Japan has stipulated the domestic principles of its 'international contribution' policies.

JAPAN'S EFFORTS FOR DISASTER-RELIEF OPERATIONS

Regarding disaster-relief operations, the Japanese government explained that the SDF would need to participate for the following reasons: 1. larger relief operation teams would be needed in some disasters; 2. the SDF should have self-sufficient capabilities; and 3. the SDF needs improved transportation capabilities. Judging from their domestic experiences in the past, the SDF's activities were limited to four areas: 1. medical services, such as first-aid medical treatment and epidemic prevention; 2. transportation of goods, patients, and disaster relief personnel by helicopters; 3. water supplies using water-purifying devices; and 4. use of transport planes and ships to carry disaster-relief personnel and equipment to the affected areas.[18]

Nevertheless, the SDF had to wait another six years before participating in its first international disaster-relief operation. In 1998, the SDF was sent to Honduras, which was devastated by Hurricane Mitch. Since then, the SDF has participated in various disaster-relief operations, as shown in Table 1.

Table 1: International Disaster Relief Operations by SDF

Period	Disaster	Unit	No. of Personnel	Work Contents
1998.11.13–1998.12.09	Hurricane (Honduras)	Medical	80	Medical and Disease Prevention
		Airlift	105	Transport Activities for Aid Supply
1999.09.23–1999.11.22	Earthquake (Turkey)	Sealift	426	Transport Activities using Ships (for Temporary Dwelling)
2001.02.05–2001.02.11	Earthquake (India)	Relief Supply	16	Relief Supply and Technical Assistance for Relief Activities
		Airlift	78	Transport Activities for Rescue Teams and Aid Supply
2003.12.30–2004.01.06	Earthquake (Iran)	Airlift	31	Transport Activities for Aid Supply
2004.12.28–2005.01.01	Earthquake and Tsunami (Thai)	Surface Force	590	Rescue Activities and Stopgap Measures
2005.01.16–2005.03.23	Earthquake and Tsunami (Indonesia)	Coordination	22	Coordination among Rescue Units
		Medical/Airlift	228	Medical and Disease Prevention/ Transport Activities
		Surface Force	593	Transport Activities for Rescue Teams and Aid Supply
		Airlift	82	Transport Activities for Aid Supply
2005.08.05–2005.08.10	Submarine Accident (Russia)	Surface Force	346	Rescue Activities

(Continued)

Period	Disaster	Unit	No. of Personnel	Work Contents
2005.10.12–2005.12.02	Earthquake (Pakistan)	Air Assistance	147	Transport Activities for Aid Supply
		Air lift	114	Transport Activities for Rescue Teams
2006.06.01–2006.06.13	Earthquake (Indonesia)	Medical	149	Medical and Disease Prevention
		Air lift	85	Transport Activities for Rescue Teams
2010.01.17 –2010.02.13	Earthquake (Haiti)	Medical	100	Medical and Disease Prevention

The data in the table were collected from the homepage of the Japan Defence Agency (http://www. jda.go.jp/).

LEARNING TO COLLABORATE WITH NON-MILITARY ORGANIZATIONS

The Japanese government as a whole has more than a decade of experience in international disaster-relief operations. However, Tokyo's involvement began long before Japan's SDF started to engage in these activities. In 1982, the Ministry of Foreign Affairs launched the Japan Medical Team for Disaster Relief (JMTDR) with the assistance of other ministries and medical organizations. The creation of the JMTDR was a response to the criticism of the lack of competent relief programmes for the refugees around the Thai-Cambodia border at the time of the 1970s Indo-China war.[19]

In the mid-1980s, the Japanese government decided to enhance its operational abilities, and to establish an integrated international disaster relief structure along with competent human resources, facilities and legal systems. The International Disaster Relief Law was enacted in 1987, and the Japan International Cooperation Agency organized Japan Disaster Relief teams (JDR). These teams, created for the purpose of emergency relief when major disasters occur overseas, especially in developing countries, are composed of three types of groups: rescue, medical and emergency management expert teams.

The SDF has been confronting the difficulties of collaborating with private organizations in disaster operations. The SDF has always been at the centre of political conflict in Japan, and, as a result, its role in domestic and international disaster-relief operations has been contentious. There has been a constant debate over how the SDF should collaborate with non-governmental organizations (NGOs) in international disaster-relief operations since the SDF joined the JDR. In 2001, Japan's Defence Agency (JDA) highlighted five challenges for international disaster-relief operations. One of the challenges was to strengthen effective collaboration with NGOs.[20] Some Japanese NGOs were clearly against the SDF's involvement in the JDR from the beginning.[21] They were sceptical about the SDF's role and capacity in 'international' disaster-relief operations, since the SDF had no experience of overseas activities since its establishment in 1954. Moreover, the SDF had not participated collaboratively very often with NGOs in domestic disaster-relief. Before the 1995 Kobe earthquake, some local governments were quite reluctant to have any political and administrative connections with the SDF. The manner in which the SDF participated in disaster-relief operations as well as its self-sufficient capabilities made it difficult to collaborate with other relief bodies. The SDF's activities in international disaster-relief operations were intentionally focused on initial responses, and their operations were not adequately coordinated with other relief groups.

Nowadays, in spite of these difficulties, there is a growing need for cooperation between the SDF and NGOs. In international disaster-relief operations, various assets held by the military or civil defence organizations are effective for the initial response phase to natural disasters. Military or civil defence organizations usually stay in the afflicted area for less than a few months, and then non-military governmental organizations and NGOs accept responsibility for the later stages of recovery. In the case of the Indian Ocean tsunami, the Indonesian government requested that foreign forces not stay in distressed areas for more than three months. In severe disaster areas, it may take more than several years to accomplish the recovery programme. The smooth transition from initial response to recovery programmes is required for quick restoration and development of devastated areas.

The SDF is still searching for a viable position within the disaster relief network. At the 10th Tokyo Defence Forum (Forum for Defence Authorities in the Asia-Pacific Region), held in June 2005, the Director-General for International Affairs of the JDA mentioned that 'the participants shared the view that coordination between many actors (including NGOs) in disaster relief...is important, in order to avoid overlapping as well as to fill the gap from the perspective of division on [*sic*] labor concerning roles, missions, and capability'.[22] It is a pressing issue for the SDF to establish a more collaborative civil-military relationship for effective and efficient operations.

Furthermore, the Japanese government has dispatched disaster relief teams (not SDF officials organized) from the Japan Fire Department to Indonesia in 2006, China (earthquake in Sichuan), and to Haiti in 2010. While the size of these rescue teams was relatively small, the Japanese government has recognized natural disasters as issues of safety and security. Although it is not easy to distinguish between these disaster relief operations and activities related to war and peace, Japan's efforts to interpret 'peace' as 'safety' will involve a variety of governmental organizations to contribute to natural disaster relief operations. Since Asia is the region with large numbers of natural disasters with high numbers of casualties, it is important for Japan to consider various aspects of international contributions.

INTERNATIONAL TERRORISM AND JAPAN'S COUNTER-MEASURES

Japan's Response to the September 11 Terrorism and the New Defence Programme Outline

The September 11 2001 terrorist attacks marked the beginning of a new century for security issues. Those who watch Japanese politics have seen the decisiveness with which Prime Minister Koizumi Junichirō acted to lend Japanese support to the US war on terrorism. While Japan's response to the 1991 Gulf War was condemned as 'too little, too late', the Bush administration, since 2001, praised Japan for its swift cooperation including the dispatch of SDF personnel.

At a press conference on the White House lawns, Koizumi made the following speech, in English:

> I am very pleased to say we are friends. We had a great talk as friends, and I conveyed what I'm thinking. We Japanese stand by the United States to fight terrorists. We could make sure of this global objective; we must fight terrorism with determination and patience – very good meeting.[23]

His excitement over the event and his friendship with the US president suggested Japan's readiness to overcome the trauma caused by the failure to make military contributions at the time of the Gulf War. At the White House meeting, Koizumi committed the dispatch of SDF personnel.

Regarding Japan's defence capabilities, the year 2004 may be considered as important for decisive changes. Premier Koizumi established a new council on Japan's security defence capabilities in April 2004, and the Council issued a report on its future vision. An 'Integrated Security Strategy' is the key term in this vision and has two goals. The first is to prevent a direct threat from reaching Japan while the second focuses more on creating a stable international environment, emphasizing the importance of 'reduc[ing] the chances of threats arising in various parts of the world...affecting the interests of Japanese expatriates and corporations overseas'. The strategy can be attained by making efforts in three areas: 1. Japan's own efforts; 2. cooperation with an alliance partner and 3. cooperation with the international community. The two goals and three efforts suggest the 'integration' of Japan's security strategy and the report argues a need for the government to apply an 'integrated decision-making mechanism'. It also emphasizes the roles of the UN Security Council, which is supposed to mix the six components of the strategy.

Along with the overreaching plan, the report also highlights the role of the defence forces to support the new security strategy, naming it a 'multi-functional flexible defence force'. The pivotal requirement of it is the ability to collect and analyse information. The overarching defence roles include: 1. responding to emergency situations; 2. strengthening intelligence capabilities; 3. reforming the defence industrial and technological base and 4. emphasizing Japan's international peacekeeping roles. The report envisioned Japan playing a more 'global' role in international security issues.[24]

In response to the above report, the JDA issued a new outline for the defence programme over the coming decade. It assumed that the primary goal was to address 'new threats' like international terrorism or weapons of mass destruction, seeking to create a stable international environment. Given that, it paid more attention to the international dispatch of Japan's SDF along with the increase in its transportation capabilities. Compared with the 1970s concept of the 'Basic Defense Force' which was influenced by *détente* between the superpowers, the new outline indicated Japan's readiness to prepare for more positive roles in international security. The outline also notes Japan's concerns about North Korea's development of nuclear weapons and China's rising military capabilities, the clear indication of which appeared for the first time since the Japanese government issued the defence programme outline in 1976.

The outline assumed Japan playing a more global role, reaching from East Asia towards the Middle East. That is, the role of the SDF is not limited to the defence of Japanese territory, but rather focused on the international aspects of security. The internationalized role corresponds to the collaborative work with the US military. The outline also emphasized the importance of Japan's alliance with the US government, while at the same time seeking to broaden both allies' security responsibilities within a wider geographic area.

While the amount allocated for the new programme will be restricted under the banner of 'administrative reform', the substantial functions and transportation capabilities of the SDF should be advanced further. The new Ministry of Defence has outlined a plan for reducing the number of SDF officials, which should be easily achieved given the current personnel shortage.

The outline also indicated a need to reexamine the principle of banning the export of arms at least to the United States. Regarding joint technological research on ballistic missile defence by Japan and the United States, the outline assumes it is necessary to uphold the philosophy of the ban, and instead pursue the enhancement of defence-related procurement and R&D.

A New Version of Japan's Alliance with the United States?

Along with the above mentioned tendency in the Koizumi cabinet to expand Japan's role in international security affairs, the 11 September 2005 election in Japan produced a more than two-thirds majority for the ruling coalition in the House of Representatives, which technically enabled it to pass new legislation.

After the victory of the LDP-Komeitō coalition, Diet members began to think of possible revisions in the Japanese Constitution. The possible revision of Article 9 will be part of the larger process of redefining Japan's role in international security. One step during the 1990s was the formulation of the US-Japan security guidelines. After the end of the Cold War, the decline of a global threat, combined with an existing regional threat of strife in East Asia, was given as one of the reasons for the formulation of the new guidelines. The parties to the deliberations on the future of the US-Japan alliance were concerned with the lingering potential for strife in the region while at the same time trying to develop a structure well suited to the less hostile post-Cold War global environment.

With the April 1996 US-Japan Joint Declaration on Security, both governments started to seek new roles for the alliance. The new US-Japan security guidelines, announced in September 1997, tried to apply the joint declaration to post-Cold War East Asia in two ways. First, an item on 'Various Types of Security Cooperation' notes that 'bilateral [Japan-US] cooperation to promote regional and global activities in the field of security contributes to the creation of a more stable international security environment.' In other words, it is the new global role of the alliance and its complex functions within the region that are being given particular emphasis. These functions include UN peacekeeping, international humanitarian relief operations, and emergency relief activities for major disasters. They also include encouraging security dialogue, defence exchanges, regional confidence building, as well as arms control and reduction – alternatives to focusing on the containment of an adversary.

Second, the US-Japan security guidelines expanded the geographical breadth and reach of the alliance. Under Article 6 of the Japan-US Security Treaty, US forces are granted the use of facilities and areas in Japan for the purpose of contributing to not only Japan's security but also the Far East region. Given this article, the guidelines sought to announce a need for US-Japan joint cooperation in areas surrounding Japanese territory. For the Japanese government, this implies the enlargement of the areas in which Japanese SDF members should conduct military operations with US personnel. That is, if a military conflict breaks out in the areas surrounding Japan, the Japanese government can legally dispatch SDF personnel for joint military actions led by the US military, although Japan's support should be limited to support-oriented logistics.

Ironically, however, one of the greatest sources of anxiety regarding the enlargement of the joint defence areas was the fear that it could dilute the alliance's ability to ensure the security of Japan. According to Douglas Stuart and William Tow, the following issues were of primary concern:

1. How is the responsibility for rear-area support and frontline battles, as well as burdens associated with military action, to be distributed between the member countries?
2. To what extent a threat can be recognized jointly by the alliance members?
3. Will collective multilateral action diminish the autonomy of a member country's foreign policies?[25]

There is also a critical conceptual question that needs addressing. It is related to the extent to which the 'areas surrounding Japan' are defined and what is included and not included. Since the late 1960s, it has been agreed in the Diet that the areas north of the Philippines belong to what was called the 'Far East'. With the inclusion of the wording 'areas surrounding Japan' in the guidelines, it is now possible for Japan to dispatch the SDF to more distant 'neighbouring areas' for the purpose of supporting US military operations. However, because the Cabinet Legislative Bureau has prohibited the application of collective self-defence rights, it is possible that the new guidelines violate the spirit of Article 9 of the Constitution.[26]

Given the above modifications in the interpretations of Article 9, it is already possible for the Japanese to conduct logistical operations for the security of the Taiwan Straits. The only difference after the revision of Article 9 will be the extent of the geographical reach for Japan's SDF, that is, how far the Japanese government can dispatch the SDF from the Japanese territories. However, the issue is already beyond the security of the Taiwan Straits. Therefore, it can be said that even with a revision to Article 9 Japan will perform a similar role for security of the East Asia-Pacific region to what it has already been doing under the current Article 9.

CONCLUSION

This chapter has highlighted how several factors have promoted Japan's contributions to war and peace in international society. What has characterized the aforementioned peacekeeping, disaster relief, anti-terrorism activities/operations from previous foreign policy controversies is precisely that it takes place in the midst of international systemic change. The end of the Cold War and the US victory in the Gulf War challenged established global relationships and opened a new range of options for the Japanese government. Japan's pursuit of a more assertive role has been expected in keeping with its formidable economic and technological capabilities. International circumstances have provided Japanese advocates for change with a chance to pursue a more proactive policy agenda[27] – one that stands in contrast to the notion of a 'declining Japan' hobbled by socioeconomic problems.

Looking back at the past two decades, this chapter has argued that Japan's response has been part of a larger process of redefining its security role in the Asia-Pacific region. Ever since it was criticized for failing to contribute militarily to the 1991 Gulf War, the Japanese government has tried to come up with alternate ways to 'contribute' to international peace and security. Foreign Ministry officials remember Japan's traumatic experience during the Gulf War.

Long-term success in this regard has required changing existing domestic political institutions. For instance, dispatching SDF officers to troubled spots has been mainly discussed within the Foreign Ministry, not the JDA or National Police Agency. Under such circumstances, SDF officers and civilian policemen are doing more than what they were originally assigned to do when they entered their organizations. Other ministries, not directly related to peace and security in the world, are usually (also intentionally) indifferent to these issues. While peacekeeping operations require a great deal of expertise in such areas as education, medicine, construction, water supply and so forth, the Foreign Ministry, which is in charge of peacekeeping operations, has dispatched quite a small number of officials to troubled areas.[28] It will take some time to change the domestic constraints that have prevented Japan from doing its part in the post-Cold War era. However, today's interdependent world and Japan's status have pressed the Japanese government to do more to achieve international peace and security.[29]

NOTES

1 K. Iwanaga, 'The UN in Japan's Foreign Policy: An Emerging Assertive UN Centrism', in B. Edstrom (ed.) *The United Nations, Japan and Sweden: Achievements and Challenges*, Stockholm: The Swedish Institute, 1998, p. 43.

2 In December 2001 the Koizumi cabinet submitted a bill to the Diet that would enable Japanese SDF personnel to conduct peacekeeping activities. In March 2002, more than 700 SDF officers were dispatched to East Timor where they monitored the cease-fire, patrolled buffer zones and inspected weapons and landmines.

[3] Y. Suzuki, 'Anpori Kamei: Gaimushō no Shosō' [Joining the Security Council: The Foreign Ministry's Views], *Bungei Shunju*, November 1994.

[4] G. D. Hook et al., *Japan's International Relations: Politics, Economics, and Security*, London and New York: Routledge, 2001, p. 323.

[5] Thus, even after the Peacekeeping Law was passed in 1992, serious constraints were imposed whenever SDF personnel would be sent to troubled regions. The Diet made a distinction between substantial, military-related operations (i.e. PKF) and less military, support-oriented peacekeeping operations, claiming that the former 'shall not be implemented until a date to be set forth by a separate law'. According to the policy of 'freezing' the substantive activities, Japanese peacekeepers would monitor elections, provide bureaucratic advice and guidance (e.g. police administration, medical care, transportation, construction), and conduct humanitarian relief operations (e.g. rescue and repatriation of war refugees). These 'rear-area support' activities would not include monitoring cease-fires, patrolling buffer zones and inspecting weapons.

[6] T. Shinyo (ed.) *Kokusai Heiwa Kyōryoku Nyūmon* [*An Introduction to World Peace*], Tokyo: Yuhikaku, 1995, chap. 2

[7] R. M. Immerman, 'Japan in the United Nations', in C. Garby and M. B. Bullock (eds) *Japan: A New Kind of Superpower?* Baltimore: The Johns Hopkins University Press, 1994, p. 185.

[8] I. Kawabe, *Kokuren to Nihon* [*the UN and Japan*] Tokyo: Iwanami, 1991.

[9] S. Kozai, *Kokuren no Heiwa-iji Katsudō* [*UN Peacekeeping Operations*], Tokyo: Yuhikaku, 1991, pp. 485–6.

[10] L. W. Heinrich, Jr., A. Shibata, and Y. Soeya, *United Nations Peace-keeping Operations: A Guide to Japanese Policies*, New York: United Nations Press, 1999, pp. 10–11.

[11] The holding of economic summits starting in the mid-1970s is a typical example. In the face of the increasing influence of third world countries on the UN general assembly, the G-5 established a small club that could discuss macroeconomic issues. I Kawabe, *Kokuren to Nihon*.

[12] S. Saito, 'The Evolution of Japan's United Nations Policy', *Japan Review of International Affairs*, 1987, pp. 1–2. Given the situation, Foreign Ministry officials started commenced efforts in the late 1970s at studying UN peacekeeping operations and considered the possibility of Japan's participation. However, the report did not attract wide attention. L. W. Heinrich, Jr. et al., *United Nations Peace-keeping Operations*, pp. 16–17.

[13] K. Iwanaga, 'The UN in Japan's Foreign Policy', pp. 39–40.

[14] A. Tanaka, 'Kokuren Heiwa Katsudō to Nihon' [UN Peacekeeping Operations and Japan], in M. Nishihara and S. Harrison (eds) *Kokuren PKO to Nichibei-anpo* [*UN Peacekeeping: Japanese and American Perspectives*], Tokyo: Aki Shobo, 1995, p. 141.

[15] Ibid., pp. 145–7.

[16] L. W. Heinrich, Jr. et al., *United Nations Peace-keeping Operations*, pp. 24–7.

[17] The evidence is taken from the IPCHQ's web page (http://www.pko.go.jp/PKO_E/rwanda_e.html).

[18] Japan Defence Agency, *Defence of Japan 2005 White Paper: English Summary*, pp. 64–71. Retrieved 18 October, 2005 from http://www.jda.go.jp/e/publications/wp2005/.

[19] Japan International Cooperation Agency (JICA), *History of Japan Disaster Relief Teams*. Retrieved 18 October 2005 from http://www.jica.go.jp/activities/jdrt/gaiyo.html.

[20] The JDA pointed out five challenges for its effective international disaster-relief operations in its *Defence of Japan 2001 White Paper*: 1. establishing information networks among ministries and agencies; 2. strengthening of collaboration with NGOs; 3. securing transportation for international disaster-relief operations; 4. capacity building of SDF and 5. enhancing publicity activities for disaster-relief operations.

[21] *Asahi Shimbun*, 29 September 1991.

[22] Japan Defence Agency, *Defence of Japan 2005 White Paper: English Summary*, pp. 64–71.

[23] Retrieved 7 January 2011 from http://transcripts.cnn.com/TRANSCRIPTS/0109/25/se.24.html

[24] The report also touched upon the need to reexamine Japan's constitution in the future. It also mentions the need to discuss the exercise of the right of collective self-defence rights with an eye to clarifying what Japan should and can do for the international roles outlined in the report.

[25] D. Stuart and W. Tow, *The Limits of Alliance: NATO Out-of Area Problems since 1949* Baltimore: The Johns Hopkins University Press, 1990, pp. 3–20.

[26] M. Sase, *Shūdanteki Jieiken: Ronsō no tame ni* [*Collective Self-defense Rights*], Tokyo: PHP, 2001, chap. 4.

[27] M. W. Doyle, I. Johnstone, and R. C. Orr (eds) *Keeping the Peace: Multidimensional UN Operations in Cambodia and El Salvador*, New York: Cambridge University Press, 1997, chap. 1.

[28] Interview with a Foreign Ministry official, New York, August 1999.

[29] M. W. Doyle, et al., *Keeping the Peace*.

5

Japan's Politics of Environment and Climate Change: From NIMBY to Global Networks

LAM PENG ER

Is Japan facing relative decline in the wake of a rising China?[1] Arguably, even when China's GDP surpasses Japan's GDP quantitatively in 2010, the Japanese GDP will still be better *qualitatively* because it inflicts less damage on the environment. While China is becoming the number two economy in the world in sheer size alone, it has also come at a tremendous cost to its environment – a polluting and painful trade-off which Japan experienced in the 1950s and 1960s. Indeed, Japan has rich experiences in environmental protection, considerable technological capabilities and resources, and is a provider of ODA (Official Development Assistance) for environmental protection to China and other developing countries. Despite Japan's economic stagnation since the bursting of its bubble economy in 1991 and impending problems of ageing and population decline, it remains a leading player in key global environmental policy areas, especially climate change.

This chapter will first look at the three major waves of environmental politics in Japan. The politics of climate change is located in the third wave and will be the main focus of this chapter. I argue that Japan's environmental politics was framed by the nexus of the then ruling Liberal Democratic Party (LDP), the economic and construction industries (with the Ministry of Environment [MOE] often playing second fiddle) and Big Business. In the case of climate change, the competing policy networks were more complicated because of the international dimension. Besides mediating between the competing economically-driven and environmentally-minded policy networks at home, the LDP government had to also consider international trends, norms and negotiations in global warming issues.

Domestically, there were competing policy networks within a one-party dominant system, with the economically-driven groups often trumping the environmentally-inspired cluster. Presumably, if there had been a rotation of political parties-in-power in post-war Japan, the presence of a significant Green Party at the national level, autonomous environmental think tanks and green NGOs with more resources and larger mass membership, then Japanese policymaking towards environmental issues including climate change would probably have been quite different and less pro-business. However, the shattering of perennial LDP one-party rule at the national level by the main opposition the Democratic Party of Japan (DPJ) in the 2009 Lower House Election will change the collusive template of conservative party, economic bureaucracies and Big Business in general and global warming policies in particular.

While Japanese environmental politics have expanded from fighting NIMBY (Not In My Backyard) disputes to forging global networks to deal with global warming, other issues such as biodiversity and conservation have been given less attention. A special pleading is often made for Japanese culture, tradition and 'exceptionalism' to hunt whales and dolphins, and foreign critics are sometimes labelled as culturally insensitive to national differences and hypocritical for accepting the slaughter of other mammals for meat and leather. While Japan pursues a leadership role to mitigate global warming, its willful indifference to international norms about protecting whales and dolphins undermines its international image.

THREE GREEN WAVES IN POST-WAR JAPAN

The first wave, most prominent in the 1950s and 1960s, comprised grassroots movements against industrial pollution best characterized as NIMBY. Typically, they were informal groups formed by residents to defend their local community from the threat of environmental degradation. However, these groups usually disappeared once they were either defeated or succeeded in attaining their goals. Their vision was local – to right the wrongs done to their immediate neighborhood, prevent pollution and claim compensation but had little ambition for a sustained and permanent organization or movement at the national let alone at the global level. Simply put, they failed to establish a national network which could become a precursor to a Green Party of Japan able to compete at the Lower or Upper House elections. However, the first wave never completely disappeared. Even today, local protests against the construction of new dams, the establishment of nuclear power stations and land reclamation of wetlands are evidence of NIMBY politics.

The key driver in post-war Japan's environmental politics was the nexus of the Liberal Democratic Party (the perennial party-in-power between 1955 and 2009), the economic and construction ministries, and Big Business in the quest for economic growth and corporate profits. In the headlong pursuit of economic growth at all costs, which catapulted Japan to the position of the second largest economy in the world, the country suffered from horrendous environmental degradation, triggering citizens or resident movements against industrial pollution. Besides severe air pollution in metropolitan areas by the 1960s, notorious cases of industrial pollution included the Minamata disease in Kumamoto prefecture caused by mercury poisoning, Yokkaichi asthma in Mie prefecture due to sulphur dioxide and nitrogen dioxide emissions, and *itai itai* disease in Toyama prefecture triggered by cadmium poisoning.

A core component of Liberal Democratic Party (LDP) one-party dominance was massive public works (including roads, bridges, dams and land reclamation), which transferred wealth from urban to rural Japan as a form of social welfare to mitigate regional disparities and helped to secure electoral support from Big Business, construction companies and farmers in the form of political donations, manpower in election campaigning and votes. But because Japan is an electoral democracy, the LDP could not ignore rising citizen protests, mounting litigation and the erosion of electoral support, in part, due to environmental pollution.

By 1970, the LDP government sought to defuse mounting public anger about environmental degradation by passing stringent anti-pollution legislation in parliament and established the Environmental Agency the following year. Due to the oil shocks of 1973 and 1979 when the price of energy more than quadrupled, Japanese industries were forced to become more energy efficient and clean. With industrial upgrading and technological advances, factories in Japan became less polluting while dirtier ones relocated abroad where environmental regulations are less stringent. Arguably, 1970 was a turning point for Japan's emergence as a green superpower.

The second wave in the 1980s and 1990s comprised citizen activists who were interested in environmental issues beyond their immediate neighbourhood and monetary compensation. Most prominent is the Network Movement comprising primarily of housewife activists interested in environmental matters such as the recycling of rubbish, opposing the use of water-polluting synthetic soap, misgivings about genetically modified food, pacifism and rights of children and disabled people.[2] The Network Movement is active in a number of major cities in the Tokyo metropolitan area (Tokyo, Kanagawa, Chiba and Saitama) and special designated cities in other regions like Sapporo and Fukuoka. However, their political boundaries are usually confined to the ward, city and prefecture and not the national level.

Supported by the social networks of regional Seikatsu (Livelihood) Club Consumer Cooperatives (with a membership of more than 300,000), around 150 women from the Network Movement have won seats in ward, city and prefectural assemblies.[3] But because the regional and decentralized Network Movement did not break out of its narrow social, gender and middle-class housewife networks and forge horizontal ties with other environmental groups, this movement has been localized to just big cities and urban prefectures and has failed to forge a national Green Party with other like-minded organizations.

Another noteworthy aspect of environmental movements in the 1990s is the exponential rise of green NGOs in Japan due to changing values in an affluent society. The environment has now become more important in the mass consciousness and spontaneous citizen self-help activities, triggered by the 1995 Kobe Earthquake and the subsequent ease for NGOs to obtain official recognition as organizational entities after the NPO (Non Profit Organization) bill was passed in 1998. Another new feature in the repertoire of environmental activism was the first local referendum in Japan in August 1996 in Makimachi, Niigata prefecture against the construction of a nuclear power station. This appeared to be a NIMBY movement but it triggered a contagion of referenda in other parts of Japan where local residents organized against public works projects such as rubbish incinerators and dams.[4] Though resistance may have been local, activists were conscious of efforts and successes in different regions of Japan thanks to the national media and new information technology.

However, environmental activists must surmount many hurdles just to hold a local referendum in Japan. They must first organize a petition with a considerable number of signatures from local residents before sending it to the local assembly which then decides whether to hold a referendum or not. Even if a local referendum is held and won by the environmental activists, the results are not legally binding. In certain cases, activists supported candidates in local and mayoral elections who were sympathetic to their green agenda to ensure that the local assembly would not ignore their plea for a referendum. While the second wave of local referenda and green-like social movement parties remain very much a part of grassroots politics in Japan, the next green wave is national and even global in its outlook.

The third wave gained prominence when Japanese NGOs became interested in the United Nations Conference on Environment and Development (UNCED or popularly known as the Earth Summit) held in Rio de Janeiro in June 1992. Besides those directly interested in climate change issues, there are other environmental NGOs in Japan which are active abroad such as planting trees in Northern China to mitigate desertification. A hallmark of the third wave is the concern beyond the parochial local and national levels to the global arena grappling with issues that do not offer any material compensation as in the case of the first wave. In this sense, the Japanese activists of the third wave are global citizens addressing the impending problem of climate change which affects all humanity. The spatial scale of environmental politics in Japan has therefore expanded from the local to the national and then the global within half a century. It is evident that Japan is a greater global player in environmental issues today compared to two or three decades ago when it was already an economic superpower.

THE POLITICS OF CLIMATE CHANGE

Even though Japan suffered from economic stagnation in the 1990s, the country succeeded in placing itself at the heart of climate change global governance by hosting the 1997 Kyoto Protocol, the only legally binding international treaty to date which limits carbon emissions. Securing the naming of a landmark international treaty after its old imperial capital can be interpreted as an effort on the part of Japan to burnish its image. Simply put, Japan remains an important global player in the key global policy area of climate change despite its relative economic decline.

The DPJ's stunning victory over the LDP in the August 2009 Lower House Election may well usher in significant changes to the country's policymaking regarding climate change.[5] In September 2009, Prime Minister Hatoyama declared at the United Nations Climate Change Conference in New York that his administration is committed to an ambitious reduction of Japan's carbon emissions by 25 per cent from the 1990 level by 2020 to mitigate global warming. From Hatoyama's proposed 25 per cent cut, 15 per cent will come from various efforts within the country, with the remainder coming from emissions trading and carbon sinks.

This numerical pledge is significantly deeper than the reduction of 8 per cent from the 1990 level announced earlier by then LDP Prime Minister Asō Tarō. By offering a sharper reduction in carbon emissions than the international community, Hatoyama sought to achieve three things: reaffirm a promise made in the DPJ's 2009 Lower House Election manifesto to the electorate; act as a catalyst to other nations to be bolder in their reduction of carbon emissions; and for Japan to take the lead once again in the global governance of climate change even after the Kyoto Protocol lapses in 2012.

However, there is a proviso to Hatoyama's policy pledge – Japan will commit to a 25 per cent reduction only if other major carbon emitters pursue significant carbon reductions too. Hatoyama's pledge is therefore only conditional because it is unclear whether the new Obama Administration in the US and the major emitters among the developing countries (especially China and India) are committed to significant cuts with mid-term numerical targets. Despite domestic and international anticipation that a new DPJ government will resolutely deal with climate change much more than its predecessor, Hatoyama's promise may turn out to be empty if Japan refuses to act unless other countries do. Even though Hatoyama also promised vigorous support for developing countries in climate technology and funding at the UN, he fell short of pledging how much Tokyo will commit financially to developing countries.

Hatoyama attended the COP15 conference in Copenhagen in December 2009. Unfortunately, COP15 failed to forge a legally binding treaty to cap emissions and replace the 1997 Kyoto Protocol. As a last ditch compromise, political leaders produced the so-called Copenhagen Accord which promised US$100 billion in yearly payments by the end of the next decade to poor nations that will suffer most from global warming. More specifically, Japan pledged US$15 billion in public and private funding to help developing countries adjust to climate change between 2010 and 2012.

In January 2010, Tokyo formally notified the secretariat of the UN Framework Convention on Climate Change (UNFCCC) of its goal to slash carbon emissions by 25 per cent from 1990 levels by 2020 if other major emitters commit to ambitious targets.[6] During his first policy speech to the Diet in January 2010, Hatoyama declared:

> Some have said that our target is excessively ambitious. However, it is the changes such targets will produce that will give us the chance to break the mould of the Japanese economy and create new demand. We will advance 'green innovation' by making maximum use of Japan's world-leading environmental technologies. We will enact a Basic Law on Climate Change Countermeasures and accelerate regulatory reforms and the introduction of new systems relating to the environment and energy. Under the 'Challenges 25' initiative, we will also mobilize all possible policy tools to transform Japan into a low-carbon society.[7]

In actuality, there is much ambivalence among politicians, the mass media and industry about the 'unfairness' of the 1997 Kyoto Protocol which obliges Japan (already a developed and energy efficient country) to reduce its emissions by 6 per cent from the 1990 level by 2012 but not 'free riding' developing countries like China and India, and the US, which abandoned the Kyoto Protocol after George W. Bush became President.

Despite Hatoyama's tentativeness at the UN Climate Change Conference, his climate change initiative marks a significant policy shift by Japan domestically and internationally. This shift was made possible only by the collapse of fifty-four years of perennial LDP rule which, hitherto, privileged the interests of a Big Business clientele opposed to mandatory cuts to carbon emissions. The new DPJ government is less beholden to industrial interest groups for financial contributions and more wary of bureaucrats (including those from the economic ministry) and is therefore prepared to remake Japan's old climate change policy framed during the period of LDP one-party dominance.

In a nutshell, this traditional policy framework can be described as: technologically-driven, nuclear power-reliant, bureaucratically-led (especially by METI [Ministry of Economy, Trade and Industry]), pro-Big Business, market-sensitive with financial incentives and subsidies from the state, societal voluntarism rather than mandatory cuts, some initiatives by enterprising local governments, and with very limited input from opposition parties, the scientific community, think-tanks, NGOs and public opinion.[8]

Until recently, the key drivers of Japan's climate change policy were METI (with heavy inputs from industries) and the Ministry of Environment (MOE), with the pro-business METI often trumping the environmental concerns of the MOE while the LDP top leadership acted as mediators between METI, MOE and Big Business domestically, and between the US, EU, G8 and other countries internationally. The Ministry of Foreign Affairs (MOFA) is supportive of a Japanese leadership role in addressing climate change to enhance the positive image of the country. There are, therefore, competing domestic policy networks in Japan's climate change policy. METI and Big Business formed an important cluster while MOE, MOFA, environmental NGOs and certain scientific think tanks formed another with the then ruling LDP acting as broker which juggled the concerns of domestic economic growth, environmental protection and Japan's international role in climate change.

The configuration of these policy networks may well be broken by the new DPJ government. The DPJ's philosophy is that elected politicians (as representatives of the people) and not bureaucrats must take the lead in policymaking. It remains to be seen whether the new DPJ government can seize the reins of policymaking in climate change from METI and its industrial clients.

TOWARDS A LOW CARBON SOCIETY IN JAPAN: MYTH AND REALITY

That Japan is globally one of the largest carbon emitters (Figure 1) is not surprising given the fact that it was the second largest economy in the world until 2010 and has a population of 127 million accustomed to the creature comforts and consumerism of an advanced industrial and capitalist society still very much dependent on fossil fuel. Japan emitted 1.34 billion metric tons of greenhouse gases in fiscal 2006 – above the 1.26 billion metric tons of 1990, far short of its Kyoto Protocol goal of 1.18 billion metric tons.[9]

Since the oil shocks of 1973 and 1979, Japan, dependent on imported oil and gas, strove to become energy efficient. That many Japanese homes are relatively small (thus requiring less energy for heating or cooling) and that a large percentage of the population stays in the great metropolitan regions of Tokyo, Osaka and Nagoya (which makes public transportation especially railways and subways more viable

Figure 1: Share of Carbon Dioxide Emission (2005)

	Emitters	Percentage
1.	US	21.4%
2.	China	18.6
3.	Russia	5.7
4.	Japan	4.5
5.	India	4.2
6.	Germany	3.0
7.	Others	42.6
	Total	100

Source: International Energy Agency in *Nikkei Weekly*, 14 July 2008.

and convenient) means that less fossil fuel is burnt than would be otherwise.

Despite the image of Japan being a high-tech and energy efficient country and the producer of commercially viable hybrid and electric cars, the reality is that it is unlikely to meet its Kyoto Protocol emissions obligations. Instead of reducing its emissions by 6 per cent to its 1990 level between 2009 and 2012, its carbon emissions have actually increased by 8 per cent above the 1990 level.[10] This means that Japan must reduce its carbon emissions by 14 per cent from the 1990 level if it is to abide by the Kyoto Protocol – which is very difficult to implement indeed. While Japanese industries have become more energy efficient, carbon emissions have escalated in the country's households, commercial buildings and transportation sectors.

Moreover, Japan has been losing its edge in renewable energy such as solar, wind and bio-fuel. Japan was a world leader in solar energy but has been overtaken by Germany after the LDP government terminated its financial subsidies to households to install solar panels. This subsidy programme to install solar panels began in fiscal 1994 and ended in fiscal 2005 and the solar market has since contracted by 15 per cent each year. However, the programme was reintroduced in January 2009 and subsequently the new DPJ government is prepared to offer subsidies as well to encourage households to rely more on solar energy.

According to the government's white paper on energy, Japan's renewable energy accounted for only 1.8 per cent of the total power generation in 2006, compared with 3.7 per cent in the US and 5.3 per cent in Germany. That will change because the new DPJ government appears to be more committed to renewable energy. Environment Minister Ozawa Sakihito boldly announced in December 2009 that the new DPJ government aims to have solar power and other forms of renewable energy account for at least 20 per cent of the nation's total energy generation by 2020.[11] If Japan can achieve this, it will reinforce its status as a leading environmental power.

Another shortcoming is the fragmentation of Japan's energy grid by ten regional electric utilities – each a monopoly in its locality.[12] Under the new DPJ government, utilities are obliged to buy back excess energy from households generated by renewal sources including solar and wind. As an incentive, the price will be raised from 28 to 48 yen per kilowatt in this 'trade-in' grid system.[13] While the previous LDP government agreed to implement a 'trade-in' based only on solar power, the DPJ administration wants to extend it to all renewable energy.

Conceivably, the DPJ government may meet its Kyoto treaty obligations if it were to increase technical and financial assistance to developing countries to mitigate climate change and earn carbon credits, and also purchase carbon credit through an international 'trade and cap' scheme from countries which have produced less carbon than their emission entitlement. Earlier, the DPJ had proposed a carbon tax as a disincentive to carbon emissions but watered down the proposal to 'consider' a carbon tax in the 2009 Lower House Election. It is uncertain when the new ruling party will implement a domestic 'trade and cap' scheme. Some of the DPJ's 2009 electoral promises also ran counter to a low carbon society: it promised to eliminate a provisional gasoline tax and highway tolls, which would increase car traffic and carbon emissions.

Moreover, Japan cannot significantly increase its nuclear energy generation as a substitute to its carbon-emitting oil and coal-based power stations because of the NIMBY syndrome. Even though the national and some local governments, METI, and utilities often seek to entice local communities with financial incentives and promises of regional economic development, there is profound suspicion among many local residents that nuclear energy is not truly safe due to man-made accidents, negligence and cover ups, damage caused by earthquakes, and the problematic disposal of toxic nuclear waste. As noted above, in August 1996, Japan conducted its first local referendum in the town of Makimachi, Niigata prefecture which voted against a nuclear station to be sited there. Any attempts to build more nuclear power stations are likely to run into social protests and referenda movements by local residents.

A LEADERSHIP ROLE IN CLIMATE CHANGE: ACTORS AND THEIR MOTIVATIONS

Despite the fact that Japanese industries are energy efficient and hostile to mandatory cuts, as well as the difficulties state, corporations and citizens are likely to face trying to implement significant carbon reduction measures, why does Japan seek a leadership role to mitigate climate change? For the Japanese political establishment, a leadership role in a new climate change regime can help satisfy the desire for Japan to play a larger diplomatic role commensurate with its status as the world's third largest economy without embarking on a military role which will contravene Article Nine – the famous no-war clause of the post-war Japanese constitution.

By 1990, Tokyo's interest in playing a global environmental role coincided with international scientific findings and trends that highlighted growing evidence that man-made greenhouse gases appear to have contributed significantly to global warming. In the same year, Tokyo joined several European countries in announcing a desire to stabilize carbon dioxide emissions voluntarily by 2000. In April 1992, former Prime Minister and powerful LDP faction leader Takeshita Noboru hosted an Eminent Persons Meeting on Global Environment in Tokyo in anticipation of UNCED in June 1992. By this time, Takeshita and many other LDP politicians had jumped on the green bandwagon in Japanese politics.

It is unclear whether prominent power brokers like Takeshita embraced a green agenda because they truly believed in it or because it was merely an expedient strategy and image change for their party to win electoral support from a public disgusted with the endemic political corruption of the LDP. Regardless of their true motivations, global environmental concerns appeared to have become a mainstream discourse in Japanese politics. By the 1990s, many Japanese in an affluent post-industrial society had become more environmentally conscious once their basic material needs had already been met.

At the 1992 Rio Conference, Japan signed Agenda 21, which included the Framework Convention on Climate Change (FCCC). However, this framework did not specify any specific measures to be taken by the signatories but left it to be negotiated in the future at annual Conferences of the Parties (COPs). Japan lobbied and won the right to host the Third COP held in Kyoto in December 1997. That the Kyoto Protocol will lapse after 2012 also forces Japan to think: what can it possibly do after that impending deadline?

While Japan enjoys the prestige of an important climate change treaty named after Kyoto, it has been ambivalent and sometimes unsupportive of the Kyoto Protocol framework. Simply put, there is a considerable gap between the rhetoric and reality of Japan's climate change policy. As explained earlier, there is a strong sentiment in Japan that the Kyoto Protocol is not fair because of 'free riders' like the US, China and India. Moreover, until September 2009, Japanese climate change policy was dominated by the nexus of the LDP, Big Business and METI which resulted in the country's failure to meet its obligations under the Kyoto Protocol.

METI is concerned about the competitiveness and profitability of Japanese businesses and that they should not be hobbled by politically-driven rather than technologically-feasible emission cuts.

METI and Japanese corporations do see the economic advantage of selling eco-friendly products and patents abroad. Their preference is for voluntary rather than mandatory carbon emissions for industries. Agreeable approaches include the certification of green products which appeal to certain consumers, state subsidies to purchase eco-friendly cars and solar panels, and 'eco-points' awarded to consumers to redeem other goods if they purchase green products.

Not surprisingly, Japanese Big Business and its METI patron have always advocated the least stringent mandatory emission cuts possible. Similarly, Big Business is cognizant that popular eco-friendly products can be profitable. Led by the Nippon Keidanren (Japan Business Federation), Big Business wants markets and government support to promote Japan's competitive edge in green technology but not to be handcuffed by 'unfair' and costly emissions standards which are not applied to its competitors abroad.

The MOE, environmental NGOs and certain think tanks are most supportive of climate change initiatives and emission cuts because these issues are their reason of existence, and opportunity to play a more prominent role domestically and internationally. The better known environmental NGOs include: Kikō (Climate) Forum, CASA (Citizens' Alliance for Saving the Atmosphere), WWF Japan (World Wide Fund for Nature) and Green Peace Japan. In recent years, environmental NGOs have also participated as members of Japanese delegations to international meetings on climate change because NGO participation has become a global norm. Nevertheless, these environmental NGOs tend to be quite small in membership and limited in resources. If they had a large and active mass membership, the ruling party would probably have taken them more seriously.

The leaders of these NGOs and environmental think tanks (such as the Institute for Sustainable Energy Policies and the National Institute of Environmental Strategies) are often quoted by the Japanese media in matters related to climate change. Although these NGOs and think tanks had a voice in the national media, it was up to the then ruling LDP to consider their views, invite them to join its advisory panels and climate change conferences abroad. Notwithstanding the passion and voices of environmental NGOs, the LDP and METI acted as key gatekeepers to the country's climate change policy.

Another feature of Japanese policymaking is the lack of strong and autonomous think-tanks on environmental and other public issues. Indeed, most established think tanks are linked to Big Business or the ministries, and the concern to secure energy supplies for a country lacking in natural resources. Environmental think tanks and advisory councils linked to the ministries are hardly neutral because their findings and recommendations tend to reflect the bureaucratic interests of their ministerial patrons. The National Institute of Environmental Studies and the Institute for Global Energy Strategies are linked to MOE; while the New Energy and Industrial Technological Development Organization, the Research Institute of Innovative Technology for the Earth, and the Global Industrial and Social Progress Research Institute are tied to METI.

In recent years, the Japanese media (regardless of the traditional ideological spectrum of left to right) has accepted the notion that 'man-made carbon emissions are a significant contributor to climate change' is a scientific fact. The media has also given much attention to Former US Vice President Al Gore and the United Nations Inter-governmental Panel on Climate Change winning the 2007 Nobel Peace Prize. Presumably, the Japanese media indirectly shape or perhaps mirror the increasing openness of the public to matters concerning climate change.[14]

The Japanese public is becoming increasingly aware of and concerned about the problem of climate change. According to one survey, the percentage of the public concerned about global warming has risen from 87.1 per cent in 2005 to 92.3 per cent in 2007.[15] When asked about the most appropriate international role for Japan today, the public has consistently ranked the country's efforts at international cooperation in environmental issues, especially global change, as number one ahead of UNPKO, peace-building and ODA (Official Developmental Assistance) (Figure 2).

Being an electoral democracy, political leaders and parties cannot ignore public aspirations for a larger role for Japan in the global governance of climate change. Since Japan's acceding to the Kyoto Protocol in 2002, LDP Prime Ministers had sought to make a mark on climate change policy and craft a better image for themselves and their country. Prime Minister Koizumi Junichirō was the poster boy for Japan's Cool Biz campaign, which sought to persuade the public, especially salary men, to surrender their coats and ties, and to dress lightly during summer to

Figure 2: Japan's Role in International Society

1. Addressing global environmental problems	58.0%
2. Conflict resolution and international peace cooperation	44.6
3. Humanitarian assistance to refugees	25.6
4. Promote universal values: rule of law, human rights, freedom and democracy	19.1
5. Contribute to a healthy economy	17.8
6. Cooperate to develop poorer countries	11.9
7. Assist in cultural exchange including the preservation of cultural artifacts	4.7
8. Others	0.2
9. Nothing in particular	0.7
10. Don't know	3.4
Multiple answers	

Source: Cabinet Office, *Public Opinion Survey on Foreign Affairs*, October 2007.

save energy by not lowering air conditioning thermostats. To METI and Big Business, such volunteerism, sacrifice, social pressure and the modification of social behavior are preferable to mandatory emission cuts.

Koizumi's successor, Abe Shinzō, advocated a 'Cool Earth 2050' target, which sought to lower Japan's carbon emissions by half in 2050. This appeared to be impressive but no mid-term targets were stipulated and the base year (whether it was 1990 or 2006 levels) was unclear. Barely a year in office, Abe resigned and was replaced by Fukuda Yasuo. The Fukuda Administration then decided on a climate change action plan that committed Japan to reducing its greenhouse emissions by 60 to 80 per cent from 'current' levels by 2050. Again there were no mid-term targets and the base year was never consistent.

In the wake of his falling popularity support, Fukuda tried to burnish his leadership image by hosting the 2008 G8 meeting in Toyoko, Hokkaido and made global warming a key issue at that meeting. Although Japan put on a brave face and claimed leadership success in moving the G8 forward to a concerted target of 50 per cent emissions by 2050, it was really an empty goal because the G8 Toyoko meeting merely stated 'serious considerations' to seek carbon reductions without any actual commitment or a roadmap to binding cuts. Moreover, it was unclear which year was to be adopted as the base year for the reduction to be calculated.

Although Tokyo aspires to act as a bridge between the EU and the US to forge a consensus on climate change policy, it was virtually impossible given the intransigence of the Bush Administration. Indeed, Japan even tilted towards the US in international climate change negotiations possibly because it was not only an ally to the US but also because it believed that an international global change regime was impractical without the US on board.[16]

At the 2007 COP13 in Bali, the Fukuda Administration appeared to move away from the obligatory carbon emission reductions set by the Kyoto Protocol for individual developed countries and proposed a complicated if not unworkable scheme whereby carbon cuts are to be made by individual industrial sectors (which have different technological capacities for reduction) within a country and then tabulated for the actual target to be attained. Presumably, such an approach was more acceptable to the US than the mandatory cuts of the Kyoto Protocol regime. In this regard, Japan led by the Fukuda Administration was rather disingenuous – seeking to burnish itself as a leader in the global governance of climate change but in reality undermining the very Kyoto Protocol that it was proud of. Not surprisingly, the EU rejected this convoluted 'cut by individual sectors' approach hatched by the Fukuda Administration.

The G8 summit at Toyoko and its centre-piece of addressing global warming did nothing to turn Fukuda's popularity rating around. Just like Abe, Fukuda quit barely a year into office and Asō Tarō became

Prime Minister but did not last longer than his two predecessors. In the wake of the global financial crisis triggered by the US sub-prime mortgage and the worst recession faced by Japan since the end of the Second World War, the Asō Administration tried to kill two birds with one stone – offering consumers 'eco-points' and rebates to purchase green products including environmentally friendly cars and household products, and to stimulate the economy through industrial production for such products.

Of particular note was the clash between the domestic policy networks for climate change during the Asō Administration in 2009. Nippon Keidanren supported a four per cent *increase* in emissions from the 1990 level; MOE favoured a goal of reducing emissions by 15 per cent from the same level while environmental groups lobbied the government to commit to a 25 per cent decrease.[17] According to the media, MOE Minister Saitō Tetsuo and METI Minister Nikai Toshihiro clashed over the appropriate emission targets during government discussions. After taking into consideration the competing domestic and external demands for carbon cuts, Prime Minister Asō compromised and settled for a 15 per cent cut from the 2005 level by 2020 (which is equivalent to only an eight per cent reduction of the 1990 base year).[18]

Unlike Germany and a number of West European countries, Japan lacks a Green Party at the national level let alone one which is a junior partner in a ruling coalition. Japan's earlier citizen or resident movements against industrial pollution had always been localized and driven by NIMBY considerations, which often fizzled out once the local problem was addressed. From the 1980s onwards, green-like local parties, especially the Network Movement, have proliferated in certain urban centres of Japan and even succeeded in capturing some seats in various municipal and prefectural assemblies.

In recent years, there have been talks about the formation of a 'rainbow and green coalition' (which include local parties) and another group, Environmental Party Greens Japan, to seriously challenge the established parties in the national Upper House elections but thus far such aspirations have not been translated into action. Presumably, the absence of a credible Green Party of Japan, with prominent leaders and a mass base of activists and voters, which can compete in national elections, means that the mainstream political parties are less subject to electoral pressure to compete on a more ambitious environmental platform.

While Japan lacks a national Green Party, it has the advantage of certain innovative local governments which have taken the lead in mitigating global warming. Indeed, some local governments headed by governors and mayors regardless of traditional ideological orientation have taken more aggressive steps than the previous LDP national government. The Presidential-like electoral system of local governments allows local residents to directly elect their mayors and governors who often run on policy platforms (including environmental protection). Governors, mayors and local governments in certain localities are also not tied to the nexus of LDP, METI and Big Business prominent at the national level. That local governments in Japan have taken the lead in addressing global warming is by no means a recent phenomenon in Japanese politics. In the 1960s, some 'progressive' governors and mayors (often with linkages to the Japan Socialist Party and Japan Communist Party) introduced innovative and aggressive anti-pollution measures ahead of the national government.

EPILOGUE

While the greening of Japanese politics has undoubtedly occurred, certain aspects of environmental protection, especially the conservation of animal species such as whales, dolphins and blue fin tuna, have not become politicized within the Japanese mainstream. The Institute of Cetacean Research (with government subsidies) continues to engage in 'scientific research', which is really commercial whaling in disguise. Recently, Ric O' Barry's documentary 'The Cove' exposed the dolphin slaughter in Taiji, Wakayama prefecture. The Japanese consume nearly 80 per cent of the world's blue fin tuna and this species may face extinction if there is no moratorium for stocks to recover.

2010 is slated to be the International Year of Biodiversity. In January 2007, Japan offered to host a conference (10th meeting of the Conference of the Parties [COP10]) on biological diversity in Nagoya in October 2010. Similar to its desire to brand an international climate change treaty after Kyoto, the Japanese government wants the prestige of hosting a conference in Nagoya. Just like its climate change policy where there is a huge gap between 'talk and walk', Japan's interest in biodiversity is laudable but it has come under international criticism for its disregard for whales and dolphins and insatiable appetite for tuna.

At the 174th Session of the Diet in January 2010, Prime Minister Hatoyama Yukio made his maiden policy speech, which also covered the issue of biodiversity:

> Of the roughly thirty million living species said to inhabit the planet, an estimated forty thousand are now going extinct each year. ... This year, Japan serves as chair of the Conference of the Parties to the Convention on Biological Diversity. In order to be able to pass on this irreplaceable Earth to the generations of our children and grandchildren, we must transcend national borders and join forces.[19]

That Japan is a leading global player in the issue of biodiversity is undeniable. However, the jury is still out on the question: is it a positive or a negative player in this matter? Perhaps one can argue that Japan has played a more positive international role to mitigate climate change than the issue of biodiversity. Hitherto, a key factor blocking a more ambitious approach to climate change was the nexus between the then ruling LDP, METI and Big Business, which privileged corporate profits and economic growth. However, that is set to change given the new DPJ ruling party, which is much more committed to climate change issues, inherently suspicious of domineering bureaucrats and not beholden to Big Business for financial and political support. Moreover, Japanese Big Business should be less resistant to stricter emission standards, especially when the world is increasingly turning to green products, and indeed should profit from the sales of its competitive hi-tech and energy efficient products.

COP15 at Copenhagen in December 2009 did not produce a new treaty framework to replace the Kyoto Protocol, which will expire in 2012. A dilemma for Japan is that no matter what it does domestically, it will not necessarily be significant from a global prospective of mitigating climate change. Given Japan's low fertility and aversion to large scale immigration from abroad, its population is projected to decline from 127 million in 2009 to around 90 million in 2055. Moreover, it will also experience an ageing population whose consumption patterns, industrial production and energy usage may weaken. Even if Japan were to continue its present climate change trajectory, its carbon emissions should dip significantly given the considerable reduction and ageing of its population within less than five decades. The global problem is that the populations of China and India are set to rise considerably over the next few decades (driven by the same consumerist patterns and high demand for energy), which will more than offset the attempts by Japan and the EU to reduce carbon emissions.

Japan's future role in mitigating climate change will therefore hinge on how it leads abroad – to have a more independent and assertive climate change policy towards the US, work closer with the EU, and provide more aid and green technology to developing countries to adopt cleaner energy and reforestation projects. While the spatial scale of Japan's environmental politics has expanded from NIMBY to global networks, it remains to be seen whether the country's state and society framed by a post-LDP regime are willing to pay the financial cost for a greener and cooler world. Whether Japan is a 'green superpower' in ascendance or decline will hinge on the country's commitment to transforming itself into a low carbon society.

NOTES

1 To be sure, Japan is not the only major country facing relative decline. The term 'decline' is a relative and comparative concept. One should ask: is X declining in comparison to Y? What about the US, Britain, France and Germany in the twenty-first century? Are these Western

countries not facing relative decline too compared to their halcyon days of imperialism and colonization? If the West is facing relative decline, then why should the relative decline of Japan be so remarkable? After all, the West and Japan are early modernizers, and China and India are catching up after many years in the economic doldrums. Is it not inevitable that the West and Japan will suffer from relative decline against the backdrop of rising China and India? However, the West and Japan are already developed countries while China and India are not. Moreover, it is conceivable that a country may face relative decline in one dimension while remaining a considerable power in another dimension.

2 P.E. Lam, *Green Politics in Japan*, London: Routledge, 1999.

3 NET in Fukuoka is supported by the F Co-Op and not the Seikatsu Club.

4 See P.E. Lam, 'Local Governance: The Role of Referenda and the Rise of Independent Governors', in G. Hook (ed.) *Contested Governance in Japan*, London and New York: RoutledgeCurzon, 2005, pp.71–89; M. Kobori, 'Referendums in Britain and Japan: Turnouts, Campaigns and Systems', *Ritsumeikan Law Review*, 26, March 2009, pp.1–26.

5 This section on climate change draws heavily from P.E Lam, 'Japan's Environmental Politics and Change', which will appear in A. Gaunder (ed.) *Handbook of Japanese Politics*, New York and London, Routledge, forthcoming.

6 See 'Japan Notifies U.N. of 25 per cent Emissions Cut Goal', *Japan Times*, 28 January 2010.

7 See 'Hatoyama's First Administrative Policy Address to Diet', *Japan Times*, 31 January 2010.

8 On Japan's climate change policy, see H. Ohta, 'Japanese Climate Change Policy: Moving Beyond the Kyoto Process', in H.G. Brauch, et al. (eds) *Coping with Global environmental Change, Disasters and Security*, Berlin, Heidelberg and New York: Springer-Verlag, 2010; M. A. Schreurs, 'Japan in the Greenhouse: The Challenge of Addressing Rising Emissions,' in B.F.D. Barrett (ed.) *Ecological Modernization and Japan*, London and New York: Routledge, 2005; and C. Holroyd, 'National Mobilization and Global Engagement: Understanding Japan's Response to Global Climate Change Initiatives', International Studies Association, 50th Annual Convention, 15 February 2009.

9 'Emissions Cuts Achievable but ...', *Asahi Shimbun*, 22 December 2007.

10 Toni Johnson, 'G8's Gradual Move toward Post Kyoto Climate Change Policy', Council on Foreign Relations, Backgrounder, 25 January 2008.

11 'Government Targets at least 20 per cent Renewable Energy by 2020,' *Daily Yomiuri Online*, 28 December 2009.

12 'Wind Power Use Hampered by Patchwork Utility Industry', *Nikkei Weekly*, 23 June 2008.

13 See A. DeWit, 'Regime Change Short-circuited: Carbon Emissions and Japan's Geed-in Tariff System', *Asia-Pacific Journal*, November 2009.

[14] The *Asahi Shimbun* notes; 'Having expressed deep remorse for its actions in the Second World War that ended following the atomic bombings of Hiroshima and Nagasaki, Japan has walked the path of peace ever since. Hiroshima was the starting point for post-war Japan. Similarly, Japan should make the Kyoto Protocol its starting point for the twenty-first century, and for global environmental conservation efforts over the century ahead.' See 'Climate Security: Kyoto the Starting Point of Global Environmental Conservation', *Asahi Shimbun*, 23 May 2007.

[15] Cabinet Office, Chikyū Ondanka Taisaku ni kansuru Yoron Chōsa [Public opinion on global warming policy], August 2007.

[16] I. Miyaoka, 'Japan's Conciliation with the United States in Climate Change Negotiations', *International Relations of the Asia-Pacific*, 4(1), 2004.

[17] 'Japan to Cut Emissions by 7 per cent by 2020', *Japan Times*, 8 June 2009.

[18] *Asahi Shimbun*, 9 June 2009.

[19] 'Hatoyama's First Administrative Policy Address to Diet', *Japan Times*, 31 January 2010.

6

National Security in Japan's Space Policy

SAADIA M. PEKKANEN AND PAUL KALLENDER-UMEZU

With the passage of the Basic Space Law in 2008, the Japanese government elevated space policy to the level of national strategy.[1] It also shifted the country's space policy focus from merely commercial and scientific aspirations to military ones that had, in principle, been governed by the Diet's peaceful purposes resolution dating back to 1969. This high-profile legal move by the government may well be taken to signal a strategic and military orientation to Japan's space policy. But the fact is that it speaks more to commercial setbacks in the market that involve some of Japan's most formidable corporate players, such as Mitusbishi Heavy Industries (MHI), Mitsubishi Electric (Melco), Ishikawajima-Harima Heavy Industries (now IHI Corporation), and NEC. As these private players made investments in the commercial space industry over time that did not lead to expected profits, they had an economic incentive to push their allies in the government to develop military space projects that required legal and institutional changes. Such projects looked increasingly legitimate, especially with regional security concerns such as the erratic behaviour of North Korea and the rise of China.

Using this reasoning as a departure point, this chapter argues that it was not so much the market as the military angle that became ever more critical to the progress of space developments in Japan. By this we mean the use of space for military purposes to support, enable, or conduct defensive, and potentially even offensive actions, to protect the homeland. The incremental militarization of Japanese space assets leaves little doubt that there is an explicit and paradigmatic shift towards national security in the contents of Japan's space policy – a theme that is at last openly and officially sanctioned by the legal and policy orientation.

However the case for a military angle in Japan's space programme is difficult to pinpoint for several reasons. First, the very idea that Japan already has the potential to be a military space power seems unreal, given that there are still controversies about the actual status of Japan even as a conventional military power. These debates implicate the actual capabilities of Japan's Self-Defence Force (SDF) and new directions in Japan's security policies, given external geopolitical changes. More fundamentally, they also implicate the 'culture of anti-militarism' and more generally pacifism that is supposed to constrain Japan's remilitarization at a general level.[2] Like reference to conventional military prowess, calling Japan a military space power today seems to be a *non sequitur* given the post-war pacifist strictures that should have constrained any such developments – that is, not to acquire power projection capabilities, not to dispatch SDF forces abroad, not to engage in collective defence, not to exceed 1 per cent of GNP on defence expenditures, not to export arms, not to share military technology, not to breach the non-nuclear principles, and of specific interest here, not to violate the peaceful uses of space.[3]

Second, the research, development, and testing of specific component space technologies was often spread across different governmental institutions and players over the post-war period, making it difficult to see a coherent whole. This lack of a coordinated and cohesive institutional base in terms of the actual developments of specific component technologies was very often pinpointed as a weakness that reflected incoherence at the national space policy level. But, at least in retrospect, the lack of national coherence turned out to be a virtue of sorts. Component by component, even highly controversial militarized space technologies, such as potential re-entry warhead ones or anti-satellite (ASAT) systems, did not draw much negative budgetary, political, or public attention. They continued to be researched, manufactured, and tested under legitimate civilian uses and goals.

Third, and in our view most important, given the emphasis on scientific and commercial dimensions in Japan's space programme as discussed below, the military angle has not been a part of the official rhetoric. Given the origins of post-war Japan's rocket science at research institutes at the University of Tokyo from 1955 onwards, most notably through what morphed into the Institute of Space and Astronautical Science (ISAS) in 1981, it is not surprising to find that there has been a strong element of public scientific research. Japan has consistently supported space science research, and engaged in noteworthy cosmic exploration and Earth observation using its space assets. Japan has also supported space commercialization, involving the fortunes of private industries in global markets. The pivotal role of corporations in promoting Japan's civilian programme on both the rocket and spacecraft front gives the impression that the story of Japan's space programme has been a story only about the market all along. Given that

Japan did not become a major competitor in the global commercial space industry, it may in fact seem even more appropriate to compare it to the country's failures in the civil aircraft industry or to the achievements of rival space players. But whether Japan's space industry is being compared to other high-tech ones or to foreign rivals, such facile comparisons merely detract serious analyses of the ways in which the underlying space technologies are dual-use. This remains true irrespective of whether they are useful in the scientific realm or make it in the commercial arena.

Despite such intellectual roadblocks, we contend that Japan has already made solid progress in developing and testing civilian space technologies that can be transposed for military uses. Rather than searching for a single overarching strategy, the more pertinent fact is that it is the law and institutions that have steadily come to reflect the progress of the militarization of the underlying space technologies, not the other way around. To make these themes clear, this chapter discusses the contemporary legal and policy shifts as well as a specific set of developed or planned spacecraft technologies – all of which mark Japan as a military space power.

The remainder of this chapter is in three parts. The first part contextualizes the militarization of Japan's space developments on two fronts that have been consistently stressed in official rhetoric: the peaceful purposes in space use reflected in the legal and policy realms, as well as the scientific and commercial prospects in global markets. The second part focuses in on a specific set of space technologies, namely satellites and spacecraft, that are currently at play in the portfolio of government agencies and that, despite claims to the contrary, can double over for military purposes. These include existing and planned communication and navigation satellite systems, reconnaissance satellites, small satellites, and ASAT systems. The third part concludes this chapter, focusing on the implications of space developments in Japan.

CONTEXTUALIZING THE MILITARY ANGLE

With incremental and painstaking steps, we believe Japan has acquired and is continuing to develop an advanced dual-use space infrastructure.[4] As with any branch of technological progression, these steps were not guaranteed to lead Japan to an elite spacefaring club that does not admit even all other advanced industrial powers such as Canada or even most individual European countries. Like only a handful of other spacepowers, Japan has independent capabilities on both the rocket and satellite side. In the former, it has sophisticated indigenous liquid- and solid-fuel space launch vehicle (SLV) technologies that equip it with independent access to space. In the latter, it also has a wide gamut of domestic satellite and spacecraft technologies that enable it to carry out advanced communications and observations especially in the Asian region.

The emerging set of technologies based on its long-standing SLV- and satellite-based knowledge also make it clear that Japan continues to keep abreast of, and sometimes leads, cutting-edge research and developments on both these fronts.

Japan has stressed only the civilian aspects of its space programme over the post-war period, and continues to do so. Yet the multi-faceted reality is that the military angle has also been a consistent part of the story virtually right from the start. With a combination of government and especially corporate efforts over time, Japan has acquired advanced military capabilities through its civilian space programme in plain sight of the public. This resonates well with the common understanding among space analysts that about 95 per cent of the underlying space technology has both civil and military applications, and that space policy itself is driven by a combination of science, commerce and security.[5] For example: rockets, launchers and missiles share fundamentals with civilian SLVs; similarly, remote-sensing and navigation satellites can be used to increase crop yields and assist aircraft transportation just as much as they can be transposed to target weapons and guide munitions. Apart from the large-scale assets like SLVs and satellites, component technologies for electronics and computers, optics, propulsion, and sensors are even more difficult to divide neatly across civilian and military uses. At a practical level, in light of the Revolution in Military Affairs (RMA), one dimension of which focuses on technical capabilities, space is considered a strategic asset and has indisputably emerged as both an enabler and primary provider of critical war-fighting capabilities.[6] From reconnaissance and surveillance, to communication and navigation systems, and onto precision strikes and networking, space assets are deemed critical to military operations.

But what specifically is meant by the militarization of space assets? As stated at the outset, this means using them for military purposes to support, enable, or conduct defensive and potentially offensive operations. In the context of space-based capabilities, these refer even more specifically to dimensions that broach the militarization–weaponization debate familiar to space analysts and also the United States military:[7] *space support* (i.e. capability to get to and maneuver in space with functioning launch vehicles and spacecraft); *space force enhancement* (i.e. capability to increase the combat and success potential of a combat force); *space control* (i.e. capability to reap advantages of space assets while others cannot, through surveillance, protection, prevention, and negation); and most controversial, *space force application* (i.e. capability to overtly engage in weaponization).

It is the first three of these dimensions that are pertinent for evaluating Japan's military capabilities in space. But such an analysis is altogether novel because officially only two dimensions have hitherto defined our understanding of developments in Japan's space programme: the legal and policy realms that continuously stressed the peaceful purposes resolution, and the official emphasis on scientific contributions for global progress and breaking into global commercial markets.

THE LEGAL, INSTITUTIONAL, AND POLICY REALM

From the time that it launched the historic *Pencil* rocket in 1955 to the end of the 2000s, the actual developments and progress in Japan's space industry took place in a legal, institutional, and policy realm that lacked coherence. To the extent that we can pinpoint the pivotal element that coloured all of Japan's official space developments, the emphasis would have to be on the peaceful uses of outer space in line with constitutional mandates. Thus, even as space assets were increasingly marked as dual-use by governments and militaries around the world, the Japanese government remained careful to stress only their civilian uses under its pacifist constraints. From 1955 to 2008, it promoted itself as being bound by legal and institutional constraints on the types, uses, and goals of space technology that it could develop as a matter of policy.

In this respect, a set of declarations and Diet resolutions in the late 1960s that explicitly attempted to block any kind of militarization of space assets were particularly relevant.[8] In 1968, Japan's Minister of State declared that although peaceful purposes had two meanings, namely non-aggressive and non-military, Japan's constitutional constraints made the use of the more restrictive latter interpretation more appropriate. In 1969, the Japanese Diet adopted the resolution that limited the development and utilization of space objects and rockets for peaceful purposes in this sense. Also in 1969, upon finding that the establishment law of the National Space Development Agency (NASDA) lacked clarity on these points, a supplementary provision by the Diet stipulated that NASDA activities were also to be circumscribed to peaceful purposes. The combined effect of these provisions was to take Japan's legal standing well beyond the provisions of the 1967 Outer Space Treaty, which has presented interpretive ambiguity over whether the practical use of outer space for exclusively peaceful purposes signifies non-aggressive or non-military uses.[9] At a practical level, this meant that, by emphasizing the latter, the Japanese government explicitly and strenuously disassociated itself from the military implications of the country's space assets – SLVs, satellites and spacecraft, as well as any associated emerging technologies – for the country's national security.

EMPHASIS ON CIVILIAN SPACE DEVELOPMENT

As noted above, the incremental but steady military progress of its space technologies was something that Japan never acknowledged outright. Indeed, over the post-war period, the legal and institutional structure focused attention on a very restrictive interpretation of the peaceful purposes provision. With this as the core, there was never any wavering of the official position: Japan' pragmatic quest for an indigenous space industry was for civilian purposes, with both scientific and commercial dimensions.

On the scientific side, Japan developed a full-fledged space science programme with an international reputation, with work that continues apace through such activities as observation of space phenomena, lunar and planetary science, cosmology, environmental and geographical monitoring, participation in the International Space Station (ISS), as well as lunar and planetary exploration.[10] It established, for example, Japan's first manned experimental facility at the ISS, known as the *Japanese Experimental Module (JEM/Kibō)*. Japan also launched the *Selenological and Engineering Explorer* (*SELENE/Kaguya*) in September 2007, billed as the world's largest lunar mission since the American Apollo programme which performed flawlessly. The Japan Aerospace Exploration Agency (JAXA) has also made overtures about mounting expeditions to the moon and even Mars. At the very least, despite budgetary and technical uncertainties, these ventures remain noteworthy.

The government's emphasis was even more strenuous on the commercial side. After all, this was a sector that would come to involve the economic fortunes of some of Japan's biggest aerospace manufacturers, namely MHI, Melco, IHI Aerospace and NEC. With an estimated $2 billion per year invested by the government for research, development, and testing from the 1990s onwards, it was expected that the industry would eventually make commercial profits in key sectors of the global space industry. But by the close of the 1990s, after forty-odd years of varying government support, the commercial prospects for Japan's space industry were still dim. Close to 70 per cent of the industry was estimated to be dependent on government demand in the 1990s, and dependence on government contracts continues to be critical at present.[11]

In 2008, the worldwide space revenues from public and private sources was estimated to be worth about $257 billion; revenues for commercial space infrastructure, including launch vehicles, satellites, ground stations, and in-space platforms totalled over $83 billion.[12] The global space industry continues to be dominated by other established players, such as from the United States and Europe, as well as ambitious newcomers, such as China and India.[13] Compared to the performance of both sets of players, Japan's market activities still remain quite lacklustre. To be sure, although they lag in the high-profile arena of SLVs and satellites, key corporate players in Japan have generated space equipment industry sales over the years totalling about $2.5 billion in fiscal 2008.[14] But even this amount was significantly less than the $3.8 billion recorded a decade earlier, suggesting a shrinking commercial share despite the appreciation for the technological sophistication of the Japanese space equipment. It was only in December 2008 that Melco scored its first overseas contract to supply a new satellite for a consortium by two telecom firms in Singapore and Taiwan.[15] Similarly, after submitting about seventy bids worldwide, it was only in January 2009 that MHI finally secured a contract for an order to launch a multi-purpose South Korean satellite on its *H-IIA* rocket, cutting costs by also launching a Japanese government satellite.

SPACECRAFT TECHNOLOGIES AND THE PLAYERS

Despite the legal and commercial limitations, Japan continued the piecemeal development of dual-use space assets to such a degree that at present we believe Japan is marked as a military space power. Through the new Basic Space Law, Japan now openly recognizes the peaceful uses of outer space as non-aggressive rather than non-military as it chose to do in 1969. This specific legal change came about not just due to the dual-use nature of space technologies. Rather, the shift can also be attributed to the fact that it offered economic benefits to the makers of such technologies who thus had an incentive to push for it.

The focus on underlying economic interests pushing for favourable changes resonates both theoretically and historically. At the theoretical level, political economists expect policy to be biased in favour of special or concentrated interests because mass publics or electorates may well lack understanding of the effect or technical complexity of such policies.[16] Thus it is not controversial to claim that, relative especially to diffuse interests, concentrated interests exert greater influence on economic policy making. At the historical level, private industry has played a key role in Japan's militarization saga, and its role across both conventional and space-based production needs to be taken into account today.[17] Thanks to the steady efforts of private industry, it is the legal and policy shifts in the late 2000s, as discussed above, that are actually catching up with the incremental and specific changes in Japan's space technologies.

This section lays out details of some of the key space technologies that form the plank of a military space infrastructure – existing and planned communication and navigation satellite systems, reconnaissance satellites, as well as small satellites and potentially advanced anti-satellite (ASAT) systems. In line with the RMA discussed earlier, in military operations, communication and navigation spacecraft are critical for relaying secure information from a constellation of satellites to ground stations, and for transmitting it to mobile terminals in the field; reconnaissance satellites are critical for obtaining information prior to, and during, any military operation; and ASAT systems may be used for protecting home satellites and, if necessary, also disabling foreign ones.

These different dimensions suggest that Japan already has a significant military space infrastructure in place.

COMMUNICATION AND NAVIGATION SATELLITE SYSTEMS INFRASTRUCTURE

Japan has been at the forefront of some of the world's most advanced communication and navigation systems, and its efforts are also poised to expand and become even more grand in the Asian region. This section briefly outlines some of the key satellites and spacecraft that are relevant to our discussion.[18] On the communication side, although little information is available about Japan's efforts to have direct access to military communication satellites, there have been calls to build a network-centric military space communications systems.[19] As in other technologies, the long-standing advances made on the civil side in the series of communication technologies from the late 1970s onwards were instrumental, beginning with *Communication Satellite/Sakura* (*CS/Sakura*) in 1977 and the *Experimental Communication Satellite/Ayame* (*ECS/Ayame)* in 1979. As the country's communication technologies began to advance, Japan's defence establishment began to make use of satellites for military communications via transponders, such as on Space Communication Corporation's (SCC) *Superbird* satellites. These moves were justified by the 'common use principle' decreed by the Japanese government in February 1985.[20] The idea was that the SDF could use those satellites that were commonly used by, or that had capabilities equivalent to, those in use by the civilian sector. Apart from opening the door to the purchase of foreign commercial satellite images for military intelligence, this statement would have far reaching implications, as it extended the range beyond just communication satellites to weather satellites, reconnaissance satellites, and navigation and timing satellites.[21]

Based on these principles, Japan has been a pioneer and leader in advancing and securing satellite communications. For governments and militaries, the new high ground for security purposes lies in optical communications – the use of lasers for optical intersatellite links (ISLs) that are speedier, more voluminous, and unjammable.[22] Japan, too, has been studying the importance of such technologies since 1985, and testing them since the early 1990s. Incremental steps were taken with the Toshiba-built *ETS-VI/Kiku-6* in 1991, which tested a number of highly advanced technologies including both S- and K-band intersatellite technologies and satellite to mobile communications.[23] Similarly, Japan's *OICETS/Kirari*, which was eventually launched in December 2005, achieved the world's first bi-directional optical ISL with the European *ARTEMIS* over a distance of about 40,000 km.[24]

Japan has also parlayed its existing technologies in other directions, such as the bus for *ETS-VI/Kiku-6* in the development of the NEC-built

COMETS/Kakehashi in 1998, which was billed as the most advanced geostationary communication broadcast satellite of its type and which carried out its tests despite initial problems.[25] *COMETS/Kakehashi* also became instrumental in advancing the Melco-built *DRTS/Kodama,* which was Japan's first data relay satellite and, given its performance, will be a pivotal technology for establishing a high-volume uninterrupted communications infrastructure for military needs.[26] Finally, both *ETS-VIII/Kiku-8* and *WINDS/Kizuna* are important in showcasing Japan's continuing regional interests in Asia, focusing not just on ultra high-speed communications in an internet society but also on satellite positioning technologies.[27] Given the technical advances, as well as military needs, Japan also plans to launch its own positioning technology that can be vital for military operations, known as the *Quasi Zenith Satellite System* (*QZSS*).[28] Akin to the US's Global Positioning System (GPS) or the European Galileo global navigation system, Japan's *QZSS* will serve as a highly precise positioning service providing constant coverage across all of Japan regardless of physical or urban terrain.

RECONNAISSANCE SATELLITES INFRASTRUCTURE

Japan's interest in building its own spy satellite network dates back to the early 1990s, and gathered pace in the late 1990s despite initial US opposition.[29] The first clear institutional indicators of Japan's quest for autonomous gathering and analysis of intelligence came with the formation of the Defence Intelligence Headquarters (DIH) in early 1997.[30] In the aftermath of the *Taepodong* incident in 1998, Japan's spy satellite saga eclipsed the importance of this institutional move, which went beyond any one event.[31]The spysat programme has become a permanent fixture of Japan's satellite programme and appears immune to budget cuts.[32] Behind Japan's rapid decision to make and launch its own satellites was the pivotal role of some of the space corporate industry heavyweights, such as NEC, and especially Melco, which rose to become the prime contractor.[33] Japan's Earth observation (EO) programme, which has advanced inexorably since the 1970s and involves the same corporate players, was a critical first step towards the evolution of the underlying technologies for national security usage.[34] While there had been moves by both public and private players to indigenize spysats, it was the evolution of the technology and the external environment that made the essential difference in the government's ability to legitimately forge ahead on its own, and to set aside calls from the US to buy American satellites.[35] Dual-use was still a reasonable cover, but the government's authorization of Japanese development for Japanese use proved to be the clearest death knell for the peaceful purposes resolution.

In March 2003, the first two *IGS* satellites, one for optimal imagery at nominally 1-metre resolution and another for radar imagery at resolutions ranging from 1–3 metres were launched.[36] Japanese public players, and especially private players, were not deterred by the problems and criticisms of the spysat's technological sophistication. The original spysats were successfully followed by a second optical satellite in September 2006, and a second radar satellite in February 2007. The Japanese government has also moved forward with ambitious plans for increasing the quality and quantity of observation satellites all around, including national security/military ones, and has specifically identified Pan-Asian observation as a top priority for EO purposes. In fact, the Basic Space Plan institutionalizes Japan's military space paradigms more clearly on this front than ever before. If all goes as planned to 2020 with no budgetary and technical hitches, estimates suggest that the total cost of public and private development for an ambitious new satellite infrastructure will be about $25 billion.[37] These ambitious plans will also include the *Advanced Satellite with New system Architecture for Observation (ASNARO),* which reflects efforts by both METI's space arm – the Institute for Unmanned Space Experiment Free Flyer (USEF) – and NEC to leverage the next-generation EO programme.[38] This involves launching high-resolution optical and radar satellites starting in 2011. At this stage, Japan's reconnaissance satellite infrastructure includes both the original *IGS* satellites and the new *ASNARO* ones, and it remains to be seen which might be favoured by the Ministry of Defence (MOD).

SMALL SATELLITES AND ASAT SYSTEMS

Space weaponry is one of the most charged aspects of space developments worldwide, and its utility is rightly questioned by many experts.[39] At the broadest level, space weaponry can be any system – including ASAT weapons – capable of damaging or destroying objects in or from space.[40] Any such weapons can harm not only a rival's military space infrastructure but also the rival's civilian space infrastructure. There is a considerable range of ASAT systems, but the high ground of ASAT weaponry rests on co-orbital small-scale or micro-satellites that use precision maneuverability and advanced guidance technology to conduct autonomous proximity operations around other satellites.[41] Any such satellites can be dual-use: on the commercial side they can service and repair satellites; on the military side they can also disable and destroy these satellites. Some components of Japan's civil satellite technologies, particularly those to do with small satellites, can be re-examined in this light.[42] The commercial prospects for such ventures were certainly reinforced by the loss of, and problems with, large satellites such as the *ADEOS/Midori* series starting in the late 1990s.[43] The commercial servicing concept later helped fuel the *Micro-LabSat* that was successfully launched in 2002 and the *SmartSat* programme that was shut down in 2008. Irrespective of whether Japan breaks into any such kind of small-satellite commercial service industry in the future, the civilian developments on this front can also, like other technologies, be transposed to serve military interests.

Japan developed and tested autonomous rendezvous and docking capabilities with the *ETS-VII/Kiku-7* launched in 1997, well ahead of the curve.[44] *ETS-VII/Kiku-7* was an extraordinary experiment for the time in that it had a 'chaser' bus and a 'target' satellite. These were designed to divide into two, fly apart, and recombine in order to test remote controlled and automatic docking technologies, thereby testing elements of complex defensive and offensive counterpace technologies. Despite some glitches, the technology, which astonishingly had been developed close to two decades earlier, worked. At present, Japan's satellite development is also moving from large-scale system spacecraft to include the worldwide trend towards small- and nano-satellites. These are not only cheaper and faster to build, but can be critical to the idea of Space Situational Awareness (SSA) on both the civilian and military side.[45] The first generation of such satellites has spread to universities and engineering students, stressing their civilian applications. These developments thus go beyond the formal space-related institutions, ministries and big corporations that have dominated space development in the past. Nevertheless, as elsewhere, the Japanese government and defence contractors are no doubt cognizant of the military applications of this trend, which are still a work in progress worldwide.

SUMMATION AND FUTURE DIRECTIONS

Although the Japanese government has emphasized the scientific and commercial aspects of its civilian space programme, the historical and emerging dimensions of Japan's space policy presented in this discussion also mark Japan as a military space power. It is difficult to believe that the trends in Japan's military space developments will reverse anytime soon, given a set of changes on doctrinal, legal and policy dimensions that now openly reflect these fundamental technological realities. Externally, Japan's security environment continues to demand military prudence and preparation, and only serves to legitimize the further militarization of the country's space assets in the interest of Japan's national security.

As it happens, these elements resonate with the concrete economic interests of Japan's major space-related contractors who, just as defence contractors everywhere, need to find ways to recoup their investments in space technologies, especially as prospects for commercial profits continue to be dim. Already internally, the legal and policy changes augur a new and visible role for space in Japan's security directions. Articles 3 and 14 in the Basic Space Law mandate a government role for promoting and developing space in the interest of Japan's national security. The follow-on Basic Space Plan is similarly clear on implementing a host of satellites for guarding national security. Like other institutions,

MOD is more focused on space as part of its military space infrastructure, some of which will no doubt fall under its jurisdiction and control in the coming years.[46] In August 2008, MOD instituted its own Committee for the Promotion of Outer Space Development and Utilization (CPSDU).[47] The CPSDU carried out a comprehensive audit of its military space needs in January 2009. Among other things, this committee made its interest very clear in terms of the key planks of a military space infrastructure as identified in this essay – better and higher-resolution imaging satellites, a dedicated military communication satellite, independent navigation and positioning capability, and small and low-cost satellites that can be launched at short notice, as well as satellite protection and SSA.

All these trends suggest that Japan's space developments, and more particularly their implications for the country's national security directions, can no longer be ignored. The efforts of public and especially of private actors involved in the progress of Japan's space developments will engender controversies as Japan continues to independently upgrade its space military infrastructure, more qualitatively than quantitatively, at least at this stage. The country's standing is all the more critical at this time in global politics, as the dynamics of military competition in space have at long last begun to shift out of the shadows.[48] Japan's positions in this game will go on to define space security discourses more openly than ever before across governments and militaries worldwide, and especially so in the Asian region.

NOTES

1 See 'Uchū Kihon Hōan' [Basic Space Law], available online through the Strategic Headquarters for Space Policy (SHSP) at www.kantei.go.jp (accessed 16 April 2009).

2 For key debates see Jennifer M. Lind, 'Pacifism or Passing the Buck? Testing Theories of Japanese Security Policy', *International Security*, 29 (1), 2004, pp. 92–121; Richard J. Samuels, *Securing Japan: Tokyo's Grand Strategy and the Future of East Asia*, Ithaca, NY: Cornell University Press, 2007; Chris Hughes, *Japan's Re-Emergence as a 'Normal' Military Power*, Oxford: Oxford University Press for the International Institute for Strategic Studies, 2004; and Andrew L. Oros, *Normalizing Japan: Politics, Identity and the Evolution of Security Practice*, Stanford, CA: Stanford University Press, 2008.

3 Hughes, *Japan's Re-Emergence*, pp. 31–40, esp. Table 1.

4 The principal arguments and evidence for these claims is drawn from Saadia M. Pekkanen and Paul Kallender-Umezu, *In Defence of Japan: From the Market to the Military in Space Policy*, Stanford, CA: Stanford University Press, forthcoming 2010.

5 For the discussion here, see especially Joan Johnson-Freese, *Space as a Strategic Asset Asset*, New York, NY: Columbia University Press, 2007, pp. 5–7, 30–4; and Kurt M. Campbell, Christian Beckner and Yuki Tatsumi,

U.S.–Japan Space Policy: A Framework for 21st Century Cooperation, Washington, DC.: Center for Strategic and International Studies, July 2003, pp. 3–4.

6 On the RMA, see Theodor W. Galdi, 'Revolution in Military Affairs? Competing Concepts, Organizational Responses, Outstanding Issues', Specialist in International Security, Foreign Affairs and National Defence Division, CRS 95–1170 F, 11 December 1995, www.iwar.uk.org, accessed 4 November 2009; Tomohiro Okamoto, 'RMA: Why is it the Revolution in Military Affairs?', *DRC Annual Report*, 2002, pp. 1–6, www.drc-jpn.org, accessed 18 August 2008; and Hughes, *Japan's Re-emergence*, pp. 83–5.

7 For military space dimensions see United States Joint Chiefs of Staff, *Space Operations*, Joint Publication 3–14, 6 January 2009, pp. ix–xi, II.1-II.10 available online via the Defence Technical Information Center (DTIC) at www.dtic.mil, accessed 28 August 2009; and US Air Force Space Command (AFSPC), *Strategic Master Plan FY06 and Beyond* (Peterson AFB, CO: Air Force Space Command, 1 October 2003), pp. 2, 17–33. On dual-use and controversies related to the militarization–weaponization divide on space assets, see Johnson-Freese, *Space as a Strategic Asset*. pp. 2–6, 27–50, 82–140; Michael E. O'Hanlon, *Neither Star Wars Nor Sanctuary: Constraining the Military Uses of Space*, Washington, DC: Brookings Institution Press, 2004, pp. 1–28; and also James Clay Moltz, *The Politics of Space Security: Strategic Restraint and the Pursuit of National Interests*, Stanford, CA: Stanford University Press, 2008, esp. p. 43.

8 See '"Heiwa"' to iu go no imi ni kan suru Nihonkoku no Kokumu Daijin no Genmei (1968 Nen Dai 61 Kokkai Kagaku Gijutsū Shinkō Taisaku Tokubetsu Iinkai Giroku)' [Declaration of Japan's Minister of State concerning the term 'peace', (Minutes of the Special Committee on Science and Technology Promotion Policy, 61st Diet, 1968]; 'Waga kuni ni okeru uchū no kaihatsu oyobi riyō no kihon ni kan suru ketsugi [Resolution Concerning Japan's Basic Development and Utilization of Space, (Plenary Session of the House of Representatives, 5 May 1969)]; and Uchū kaihatsu jigyōdan hō ni tai suru Kokkai no futai ketsugi [Supplementary Resolution by the Diet Concerning the National Space Development Agency Law] (Special Committee on Science and Technology Promotion Policy, House of Representatives, 13 June 1969). All three instruments are available via the official index on 'Uchūhō' (Space Law) online through the library at JAXA at www.jaxa.jp, accessed 5 November 2009. For background see Setsuko Aoki, 'Tekitō na uchū gunji riyō kettei kijūn toshite no Kokkai ketsugi no yūyōsei' [The significance of the Diet resolution on the legitimate standards for the weaponization of outer space], Sōgō Seisakugaku Working Paper Series, 68, Keio University, April 2005, esp. pp. 5–6, 16–22; Tetsuo Tamama, 'Japanese Space Policy Revision and Future of National Security', DRC Annual Report, 2002, www.drc-jpn.org (accessed 28 October 2008); and Maeda Sawako, 'Transformation of Japanese Space Policy: From the "Peaceful Use of Space" to "the Basic Law on Space"', *The Asia-Pacific Journal*,

44-1-09, 2 November 2009, www.japanfocus.org, accessed 5 November 2009.

9 See Outer Space Treaty, Article IV, ¶2. For an overview, see Paul G. Dembling and Daniel M. Arons, 'The Evolution of the Outer Space Treaty', reprinted in Francis Lyall and Paul B. Larsen (eds), *Space Law*, England/USA: Ashgate, 2007, pp. 164–7; Christopher M. Petras, 'Military Use of the International Space Station and the Concept of 'Peaceful Purpose', *Air Force Law Review*, Spring 2002, findarticles.com (accessed 6 October 2007), esp. ¶IV; and Johnson-Freese, *Space as a Strategic Asset*, pp. 107–109.

10 For an overview of these mission areas see, Japan Aerospace Exploration Agency (JAXA), 'Space Science Research', Satellite and Spacecraft: *SELENE/'Kauguya'*), 'International Space Station (ISS) and Human Space Exploration*: JEM/'Kibo'*; all available online at www.jaxa.jp, accessed 28 October 2009. See also JAXA, 'Japan's Mars Exploration Plan: MELOS', March 2009, mepag.jpl.nasa.gov, accessed 28 October 2009.

11 For earlier assessments on the commercial side, see K. Tatsuzawa, 'Space Commercialization Law and Policy in Japan', *Bulletin of the European Centre for Space Law*, 16, May 1996, pp. 5–6; Saadia M. Pekkanen, *Picking Winners? From Technology Catch-up to the Space Race in Japan*, Stanford, CA: Stanford University Press, 2003, pp. 170–85; and Kazuto Suzuki, 'Administrative Reforms and the Policy Logics of Japanese Space Policy', *Space Policy*, 21, 2005, esp. p. 12.

12 Space Foundation, *The Space Report 2009 – Executive Summary* (Colorado Springs and Washington DC: Space Foundation, 2009), www.thespacereport.org, accessed 28 October 2009, pp. 5–6.

13 See, for example, United States Department of Transportation, Federal Aviation Administration (FAA), *Commercial Space Transportation: 2008 Year In Review*, Washington DC: US Department of Transportation, January 2009, esp. pp. 8, 11, 17, www.faa.gov, accessed 28 October 2009) and the Satellite Industry Association (SIA), *State of the Satellite Industry Report June 2009*, www.sia.org, accessed 28 October 2009, esp. p. 14.

14 Yukihiro Kawana, 'Space Industry Looks for Business', *The Nikkei Weekly*, 5 October 2009; and 'Japan Aerospace Firms Hope Business Takes Off Overseas for Spacecraft Components', *The Nikkei Weekly*, 24 September 2009.

15 Toru Sugawara, 'Aerospace Firms Target World Market', *The Nikkei Weekly*, 26 January 2009.

16 For a succinct summary, see Jeffrey Frieden and Lisa L. Martin, 'International Political Economy: Global and Domestic Interactions', in Ira Katznelsona and Helen V. Milner (eds), *Political Science: The State of the Discipline*, New York: W. W. Norton & Company, 2002, pp. 126–36.

17 See Richard J. Samuels, *'Rich Nation, Strong Army': National Security and the Technological Transformation of Japan*, Ithaca, NY: Cornell University Press, 1996, pp. 99–100; Andrew L. Oros, 'Explaining Japan's Tortured Course to Surveillance Satellites', *Review of Policy Research* 24 (1), 2007, pp. 33–4,

and Christopher W. Hughes, *Remilitarizing Japan*, London: Routledge for the International Institute for Strategic Studies, 2009, pp. 67–77.

18 Unless otherwise indicated, all details and background in this section on the actual communication and navigation satellite and spacecraft systems, as well as the general trajectory of events, are taken from JAXA, 'Satellites and Spacecraft', www.jaxa.jp, accessed 1 July 2009. Additional general background information is from Oros, *Normalizing Japan*, p. 137; Johnson-Freese and Gatling, 'Security Implications of Japan's Information Gathering Satellite (IGS) System', pp. 544–7; and Johnson-Freese, 'Space as a Strategic Asset', pp. 34–7.

19 Takashi Iida, 'National Security: How We Should Push Forward R&D of Satellite Communications Technology As a Nucleus of Network Centric Defence System', *Space Japan Review*, 12 (1–3), 59–60, December–March 2009, pp. 1–13, satcom.nict.go.jp, accessed 12 July 2009.

20 MOD, 'Space-Related Defence Policies and Future Topics for Consideration', Tokyo, MOD, November 2008, p. 1.

21 Oros, *Normalizing Japan*, p. 137.

22 See generally Berry Smutny et. al., '5.6 Gbps Optical Intersatellite Communication Link', *Proceedings of the International Society for Optical Engineering* (SPIE), 7199, 24 February 2009 (online publication), pp. 1–8 (esp. introduction), available online via the Smithsonian/NASA Astrophysics Data System at adsabs.harvard.edu, accessed 28 August 2009; and also Peter de Selding, 'Space-to-Ground Laser Link Tests Set for 2007', *Space News*, 6 April 2006, www.space.com, accessed 1 July 2008.

23 On *ETS-VI*, see also JAXA, 'Laser Communication Experiment Using ETS-6 Satellite', and 'Engineering Test Satellite VI Kiku No. 6 (ETS-VI)', www.jaxa.jp, accessed 1 July 2008.

24 On *OICETS*, see Yuuichi Fujiwara et. al., 'Optical Inter-Orbit Communications Engineerings Test Satellite (OICETS), *Acta Astronautica*, 61 (11–12), 2007, pp. 163–75; and JAXA, 'Toward the Era of Optical Communication in Space. Success of the Optical Inter-orbit Communication Experiment between the Optical Inter-orbit Communications Engineering Test Satellite "Kirari" (OICETS) and the Advanced Relay and Technology Mission (ARTEMIS)', Press Release, 9 December 2005.

25 See JAXA, 'Communications and Broadcasting Engineering Test Satellites 'Kakehashi' (COMETS)', www.jaxa.jp, accessed 1 July 2008; and Craig Covault and Eiichiro Sekigawa, 'Japanese H-2 Failure Ruins Satcom Research Mission', *AWST*, 2 March 1998, p. 34.

26 See JAXA, 'Data Relay Test Satellite "KODAMA" (DRTS)'; JAXA, 'Overview: "KODAMA" Data Relay Test Satellite (DRTS) to Dramatically Extend Contact Time and Areas'; and JAXA, 'DRTS: Data Relay Test Satellite'; with all documents available online at www.jaxa.jp, accessed 1 July 2008.

27 JAXA, 'ETS-VIII: Engineering Test Satellite-VIII Kiku No. 8"; JAXA, 'Deployment Result of the Large Deployable Antenna Reflectors of the ETS-VIII Kiku No. 8'; Press Release, 26 December 2006; JAXA, 'WINDS: Wideband InterNetworking Engineering Test and Demonstration

Satellite Kizuna'; JAXA, '"KIZUNA" Carries out World's Fastest Satellite Data Communication at Speed of 1.2 Gbps', Press Release, 12 May 2008; with all documents available online at www.jaxa.jp, accessed 3 Sept 2009. See also Paul Kallender, 'Japan Develops Mobile System', *Space News*, 12 May 1997; and Paul Kallender, 'Japan to Develop Next-Generation Gobal Stellite Communication Constellation', *Japan Press Network*, 13 May 1997.

28 See Strategic Headquarters for Space Policy (SHSP), *Uchū Kihon Keikaku; Nihon No Eichi ga Uchū o Ugokasu [Basic Space Plan: Wisdom of Japan Moves Space]*, Tokyo: SHSP, 2 June 2009, pp. 19–20, 28–9. For a description and details of the QZSS see JAXA, 'Jyun tenchō eisei shisutemu' [Quasi-Zenith Satellite System], with all JAXA items available online at www.jaxa.jp, accessed 29 July 2009.

29 'Hata Supports Future Possession of "Spy Satellites"', *BBC Summary of World Broadcasts*, 9 June 1994; Eiichiro Sekigawa, 'Japan Ponders Building Military Recon Network', *AWST*, 10 June 1996, p. 38; 'USA Reported Opposed to Japan's Plan for Spy Satellites', *BBC Summary of World Broadcasts*, 8 January 1998.

30 Norihide Miyoshi, 'Integrated Security HQ Set Up by Defence Agency to Enhance Operations', *The Daily Yomiuri*, 25 January 1997; Nao Shimoyachi, 'Spy Satellites Part of Intelligence Quest', *The Japan Times*, 27 March 2003. For an overview of Japan's intelligence trends and policy structure, see Andrew L. Oros, 'Japan's Growing Intelligence Capability', *International Journal of Intelligence and CounterIntelligence*, 15, 2002, pp. 1–25.

31 The general background information and details on the *IGS* in this section are drawn from Johnson-Freese and Gatling, 'Security Implications of Japan's Information Gathering Satellite (IGS) System'; Oros, 'Explaining Japan's Tortured Course to Surveillance Satellites'; Oros, *Normalizing Japan*, esp. pp. 139–46; Hughes, *Japan's Re-emergence*, pp. 85–8; Christopher W. Hughes, '"Supersizing" the DPRK Threat: Japan's Evolving Military Posture and North Korea', *Asian Survey*, 49 (2), 2009, esp. p. 198; Paul Kallender, 'Japan Aims for Operational Military Space Systems by 2006', *Space News*, 2 September 2003, www.space.com, accessed 1 July 2008.

32 Eiichiro Sekigawa, 'Recce Recovery', *Aviation Week & Space Technology* (hereafter *AWST)*, 7 February 2005, p. 38.

33 'Tamokuteki eisei de dokuji kōsō – NEC to Mitsubishi Denki – 1 meetoru no buttai mo shikibetsu' [Independent scheme with multi-purpose satellites – NEC, Melco – distinguishing objects at 1 Meter], *Nihon Keizai Shinbun*, 12 September 1998; Paul Kallender, 'Firms Vie to Win Japan's Biggest Satellite Deal', *Space News*, 8 February 1999; and Paul Kallender, 'Spy Satellite Launch Marks New Era for Japan in Space', *Space News*, 9 April 2003; with all *Space News* articles available online at www.space.com, accessed 1 July 2008.

34 This section draws on the following sources: JAXA, 'JAXA no chikyū kansoku no ayumi [The path of JAXA's earth observation]', available

online at www.jaxa.jp, accessed 1 July 2008; Isamu Mishima, 'Technology Ready for Observation Satellites', *The Daily Yomiuri*, 16 December 1998; Paul Kallender, 'Prime Minister Seeks More Funds To Speed Japan's ALOS effort', *Space News*, 30 November 1998; Paul Kallender, 'Satellites Key to Japanese Disaster Management Plan', *Space News*, 17 February 2003; Paul Kallender-Umezu, 'Japan Lofts Newest Earth Observing Satellites', *Space News*, 30 January 2006; with all *Space News* articles available online at www.space.com, accessed 1 July 2008.

35 'Cabinet Gives Go-Ahead to Recon Satellite Plan', *The Daily Yomiuri*, 7 November 1998; and Akinori Uchida, 'Washington Asks Tokyo to Buy U.S. Satellite', *The Daily Yomiuri*, 15 May 1999.

36 Eiichiro Sekigawa, 'And So It Begins', *AWST*, 7 April 2003; and Paul Kallender, 'Spy Satellite Launch Marks New Era for Japan in Space', *Space News*, 9 April 2003; Craig Covault, 'Launch of Japan's Second Pair of Reconnaissance Satellites Delayed', *AWST*, 6 October 2003, p. 33; Frank Morring, Jr., 'Reconnaissance Launch', *AWST*, 18 September 2006, p. 15; 'Japan's First Reconnaissance', *AWST*, 2 April 2007, p. 24; Frank Morring, Jr., 'Watching North Korea', *AWST*, 5 March 2007, p. 15; and Paul Kallender, 'Rocket Problems Postpone Japanese Spy Satellite Launch', *Space News*, 20 October 2003; with all *Space News* articles available online at www.space.com, accessed 1 July 2008.

37 SHSP, *Uchū kihon keikaku* [Basic space plan], Appendix 2.

38 See USEF, 'ASNARO', www.usef.or.jp, accessed 27 July 2009; and generally also Paul Kallender-Umezu, 'Japan Moving Ahead with Smaller Earth Imaging Satellites', *Space News*, 10 August 2009.

39 See, for example, Bruce M. DeBlois, Richard L. Garwin, R. Scott Kemp, and Jeremy C. Marwell, 'Space Weapons: Crossing the US Rubicon', *International Security*, 29 (2), 2004, pp. 50–84; and Michael Krepon (Co-Founder, The Henry L. Stimson Center), Testimony of Michael Krepon Before the House Committee on Armed Services Subcomittee on Strategic Forces, Space Security, 18 March 2009, www.armedservices.house.gov, accessed 1 August 2009.

40 Clay Moltz, *The Politics of Space Security*, p. 43.

41 Theresa Hitchens, 'Space Wars – Coming to a Sky Near You?', *Scientific American*, 18 February 2008, www.sciam.com, accessed 1 July 2008; Elaine M. Grossman and Keith J. Costa, 'Small, Experimental Satellite May Offer More Than Meets the Eye', *Inside the Pentagon*, 4 December 2003, www.globalsecurity.org, accessed 1 July 2008); and Leonard David, 'Military Micro-Sat Explores Space Inspection, Servicing Technologies', *Space.com*, 22 July 2005, www.space.com, accessed 1 July 2008.

42 On Japan's efforts, see the overview by Uchū Tsūshin Nettowaaku Guruupu [Smart Satellite Technology Group (SSTG)], 'Kidōjyō hozen shisutemu ni kan suru kenkyū [Research related to OMS], sstg.nict.go.jp, accessed 30 August 2009.

43 Paul Kallender, 'ADEOS Loss May Force Redesign', *Space News*, 14 July 1997; Paul Kallender, 'Failure of Adeos Fuels Debate on Size of Satellites',

Space News, 7 July 1997; and Paul Kallender, 'Japan's Adeos-2 Suffers Catastrophic Loss', *Space News*, 11 November 2003; with all *Space News* articles available online at www.space.com, accessed 1 July 2008.

44 See JAXA, 'Engineering Test Satellite VII "Kiku No. 7" (ETS-VII).' www.jaxa.jp, accessed 1 July 2008; 'Japan's *ETS-VII/KIKU-7* Spacecraft', *AWST*, 17 August 1998, p. 25; 'Japan's National Space Development Agency', *AWST*, 7 September 1998, p. 52; Bruce A. Smith, 'Experiments Completed', *AWST*, 8 November 1999, p. 21; Sumiko Oshima, 'Satellites to "Dance" in Orbit', *The Japan Times*, 7 July 1998; 'Tokyo First to Achieve Unmanned Docking in Space', *BBC Monitoring Asia Pacific*, 7 July 1998; Paul Kallender, '*ETS-VII/KIKU-7* – Orbital Rendezvous and Robotic Mission', *Japan Space Net*, 2 April 1997; Paul Kallender, '*ETS-VII/KIKU-7* Achieved Goals Despite Glitches', *Space News*, 17 August 1998, www.space.com, accessed 1 July 2008.

45 Paul Kallender, 'Japanese Lab Forms Unit to Developing Microsatellites', *Space News*, 14 October 2002; and Paul Kallender, 'Japanese Group Sees Important Role for Microsatellites', *Space News*, 29 April 2003; with all *Space News* articles available online at www.space.com, accessed 25 March 2006.

46 MOD, 'Space-Related Defence Policies and Future Topics for Consideration', Tokyo, MOD, November 2008, p. 1.

47 MOD, *Nihon no bōei* [Japan's Defence], Tokyo: MOD, 2009, p. 105; CPSDU, 'Uchū kaihatsu riyō ni kan suru kihon hōshin ni tsuite [Concerning the basic policy on space development and utilization], 15 January 2009, pp. 1–13, www.mod.go.jp, accessed 27 July 2009; and CPSDU, 'Uchū kaihatsu riyō ni kan suru kihon hōshin ni tsuite (gaiyō) [Concerning the basic policy on space development and utilization (outline)], 15 January 2009, www.mod.go.jp, accessed 27 July 2009; and MOD, 'Space-Related Defence Policies and Future Topics for Consideration', Tokyo, MOD, November 2008; slides 2–7. See also Paul Kallender-Umezu, 'Japan Military Space Guidelines Identify Capabilities But Lack Planning Specifics', *Space News*, 16 February 2009.

48 See, for example, Kathrin Hills, 'China Chief Foresees Military Space Race', *Financial Times*, 4 November 2009.

7

Japan's Regional Engagement: Network Diplomacy

PURNENDRA JAIN AND ALEX STEPHENS[1]

INTRODUCTION

The first years of the twenty-first century have seen Japan engage in the Asia-Pacific region more extensively, vigorously and strategically than ever before. While shifts in both sources and types of power now ineluctably reshape the regional and global strategic environments, Japan is taking astute strategic action to maintain its strength through a discernible approach to managing international relationships, especially since Japan's economy, the primary source of its regional influence, has lost some of its earlier allure. In this chapter we use a new theoretical concept of strategic networking to explain how Japan approaches its engagement with this region. In examining Japan's strategic approach, we detect signs of how the nation's policymakers envision Japan's present and potential future strategic leverage, and thus their perceptions of Japan's regional status. We see recognition within Japan's foreign policy community that Japan is no longer *the* key regional player but it is still *a* key player in Asia-Pacific today.

As we explain in this study, Japan's foreign policy community understands that the considerable influence Japan still exercises in the region continues to enhance the nation's appeal to other regional players. So while Japan's national power still has co-optive pull, the diplomatic approach is to harness this strategically valuable appeal for formation and adhesion of regional 'networks' around or including Japan, to deal with issues on which like-minded network members share interests. Importantly, the approach also has potential to help sustain Japan's strategic influence for the longer term through shaping the normative architecture of these regional networks, especially through Japanese involvement in institutionalizing networks as regional organizations. We call this approach 'network diplomacy'.

It uses collective problem-solving principles familiar to Japanese people to address regional issues and maximize the inherent strategic value of Japan's regional strength. It is a pragmatic response to transformation of the strategic landscape across Asia-Pacific and beyond.

Japan's strategic dilemma in the face of this transformation of regional power has forced its foreign policy community to re-conceive the approach to managing the nation's foreign affairs. This means not only *who* to engage with but also *how* to engage. The United States, on which Japan has depended for the past sixty years for its own national security, is on a trajectory of relative decline, Asia's new giant China is emerging as a great power on Japan's doorstep, and India's surge in economic and political power suggests it is becoming Asia's second 'new giant'. We see Japan seeking to position itself more independent of the US, more favourably disposed towards China, and more interested in engaging with India. One way to understand Japan's strategic approach to the Asia-Pacific region, largely because of these three key players, is through the conceptual framework of 'networks'.

Before we discuss network diplomacy as a concept and why it is useful for explaining Japan's engagement with the region, let us clarify what we mean by 'Asia-Pacific region'. The Asia-Pacific Economic (APEC) forum comprises twenty-one Asia-Pacific economies from the North and South Americas, East and Southeast Asia, Russia and Oceania. We do not deal with Russia or South America in this discussion. We do, however, include India, given its great economic significance, its contribution to shifting the region's strategic landscape, and Japan's consequent new interest in pursuing more active and extensive engagement.

This chapter has three parts. The first explains network theory and the utility of this concept for understanding Japan's current approach to regional engagement. The second analyses Japan's involvement in economic and financial networks in the Asia-Pacific region. The third analyses Japan's involvement in security networks in this region since the end of the Cold War and particularly in the aftermath of 9/11. We conclude with some views on how the regional networking concept best captures the evolving foreign policy posture that Japan is developing in Asia-Pacific and beyond.

EXPLAINING JAPAN'S REGIONAL ENGAGEMENT: NETWORK DIPLOMACY

Contributions from all three mainstream dispositions in international relations scholarship – realism, liberal institutionalism and constructivism – have sought to explain Japan's engagement within the Asia-Pacific region that surrounds it. Yet all three have shortcomings. Katzenstein and Okawara made this clear in a well-regarded article advocating 'analytical eclecticism'[2] for understanding the distinctive aspects of politics and security in the Asia-Pacific. Realist approaches have difficulty explaining Japan's interest in multilateralism, while liberal institutionalists struggle to explain the primacy of the US alliance in Japanese politics. Constructivist approaches offer interesting insights into the role of ideas, norms and identities in influencing the terms of the debate on regional dynamics, but they fail to deal with the realities of regional power balances and incentives for cooperation and change.[3]

The analytical picture of Japanese foreign policy towards the region and beyond is therefore confused and confusing. Kang has rightly rejected the unhelpful binaries that mark this scholarship, noting 'Japan is neither normal nor abnormal, militaristic nor pacifist. Its survival and economic health are best provided by a stable order.'[4] Kang is also right to suggest that in conducting international relationships, Japan has not followed a clearly defined theoretical path. Japan kept a very low strategic profile for several decades post-war while concentrating narrowly on economic growth. Then, while flush with economic strength but without constitutional legitimacy to contribute to military efforts, 'chequebook diplomacy' was one of Japan's common responses to maintain and protect national interests.[5] Particularly from the 1990s, Japan has taken up more diverse approaches to this end, through bilateral, regional and global initiatives.

In recent years, however, Japan faces an unprecedented and unforeseen strategic scenario with huge import for the nation and its standing within the region. Here Japan finds itself in some ways strategically sandwiched as the region and the world adjust to what appears to be the rise and fall of great powers. The ascendance of China and emergence of India as powerful Asian nations on the world stage coincide with the relative decline of the US leading a unipolar world order. Japan's ultimate concerns in managing international affairs in the region therefore hinge on the three core themes involving these players. One is preventing China's domination of the region while avoiding tension with this huge and powerful neighbour that shares a troubled history with Japan. Another is reducing reliance on the US, while retaining this principle ally as the centre-piece of its national security. The third is drawing a hitherto neglected India into its regional policy net partly as counterweight to developments with China and the US.

These circumstances demand of Japan something like a diplomatic juggling act to sensitively maintain working relations with all three nations and with other nations across the region while retaining and demonstrating its own regional strength. They require an approach to conducting international relations that gives Japan some capacity to inoculate relationships that need to be kept solid. Containing some issues and their consequences, if possible, within the diplomatic scope of a group that shares interest in specific or related issues enables Japan to minimize the spillover of negative consequences to other issues and other players and achieve most strategically comfortable outcomes for Japan. This is why our analytical lens has been drawn to the concept of strategic networking. It provides Japan with some much-needed flexibility to be defensive, hedging, cooperative, constructive – and influential – depending on the circumstances Japan confronts. We find 'network diplomacy' the most useful explanatory tool for understanding Japan's diplomatic strategy in the current context of a transforming regional order.

Networks – Concept and Context

Berger's 2007 study argues that Japan should be seen as an adaptive state that pursues liberal goals through operating in multilateral institutions, increasing linkages between states and fostering the spread of human rights and democracy. He identifies Japan's ability to build networks, either unilaterally or multilaterally, at the heart of its postwar diplomacy.[6] This framework offers a corrective to earlier studies in acknowledging Japan's networking approach but it is misguided in insinuating that driving Japan's foreign policy is a particular ideology rather than a strategy for pursuing Japanese national interests, which are fluid just like the international and regional environments in which Japan co-exists with others.

At its heart, network theory as an analytical tool explains the pattern of linkages between actors in a system. As Shiraishi and Hau describe:

> A network, in general terms, consists of nodes and links. Ordinarily we use this word loosely to refer to the netlike web of connections among people. In this case, we think of a network as something static, consisting of a certain number of nodes and random connections among them. But a static, or synchronic, view does not allow us to understand the network. According to Albert-Laszlo Barabasi, networks are governed by two laws: growth and preferential attachment. 'Each network starts from a small nucleus and expands with the addition of new nodes. Then these nodes, when deciding where to link, prefer the nodes that have more links.' Through this process, he explains, nodes with many links develop into hubs. If one or more of these hubs are eliminated, the network changes shape and in some cases breaks up. In other words, networks are highly dynamic systems, with new nodes making new links, links being cut, nodes developing into hubs, and hubs being eliminated.[7]

Building networks is a continual process of developing links between two or more actors. A primary appeal of this approach for conducting international relations is the flexibility it affords. First, links are fluid; actors seek to expand, strengthen, diversify, or to shrink or end these links according to how actors perceive their own interests and in what capacity and with what priority to pursue these interests. Second, links are not mutually exclusive, which allows actors to come together on the basis of their shared interest in a particular issue without needing to share interests or views on other matters. Flexibility, however, contributes to uncertainty. Network actions may have unforeseen consequences and states that create links may not be the ones to take greatest advantage of their benefits. The dynamism of a series of interlinked networks that have varied scope, purpose, complexity and benefit is today mirrored in Japan's moves to build links that form nodes/hubs or networks, across the region and beyond.

The networking strategy involves promoting connections not just between and among interested actors but also between and among contested issues and contesting actors. Taking the initiative to establish networks, cultivating nodes and hubs, and steering the choices of members and issues can yield valuable strategic advantage in international diplomacy – symbolically and practically. Symbolically, involvement in initiating, constructing and maintaining networks signals that Japan is still deeply engaged and an influential player in the region, a national player that strategically shapes outcomes rather than simply responds to the consequences of others' actions. Networking activity therefore bolsters perceptions of Japan's power and status in the region. Practical benefits are less perceptible in the short term. Being instrumental in the process of constructing formal and informal networks within the region involves Japan in establishing state norms, especially through its moves to institutionalize networks as formal organizations. Because these norms and rules shape the actions – and sometimes also the perspectives – of other regional actors, they help to create a regional environment more conducive to Japan's interests and therefore help to alleviate some concerns about Japan's vulnerability to this evolving environment.

But another benefit, effective in both short and longer terms, has particular significance given the diplomatic juggling act Japan now struggles to perform. The flexible and eclectic nature of networking strategy enables Japan to effectively form networks with like-minded nations in areas where interests coalesce, but also leaves Japan, and all other network players, well positioned to disagree strongly where national interests diverge, as discussion below illustrates in relation to China in particular. In this way the networking strategy provides a valuable conduit for diplomatic fallout, which Japan finds diplomatically very useful while in its strategically 'sandwiched' position.

The networking approach therefore enables Japan to keep open the lines of communication with its strategic competitors, such as China, with which Japan has strong trade networks, but weak security networks. It also enables Japan to spread risk. This is why Japan works broadly on networks that incorporate not just the US as it primary economic and strategic partner, but also China, South Korea, ASEAN and India, with which Japan shares strong interests in economic and strategic wellbeing.

With this understanding of network approach, let us turn our lens to two areas: economics (particularly finance) and politico-security. In both Japan has used various frameworks to pursue objectives conducive to Japan's interests, which include economic development and regional stability that also serve the region at large. In terms of economics/finance, Japan has facilitated networks to build regional capacity in governance and infrastructure of economic institutions, to serve Japanese companies and other actors in the region as well as the region's economic wellbeing. In terms of national security, Japan continues to try to institutionalize linkages beyond the US, reaching to countries such as India and Australia. Overall, Japan's recent actions in both areas reveal the nation is trying to harness the appeal of the power it still has to draw cooperation across the region, strategically cultivate shared interests, and in some instances formalize cooperative arrangements in regional institutions, as discussion in the following two sections illustrates.

NETWORKS IN JAPAN'S REGIONAL ECONOMIC POLICY

Networks can be created through both informal (non-government and semi-government initiatives) and formal (government) channels, and historically Japan has used both channels to develop networks. Sometimes semi-government initiatives lead to government networks. For example, in the case of the Asia-Pacific Economic Cooperation (APEC) forum, its creation in 1989 was the result of a widespread desire to develop better business–government relations in the region. This official body arose from the formation of the Pacific Basin Economic Council (PBEC) in 1967, followed by the Pacific Economic Cooperation Council (PECC) in 1980. The need for flexibility and informal networks beyond direct business relationships became clear quickly in the post-war period after 1945. Informal networks could go where Japan's government could not go due to post-war sensitivities on both sides.[8] Japan's motivation in taking the initiative and working hard to establish these institutions derived from its interest in fostering a regional business environment that benefited the commercial interests of Japanese corporations.[9] However the effort to create this network of regional bodies to facilitate economic relations across the region has proved to be a great success for Japan and for the Asia-Pacific region. Most states in East Asia and the Pacific now see their own domestic programmes of economic development in regional terms. Japan can take credit for driving much of this effort.

Japan's earliest links to networks in economic policy centred on trade. At various points since 1945, Japan sought different networks to pursue its national interests of economic development and regional stability. Japan's inherent vulnerability to external shocks led it to seek admission as early as possible to the General Agreement on Tariffs and Trade (GATT) process, which it obtained in 1955. When the GATT process slowed during the mid-1980s, Japan sought to push the APEC forum as a way of pursuing free trade in Asia-Pacific. And, as APEC struggled to achieve progress on its trade goals, Japan moved to develop bilateral trade agreements, which drove a regional move to build a network of bilateral trade deals in 1999. Japan began to formalize bilateral economic partnerships beginning with an Economic Partnership Agreement (EPA) with Singapore in 2002, followed by one with Mexico in 2005 and one with Malaysia in 2006.[10] By 2009 Japan had nine EPAs (with most ASEAN states, Mexico and Chile) and is negotiating agreements with Australia, South Korea and India.[11] Japan has also sought to reach beyond bilateral agreements to a regional arrangement in the form of a Japan–ASEAN free trade area.

The election to power of Hatoyama Yukio of the Democratic Party of Japan (DPJ) in September 2009, after decades of LDP rule, reiterated this position. In a number of statements as the new national leader, Hatoyama urged the construction of an East Asian Community to more effectively integrate the individual countries of East Asia. He has argued that a complex network of institutional interactions will help to protect the region against the excesses of nationalism and to strengthen political and economic relations between East Asian nations.[12] His claims affirm Japan's continued interest in establishing a variety of networks with various trade partners in different contexts. The recent moves by the Kan government in November 2010 to express interest in the Trans-Pacific Partnership (TPP) free trade area is also consistent with the desire to tie Japan into networks.

Japan, Networks and Growth in Regional Financial Cooperation

While trade and manufacturing constituted the bulk of activity in Japan's economic network activism, financial and other forms of economic cooperation have also been targeted in recent times. Japan's suggestion to offer crisis funds to countries suffering during the Asian financial crisis in 1997 by establishing an Asian Monetary Fund (AMF) was the starting point of what may evolve into an institutionalized regional financial network. The Japanese initiative was not successful, but it helped to stimulate awareness of the need for greater regional cooperation in monetary and financial matters. Since the Asian economic crisis and Japan's proposal for a regional solution, regional economic and financial cooperation has grown quite markedly. This growth in cooperation is important in two major respects. One is its fast pace. The other is its geographic location, centred around East Asia. Efforts were generated and pursued within this region and every nation in the region is now interested in developing a regional political and economic environment that is open to competition and regulation. Two major elements are the Chiang Mai Initiative (CMI) led by ASEAN+3 and with Japan as a key member, and the development of an Asian Bond Market (ABM) under the auspices of the Executive Meeting of East Asia and Pacific (EMEAP) Central Banks.[13] Japan has continued to push through integration with network diplomacy, despite ongoing problems with others' perceptions of Japan's role in the region.[14]

The AMF and Japan's Role in Regional Financial Cooperation

Japan offered its proposal for an Asian Monetary Fund (AMF) largely in response to perceived mismanagement of the Asian financial crisis by the IMF. Experienced observers claimed that by increasing interest rates, slashing public spending and liberalizing portions of the economy, the IMF turned a moderate economic 'correction' into a full-scale crisis.[15] Japan claimed that the AMF it proposed would solve three problems that underlay the crisis. An AMF would deploy funds when a currency was under sustained, massive speculative attacks. It would provide a 'cooperative framework for the region', which was noticeably absent from Northeast and Southeast Asia. And it would increase international liquidity, an important move given that the IMF had demonstrated it was too slow and its rescue package too small to satisfactorily aid Thailand in the early stages of the crisis.[16] As Hughes argues, Japan's initial proposal of a US$100 billion AMF was used as a means to bridge the gap between the positions of East Asian states and the IMF–Washington Consensus during the crisis.[17] This initial proposal has subsequently been replaced by one in which the region as a whole, rather than just Japan, has pushed for greater regional cooperation in financial affairs.

Japan consulted within the region after its initial proposal for an AMF to a meeting of ASEAN members in August 1997, and the idea gained widespread support for its potential role in the regional economy. The US and Europe, however, expressed strong opposition to the AMF proposal, fearing it would undermine the IMF and strengthen Japan's regional economic position. The proposal ultimately failed despite Japanese efforts to find compromises.[18] In the face of criticism over its AMF proposal, Japan tried a more pragmatic, low-key approach, with other nations taking on the burden of driving economic cooperation. This time Japan's proposal resulted in a larger role for East Asian countries in IMF decision-making, a development called the 'Manila Framework'.[19] But although this addressed some of the pre-crisis concerns of East Asian nations about the nature of regional capital markets and movements, these nations continued to seek a regional network to support regional economic stability. Japan also sought to build a financial network unilaterally through the Miyazawa Initiative in December 1997 and subsequent establishment of a US$5 billion Special Yen Loan Facility in 1998 to assist countries and businesses affected by the crisis. While these moves were useful, they underlined Japan's inability to persuade other countries (particularly the US and China) of the merits of Japanese initiatives. However, this setback provided Japan with a valuable strategic lesson, proving the importance of networks not just for building a stable regional environment, but also for persuading other countries of the long-term merits of Japanese ideas even if they distrusted Japan's motives.

In the aftermath of Japan's proposal, many observers debated the nature of the AMF and its possible utility in the post-crisis economic environment.[20] Positive views valued the stabilizing effect of a regional crisis fund on market confidence, while negative views claimed an AMF would introduce too much 'moral hazard' into the market and upset the regional institutional architecture by undermining the IMF. The proposal's failure to include the US as a partner also renewed fears that Asia was seeking to retreat into a closed regional body, with the AMF as a first step towards a regional central bank of a closed regional organization.[21] The proposal of South Korean Prime Minister Kim Jong Pil, while visiting Japan, to revive the AMF idea showed a 'degree of latent diplomatic support for resurgent Japanese financial leadership' across the region. Encouraged by signs of new East Asian support for a regionally based response to the currency and economic crises, Japanese Finance Minister Miyazawa Kiichi hinted at a new AMF plan in December 1998, this time in a different form.[22]

The end result of the 'politics of resentment'[23] was the Chiang Mai Initiative (CMI), a series of currency swap agreements that became the centerpiece of ASEAN+3 – a meeting of ASEAN, South Korea, China and Japan inaugurated in Malaysia in December 1997 at the height of the crisis.[24] The CMI was brought forward from Chinese suggestions at a Japan–China–South Korea meeting on the sidelines of the 1999 ASEAN+3 meeting, based on China's fear that the ten ASEAN nations would be concerned with China's threat to them as a strong economic competitor. This network of regional reserves served a dual function. It not only made use of Japan's expertise in international finance to improve capacity within the region to manage regional markets, but also managed to stimulate greater reliance on the regional economy for assistance.

Although China was publicly supporting the CMI, it took a backseat to Japan in efforts to build a network of swap agreements, first under the New Miyazawa Initiative and then as an unofficial arbitrator of bilateral swap agreements in ASEAN+3.[25] Japan was also conscious of the political effect such programmes would have on the region, recognizing that helping neighbours when under considerable stress was 'an effective way for Japan to build goodwill in a region still characterized by sensitive bilateral relations'.[26] This can be seen recently following the Global Financial Crisis (GFC), which started in mid-2008. With the arrival of the GFC, Japan has continued to expand its involvement in the CMI and plans to expand its involvement further. In 2009, Japan expanded its bilateral swap agreements with South Korea (from US$3 to $20 billion) and with Indonesia (US$6 to $12 billion) to help bolster these nations in the face of global financial instability.[27] The CMI has also grown with the effort to further multilateralize these swap agreements, culminating in an agreement to expand the total agreements to reach $120 billion in 2009, with a commitment by the participants to expand the CMI further.[28] Japan also signed a bilateral swap agreement with India in June 2008 worth $3 billion.[29] This agreement shows that Japan continues to actively pursue building its networks in finance, a point highlighted by the fact that this agreement was one of the first to expand the CMI framework beyond ASEAN+3.

The Newest Extensions of Japan's Economic Networks: The Asian Bond Fund (ABF) and an East Asian Common Currency

The other big area of collaboration within Asia has been dialogue on a regional bond market. Here too Japan has played an important role. As 40 per cent of the world's savings are generated in Asia and are currently invested in the OECD, a regional bond market may be better placed to use these savings to serve the region. The regional bond market initiative was floated at the 1996 APEC Finance Ministers' Forum, but the US was not interested in it until the Asian financial crisis erupted the following year. Here we see another important aspect of networks in their capacity to generate acceptance of, or at least positive disposition towards, new ideas. The desire to find another source of funding apart from short-term bank lending, as well as the positive impact of the CMI on regional thinking about cooperation, helped to foster a more positive view of financial cooperation, although such cooperation would involve complex deregulation and harmonization across the region.[30] With many Japanese businesses spread throughout Asia-Pacific, Japan's involvement in developing this network has been crucial.

The Executive Meeting of East Asia and Pacific (EMEAP) constructed the first Asian Bond Fund (ABF1) in June 2003 as a small fund trading in governmental securities, while the ASEAN+3 Finance Ministers Meeting set up the Asian Bond Market Initiative (ABMI) in August 2003 to oversee the infrastructure required to form a regional bond fund. The ABF1 was a US$1 billion bond fund limited to some EMEAP members, whereas the second stage of the Fund (ABF2) established in December 2004 was a $2 billion investment fund in a basket of regional currencies, which was open to the public.[31] Japan had a strong interest in the ABF, primarily as a way for Japanese companies to finance their in-country operations. Given the large number of Japanese businesses in Thailand and Malaysia, Japan helped these two countries participate in this mechanism. By acquiring finance through local funding, businesses could cut business costs by avoiding the need for insurance ('hedging') on the transfer of funds from yen to the local currency. Japan also was closely linked to the development of the ABMI. The scope of the ABMI was expanded in 2008 as the push for regional financial integration moved to ASEAN+3 and to the Asian Development Bank (ADB), where Japan is a major player.[32] The comparatively sophisticated nature of Japan's bond markets makes Japan the only country to co-chair two (out of four) of the task forces linked to the expansion of the ABMI.

In October 2009, the Japanese President of the ADB, Kuroda Haruhiko, suggested that initiatives like the CMI and ABMI could be used to help develop a regional consensus on financial cooperation.[33] Japan's regional policy of incrementally building coalitions through networks and giving impetus to institutional development is helping to define to what extent an Asian region will set its own reform and agenda for economic integration. The development of a regional currency unit offers an instructive example. While currency swaps and regional debt markets have become a part of the regional network in economic cooperation, these are not the only areas where cooperation is taking place. At the 2001 Asia–Europe Meeting (ASEM), the Japanese government put forward to the rest of Asia its suggestion concerning efforts to share information on regional currency cooperation, using the EU as a potential model. In 2006, ASEAN+3 finance ministers began to consider the idea, although China's ongoing worries that a shared Asian currency would privilege Japan at the expense of its own economic interests has delayed the proposal.[34] Yet lack of interest has not dissuaded Japan from seeking to build a new network opportunity. In his manifesto published just before his election as prime minister in September 2009, Hatoyama suggests that currency cooperation is 'a natural extension' of the ongoing efforts at economic development throughout East Asia, and that ultimately the European Union (EU) model of regionalism offers insight into the frameworks required to boost economic cooperation in the East Asian region.[35]

This discussion of regional networks in Japan's international economic policy reveals the utility of diplomatic networking as a strategic approach for pursuing Japan's national interests, a vital one of which is the economic strength of the Asia-Pacific region on which Japan's own economic strength depends. We see here how Japan has used networks for many years to advance regional economic cooperation, to the point where a regional currency is being considered as a future goal. We see the veracity of Barabasi's claim that networks are governed by laws of preferential attachment and growth; regional status as an economic giant has drawn prospective network members around Japan to pursue their shared interests. We see a preference to institutionalize key regional economic networks, often, it seems, at Japan's initiative or with strong Japanese urging, and thus with the potential for longer term benefits for Japan as the normative architect of these new organizations. We also see that while networking has been a successful approach for Japan to manage economic relationships in Asia-Pacific for roughly half a century, this approach is still working effectively even under the quite different economic and strategic circumstances that mark the region today.

POLITICO-SECURITY NETWORKS

As in the financial and other economic domains discussed above, trends towards institution building and other cooperative arrangements through regional networking are evident in the politico-security arena. The East Asian Summit (EAS) and Japan's proposal for an East Asian community are the two key examples. The process to establish the EAS was very important for Japan in its struggle to curb China's domination in regional institutions and secure a balance between the two powers so that Japan can pursue its national interests without incursion by a powerful China (and the complex strategic and financial costs this would entail for Japan). To this end, Tokyo successfully argued that India, Australia and New Zealand should be admitted to the Summit in addition to the 13 members of ASEAN+3. Japan did not propose US membership, recognizing that such a move would both harm its own *bona fides* and weaken its position in this very important project. China resisted Japan's move, particularly because it saw that the inclusion of India would substantially dilute China's position within the EAS. However through able diplomacy, using the support of many of the ASEAN members in a politico-strategic network, Japan was successful in drawing India into this grouping.

In 2006, then Japanese Foreign Minister Asō Tarō noted Japan's place as part of not only a growing Asian society but also of a multidimensional network. In September 2009, the new Prime Minister Hatoyama Yukio resuscitated the idea of an 'East Asian Community', proposing frameworks for ongoing economic development and security. This most recent proposal demonstrates the importance of networking within Japan's regional foreign policy given Japan's regional position and national aspirations at this historical moment. First, Japan sees the utility and therefore the strategic value of creating links with other national actors – networking – as a particularly important strategy for pursuing its foreign policy goals. Second, as Hatoyama's pronouncement highlights, networking is promoted as an effective means to address Japan's vulnerability to external harm, whether the consequences of the relative decline of its alliance partner the US or itself as regional giant, or of the rapid rise of Asia's new giant, China. Third is regional identification; the Asia-Pacific region is Japan's primary geographic interest and regional networking is intrinsic to Japan's national wellbeing and security since Japan is *part of this larger regional collective*. As Hatoyama argues, Japan should commit:

> to work continually and unceasingly towards the goal of establishing a system of permanent and universal economic and social cooperation and a system of collective national security in the international community, particularly in the Asia-Pacific region.[36]

The need to maintain Japan's importance to the regional economy has been, and continues to be, the primary national interest. Hatoyama's strong endorsement suggests that network diplomacy in all its forms and with all influences will continue to drive Japan's strategic engagement in East Asia. It will be Japan's foreign policy approach to not only mitigate the threat and actual consequences of regional power competition but also to generate new dynamism in Japan's regional relationships as it tries to create a regional economic and security environment where Japan and other countries can potentially cooperate with each other in peace and for mutual prosperity.

Japan's National Security

In recent years, Japan has sought actively to expand security linkages beyond the US as its sole security provider to a range of other partners in Asia-Pacific. Here, too, Barabasi's two laws of growth and preferential attachment are at work. Tokyo retains the US as the hub of Japan's security, but has attempted to add other nodes to this hub, some attempts successful, others not so. These attempts to expand Japan's security networks are clearly motivated by the regional power shift now under way, which has major consequences for Japan. This 'shift' involves of course the apparent fall of the US and unmistakable rise of China on Japan's doorstep.

The US, Japan and Australia Trilateral Security Dialogue (TSD) exemplifies moves by Japan to expand and solidify its national security networks. The TSD began with official meetings in 2001, which were upgraded to ministerial dialogues in 2005. The TSD has linked the two security 'nodes' (Australia and Japan) to the US 'hub', providing opportunities for the three national leaders to meet personally to discuss a range of security-related matters at ministerial level. In upgrading the TSD to ministerial level, Japan sought to draw in Australia as a new node to its security network, particularly to signal to the region that the days of Japan as simply an attachment to the US security system are gone. Tokyo is no longer the bystander in regional security matters that it was for roughly fifty-five years since the end of the Second World War, and now acts proactively to ensure a position more independent of the US and focused on Asia-Pacific. The power transition we have noted exerts an ever greater pull on the standing of the region's powerful players.

Japan also pushed the idea of a quadrilateral security arrangement involving the US, Australia, India and Japan. Former Prime Minister Abe Shinzō (2006–7) favoured the move. Abe's successor and former foreign minister Asō Tarō even favoured an expanded form of such a network, with the group seeking to establish an 'arc of freedom and prosperity'.[37] But realization of the quadrilateral framework became increasingly difficult for Japan in the face of China's opposition and the subsequent lack of interest among other partners. With Australian Prime Minister John Howard and US President George W. Bush replaced by leaders of different political persuasions, Tokyo's wish for a quadrilateral framework remains unfulfilled. Australian Prime Minister Kevin Rudd and US President Barack Obama appear to have decided already that China's entry into a strong regional position cannot be balanced by a regional network, instead concentrating on bilaterally influencing China's interaction with the region.

But Japan has not ended its quest for establishing other types of security networks with the failure of the quadrilateral framework. Tokyo was instrumental in creating two new bilateral relationships to strengthen and reinforce its security networks. In March 2007, Japan signed a joint Declaration on Security Cooperation with Australia and in October 2008 it signed a similar declaration with India.[38] We may question whether the new government in Tokyo led by DPJ leader Hatoyama Yukio will add further flesh to such security networks that China perceives to be 'anti-Beijing'. Although its approach is more inclusive and less nationalistic than that of his predecessors such as Koizumi, Abe and Asō, Hatoyama's government has also signalled its desire to deal with the US on an 'equal basis' and to renegotiate some existing bilateral agreements to relocate US troops stationed in Okinawa.

Japan still regards – and treats – the US as the hub of its security ties. But the new nodes it has sought to add to its security arrangements confirm Japan's readiness to move beyond its principal security linkage with the US, which was unthinkable hitherto. The move signals Japan's new political will to be strategically proactive in the region. India and Australia are not the only two nations with which Japan is expanding security ties. South Korea is another. Although Japan carries historic baggage in its relations with South Korea and politico-security ties remain fragile, Japan is trying to nurture strategic links with South Korea via the key security provider that the two nations share, the United States. Japan has initiated a security dialogue with the US and South Korea that is similar to the trilateral security dialogue process between the US, Australia and Japan. But it appears that the political will of both parties to develop the process is weaker than in the US–Japan–Australia security network.

Japan remains committed to a larger security community in the Asia-Pacific and is playing a key role in such institutions as the ASEAN Regional Forum (ARF) and track two processes such as the Centre for Strategic and International Studies (CSIS), the International Institute for Strategic Studies (IISS), the Shangri-La Dialogues and the Council for Security Cooperation in the Asia-Pacific (CSCAP). These moves by Japan further signal Tokyo's desire to reduce Japan's dependence on the US for its own national security. Instead it aims to strategically engage partners such as Australia, India and South Korea beyond long-standing trade relations in a more complex relationship that includes national security. All three partners have strong relations with the US, which appears to be a vital consideration. Shared interests and strategic preferences such as these are the basis on which Japan is cultivating security networks for mutual and regional security and for positioning Japan as a powerful strategic player in Asia-Pacific.

The immediate neighbourhood is inevitably a key concern and why Tokyo is now networking on security matters with China as well as with South Korea. Both are Japan's nearest neighbours geographically and both have long expressed concerns about Japan's unwillingness to apologize to them for past military behaviour and more recently, about Japan's future military designs. Because of these concerns of its nearest neighbours and Japan's own uneasiness over China's growing military prowess, Tokyo seeks to maintain engagement with them through low-key linkages, if not true 'networks' in non-traditional security areas. For example, trilateral ministerial-level meetings were held in November 2009 in the Japanese city of Kobe to liaise on cooperation in disaster readiness and control. The three agreed to hold regular meetings in a rotating fashion, with the second scheduled in China in 2011. Japan and China are also planning to hold joint military exercises in the future to build a 'soft' security network, unthinkable only a few years ago.[39] Managing its relations with China though is not an easy task for Japan as events following the arrest of a Chinese trawler captain by Japanese authorities in September 2010 would make it abundantly clear.

CONCLUSION

Historical, constitutional and legal constraints upon Japan serve to complicate and partly disable the effectiveness of conventional approaches to managing international relations and thus the suitability of the conventional theoretical frameworks for explaining Japan's approaches. Conventional theoretical frameworks that conceive of Japan's foreign policy behaviour in terms of the primacy of the bilateral relationship with the US are no longer appropriate for explaining current geo-strategic realities and Japan's intentions in response to them. The rise of two new Asian giants, while Japan struggles to maintain leverage by whatever means it can, presents a contemporary foreign policy scenario quite different from the familiar earlier period that now belongs to history. Japan was then Asia's new and only giant, and the type of giant that Japan had so quickly become exuded economic rather than geo-strategic strength, or even serious geo-strategic interest in its region until quite recent times.

In this chapter we have introduced a new concept, which we have termed network diplomacy, to explain Japan's approach to managing international affairs under present conditions. Our discussion of Japan's two most important types of networks – economic and politico-strategic – has revealed how and why Japan uses network diplomacy as an effective foreign policy strategy to help secure its position as an influential and respected regional power. In both economic and politico-strategic areas, building networks has enabled Japan to steer membership and issues, to help shape a regional environment that is more conducive to Japan's interests and to signal Japan's strategic clout.

These reasons help explain why now more vigorously and determinedly than before, Japan is using formal and informal channels to cultivate linkages. These are to build networks of like-minded regional actors on which Japan can draw and to which Japan must respond as strategically required. Tokyo wants to draw into these networks through separate nodes those that are not Japan-inclined, such as South Korea and China, but here has had less success. Now there is a particular imperative. A new challenge for Japan's foreign policy is to staunch the decline in Japan's capacity to influence others and thus in its status as a regional leader cum Asian giant. This challenge requires diplomatic savvy; Japan is strategically caught in the tide, as power pulls eastward to mainland Asia, away from the US that for a long time had pulled it westward across the Pacific.

The growing impact of China and India upon the Asia-Pacific region economically and strategically, and the concomitant decline in Japan's economic clout have served to diminish the central position in regional organizations and global affairs that Japan had assumed with its own ascendance as an Asian giant from the 1970s. In response, as our discussion of Japan's regional network diplomacy has explained, Japan is working to retain regional strength and position itself for future strategic leverage which will have particular importance if Japan's economic decline continues. Japan is searching for new niches of influence through interlinked networks of regional actors to boost its regional profile and its capacity to achieve national interests, particularly in regional economic development and security. Engaging the region through establishing and cultivating different kinds of networks is a pragmatic response to extend the strategic leverage of its status, while positioned as 'a' rather than 'the' economic powerhouse of Asia.

NOTES

[1] Research for this paper was carried out as part of Purnendra Jain's larger research project on Japan's network diplomacy funded by the Australian Research Council under its Discovery Grants scheme. This is a revised version of our paper presented at the 'Japan in Decline?' workshop held at the University of Adelaide, 23–24 November 2009. We have benefited from feedback and comments provided by the symposium participants, especially from Saadia Pekkanen, Lam Peng Er, Shoko Yoneyama and Maureen Todhunter. We alone remain responsible for the information, interpretation and the analysis presented in this paper

[2] P. Katzenstein and N. Okawara, 'Japan, Asian Pacific Security and the Case for Analytical Eclecticism', *International Security*, 26 (3),Winter 2001/02, pp. 153–85.

[3] For an overview of this debate, see D. Kang, 'Getting Asia Wrong: The Need for New Analytic Frameworks', *International Security*, 27(4), Summer 2003, pp. 57–85; and D. Kang, 'Hierarchy, Balancing, and Empirical Puzzles in Asian International Relations', *International Security*, 28(3), Winter 2003/04, pp. 165–80; and A. Acharya, 'Will Asia's Past Be Its Future?', *International Security*, 28(3), Winter 2003/04, pp. 149–64.

4 Kang, 'Getting Asia Wrong', p. 79.

5 Checkbook diplomacy describes policy openly using economic aid and investment between countries to curry diplomatic favour. The term has commonly been used to refer to Japan's approach to foreign affairs, especially since contributing financially during and after the First Gulf War (1990–91), although it is one that aggrieves many Japanese people.

6 T. Berger, 'The Pragmatic Liberalism of an Adaptive State', in T. Berger, M. Mochizuki and J. Tsuchiyama (eds), *Japan in International Politics: Foreign Policies of an Adaptive State*, Boulder: Lynne Reiner, 2007, pp. 268–9.

7 T. Shiraishi and C. Sy Hau, 'Beyond the Spell of Asianism.', *Japan Echo*, June 2009, p. 34. See also Albert-Laszlo Barabasi, *Linked: How Everything is Connected to Everything Else and What it Means for Business, Science and Everyday Life*, London: Plume, 2003.

8 T. J. Pempel, 'Gulliver in Lilliput: Japan and Asian Economic Regionalism', *World Policy Journal*, 13(4), Winter 1996/97, p. 17.

9 W. Hatch, 'Japan's Agenda for Asian Regionalism: Industrial Harmonization, Not Free Trade', paper for the ISA Conference, 17 March 2004, Montreal, pp. 1–17; and D. J. Encarnation (ed.), *Japanese Multinationals in Asia: Regional Operations in Comparative Perspective*, New York: Oxford University Press, 1999.

10 T. Terada, 'The Making of Asia's First Bilateral FTA: Origins and Regional Implications of the Japan–Singapore Economic Partnership Agreement', *Pacific Economic Papers*, 354, 2006, p. 9.

11 Japanese Ministry of Foreign Affairs, 'Japan's Current Status and Future Prospect of Economic Partnership Agreement (EPA)', www.mofa.go.jp/policy/economy/fta/effort.pdf, October 2007, accessed 12 July 2009.

12 See Y. Hatoyama, 'My Political Philosophy', http://home.kyodo.co.jp/modules/fstStatic/index.php?pageid=24&&, accessed 17 September 2009.

13 E. Lincoln, 'Adapting to Global Economic Change', in T. Berger, M. Mochizuki and J. Tsuchiyama (eds), *Japan in International Politics: Foreign Policies of an Adaptive State*, Boulder: Lynne Reiner, 2007, p. 129.

14 See B. Singh, 'ASEAN's Perceptions of Japan: Change and Continuity', *Asian Survey*, 42(2), 2002, pp. 276–96.

15 See S. Radelet and J. Sachs, 'The East Asian Financial Crisis: Diagnosis, Remedies, Prospects', paper for the Harvard Institute for International Development Conference, 20 April 1998, initially presented to the Brookings Panel, Washington D.C., 26–27 March 1998.

16 J. S. Enia and M. P. Karns, 'Testing the Strength of Regional Cooperation: The Asian Financial Crisis as Threat or Opportunity?', http://pro.harvard.edu/abstracts/016/016001KarnsMarga.html, March 2000, accessed 13 February 2010.

17 C. Hughes, 'Japanese Policy and the East Asian Currency Crisis: Abject Defeat or Quiet Victory?.' http://www.warwick.ac.uk/fac/soc/CSGR/wpapers/wp2499.pdf February 2000, accessed 13 February 2010.

[18] J. Amyx, Moving Beyond Bilateralism? Japan and the Asian Monetary Fund', *Pacific Economic Paper*, 331, September 2002, p. 2.

[19] 'Japanese Policy and the East Asian Currency Crisis: Abject Defeat or Quiet Victory?', http://www.warwick.ac.uk/fac/soc/CSGR/wpapers/wp2499.pdf, accessed 13 February 2010

[20] For example, see Fred Bergsten, 'Reviving the "Asian Monetary Fund"', http://www.iie.com/NEWSLETR/news98-8.html, December 1998; *The Economist*, 'The Case for an Asian Monetary Fund', November 1998, p. 18; Jeffrey Lewis, 'Asian vs. International: Structuring an Asian Monetary Fund', http://www.fas.harvard.edu.au/%7Easiactr/haq/199903/9903a005.html, July 2000; J. Mathews and L. Weiss, 'The Case for an Asian Monetary Fund', *Japan Policy Research Institute Working Paper*, 55, March 1999; and J. Amyx, Moving Beyond Bilateralism? Japan and the Asian Monetary Fund', *Pacific Economic Paper*, 331, September 2002.

[21] Mathews and Weiss, 'The Case for an Asian Monetary Fund', pp. 1, 3; and Bergsten, 'Reviving the "Asian Monetary Fund",'.

[22] Hughes, 'Japanese Policy and the East Asian Currency Crisis'.

[23] R. Higgott, 'The International Relations of the Asian Economic Crisis: A Study in the Politics of Resentment', in R.. Robison, M. Beeson, K. Jayasuriya and H. Kim (eds), *Politics and Markets in the Wake of the Asian Crisis*, London: Routledge, 2000, pp. 261–82.

[24] J. Henderson, 'Reassessing ASEAN', *Adelphi Paper*, 328, London: International Institute of Strategic Studies, 1999, p. 64.

[25] J. Amyx, 'Regional Financial Cooperation in East Asia since the Asian Financial Crisis', in *Crisis as Catalyst: Asia's Dynamic Political Economy*, in A. MacIntyre, T. Pempel and J. Ravenhill (eds), Ithaca and London: Cornell University Press, 2008, pp. 120–1.

[26] M. Castellano, 'Japanese Foreign Aid: A Lifesaver for East Asia?', http://www.jei.org/Archive/JEIR99/9906f.html, 5 September 2000, accessed 21 January 2010.

[27] Japanese Ministry of Finance, 'Japan's Bilateral Swap Arrangements (BSAs) Under the Chiang Mai Initiative (CMI)', http://www.mof.go.jp/english/if/pcmie.htm, October 2009, accessed 21 Janury 2010.

[28] See Japanese Ministry of Finance, 'Joint Media Statement of the ASEAN+3 Finance Ministers' Meeting: Action Plan to Restore Economic and Financial Stability of the Asian Region, 22 February 2009, Phuket, Thailand', http://www.mof.go.jp/english/if/as3_090222.pdf, 29 October 2009; and Bank of International Settlements (BIS), 'Regional Financial Integration in Asia: Present and Future', BIS Papers, 42, http://www.bis.org/publ/bppdf/bispap42.htm, October 2008, 29 October 2009, all accessed 21 January 2010.

[29] Japanese Ministry of Finance, 'Joint Press Release: Signing of the Bilateral Swap Arrangement between Japan and India', http://www.mof.go.jp/english/if/080630press_release.htm, accessed 29 October 2009.

[30] Amyx, 'Regional Financial Cooperation in East Asia since the Asian Financial Crisis', pp. 120–2

[31] Ibid., p. 129.

[32] ADB Asian Bonds Online, 'Asian Bond Market Initiative ASEAN+3 New ABMI Roadmap', http://asianbondsonline.adb.org/features/abmi_roadmap/080731_ABMI_Roadmap_Publication_Final.pdf, accessed 29 October 2009.

[33] Haruhiko Kuroda, 'Designing a Framework for Effective Governance', Keynote Address at the ADB/ADBI Conference on Asian Architecture and Global Governance, 29 October 2009, Mandaluyong City, Philippines, http://www.adb.org/Documents/Speeches/2009/ms2009086.asp, accessed 30 October 2009.

[34] Amyx, 'Regional Financial Cooperation in East Asia since the Asian Financial Crisis', pp. 133–4.

[35] Hatoyama, 'My Political Philosophy', accessed 17 September 2009.

[36] Ibid.

[37] Asō Tarō, *Jiyū to hanei no ko* (The arc of freedom and prosperity), Tokyo: Gentosha, 2008.

[38] For details, see P. Jain, 'Japan's Expanding Security Networks: India and Australia', *Indian Journal of Asian Affairs*, June-December 2009.

[39] 'China, Japan Plan first Joint Military Exercise', http://www.reuters.com/article/idUSTRE5AQ2EY20091127, accessed 26 January 2010.

8

Can Japan Engage Northeast Asia? Overcoming Perceptual and Strategic Deficits

JONG KUN CHOI

INTRODUCTION: JAPAN'S PLACE IN NORTHEAST ASIA

The unstoppable rise of China itself heralds a future that may be marked by a potential power transition from the United States in which Japan may find it even more difficult to find its own role in Northeast Asia. While Northeast Asia has recently become the epicentre of International Relations (IR) debates from a power transition perspective where a rising China may challenge American hegemony,[1] studies on Northeast Asia's international relations have focused on China's growing economic and military influence in the region. North Korea's nuclear development and South Korea's persistent challenge to Japan's economy have also featured in scholarly and media outlets. In this vein, the lack of academic and policy discussions about Japan's roles in Northeast Asia, especially in the 2000s is rather puzzling considering Japan's formidable presence in the region. Japan is still the world's second (although soon to be third) largest economic power. Its military capabilities, especially air and naval power, may be ranked second only behind the United States.[2] Its production networks are densely dispersed throughout the world but concentrated in East Asia.[3] It is one of the largest Official Development Assistance donor countries in the world. In terms of its place in regional security, more attention should be paid to Japan given that a rising China and a nuclear-proliferating North Korea are direct threats to its national security. However, there seems to be a lack of scholarly focus on Japan's prescribed regional roles in major IR journals. It thus seems that Japan's place in Northeast Asia is not highly appreciated even among Northeast Asian states. In short, Japan is undervalued in many discussions of Northeast Asian security.[4]

The Democratic Party's inauguration as the ruling party of Japan and Hatoyama's Asian vision has signalled a more engaging approach towards the region, which may have surprised many Northeast Asian security observers normally accustomed to its dormant regional role in Northeast Asia. What haunts Japan has been historical and territorial disputes with neighbouring states such as China and South Korea. From the Chinese and Korean perspectives, perhaps, their dealing with Japan in terms of memory politics may have been as challenging as their dealing with North Korea's nuclear venture.

Against these backdrops, this chapter addresses the following questions. What constrains Japan's influence in the region? Why have we not seen Japan playing a political and security role commensurate with its economic status? What does a new Japan have to do in order to engage Northeast Asia to contribute to what Hatoyama envisions as an East Asian Community? What can Japan do to enhance its regional role and contribute to a more stable Northeast Asia? For Japan to contribute to forming an East Asian Community (i.e. ASEAN + China, India, Australia, New Zealand and Japan), its cooperation with South Korea and China is quite essential for achieving integration among extremely heterogeneous countries. Without China's and South Korea's cooperation, Hatoyama's vision will remain as political and diplomatic rhetoric. In short, this chapter examines the future prospects for Japan and whether it can engage more actively with Northeast Asia.

This chapter argues that Japan suffers from perceptual and strategic deficits in Northeast Asia, and that these deficits have constrained Japan's role and influence in dealing with its neighbours. The perceptual deficit derives from its unresolved historical disputes that have continued to create diplomatic standoffs with South Korea and China. The strategic deficit is a product of Japan's position on the abductions issue with North Korea which hindered its participation in the Six Party Talks. These two deficits essentially have constrained Japan's role in Northeast Asia.

PERCEPTUAL DEFICIT IN THE POLITICS OF HISTORY

Politics of Memory in Northeast Asia

The unique aspect of the Northeast Asian history dispute is that South Korea's and China's perceptions of Japan's neo-imperial intentions are confirmed when Japan makes territorial claims over what they believe to be their territory. In 2006, the textbook issues became more explosive when it was linked with Japan's claim over South Korea's Dokdo island. The Shimane Prefectural Assembly's proposal for a 'Takeshima Day' in February 2006, to celebrate the 100th anniversary of Takeshima's incorporation into Japan, intended to proclaim this island as an inalienable part of Japanese territory. Moreover, on 23 February, Takano Toshiyuki, Japan's Ambassador to South Korea, also expressed at the

Korean Press Centre, that 'historically Takeshima is Japanese territory', which provoked public outrage in South Korea.[5] On 16 March, the Shimane Prefectural Assembly enacted a 'Takeshima Day' ordinance despite South Korea's explicit demand to the central government of Japan to stop such a move. In the midst of this, the Japanese Ministry of Education announced that the Committee for Re-writing History Textbook's textbook passed the screening process on 5 April 2006.

The Japanese government has argued that South Korea and China should recognize Japan's post-war pacific behaviour. Regarding the Yasukuni Shrine, some local supporters argue that visits to the shrine symbolize Japan's bid for peace by mourning those who sacrificed their lives during the war.[6] Koizumi occasionally counter-criticized the neighbouring states' opposition by expressing doubts as to how the visits to Yasukuni violate the Constitution and emphasizing that he was merely paying his respects to those who died in the war, 'with the conviction that we must never wage a war again'.[7] He characterized South Korea's and China's criticisms as 'temporary confrontations and differences of opinion',[8] and emphasized the relational interdependence from which the three states have benefited. Koizumi also frequently asserted that 'Other countries should not interfere with the way countries pay tribute to the war dead.'[9] Many in Japan also maintain that the country has become an economic superpower, not a military state, that consciously engages in peaceful diplomacy as a reflection of its bitter wartime experiences. Moreover, occasionally the Japanese government has criticized the governments of China and South Korea by pointing out that 'Every day they [Chinese and South Korean citizens] are reminded of the brutalities in the war. They don't know or appreciate Japan's efforts to become a peaceful nation after the war.'[10] Japanese leaders have dismissed South Korea's and China's warnings to Japan as being designed for domestic consumption to appease nationalists in each state.[11] Regarding the history textbook issue, Japan has argued that if draft textbooks submitted by publishing companies to the Ministry of Education fulfil certain criteria, the government cannot prevent publication because of freedom of speech. Despite growing criticism from its neighbours, Japanese right-wingers believe that Japan has its own sovereign right to interpret and teach its own history and neighbouring countries should not interfere with Japan's domestic affairs. Japanese top leaders have also often complained that South Korea and China are 'the only two countries in the world problematizing Koizumi's visit to the Yasukuni Shrine'.[12] Recently, Japan's then Foreign Minister Asō Tarō stated that 'Japan may not have to pay much attention to South Korea and China's warning about Japan's isolation because it is simply not true.'[13] It is clear that many key Japanese leaders are annoyed by what they consider their neighbouring states' endless whining about issues only related to its dark history while downplaying Japan's positive contributions to regional peace and security.

Perceptual Deficit from China's and South Korea's Perspectives

The recurrence of acrimonious relations, especially between Japan, on the one hand, and China and South Korea, on the other, has been a familiar theme in the regional IR literature.[14] Differences over historical memory have been treated as the decisive factor in the lack of trust and a multilateral institution in the region akin to the European Union. The prevailing argument is that the failure of the regional states to resolve the history dispute contributes to the pessimistic outlooks for regional cooperation. Regarding Sino-Japanese relations, for example, the lack of trust rooted in history has bedeviled other aspects of their relationship: mutual suspicions that each is enhancing its military capabilities, differences over the Taiwan issue and Japan's alliance with the US. Both South Korea and China perceive that Japan has not shown any true contrition for its past, and has failed to match its repeated but abstract apologies with corresponding behaviour.

Recurring exchanges of invective over the historical past, especially Japan's aggression during the early twentieth century, the reinforced mutual, negative images of the other and historical animosity certainly have been the usual themes of the Northeast Asian history dispute, which has certainly generated emotional interactions in the region. These emotional elements have perpetuated the recurrence of ebbs and flows in regional cooperation. Former Prime Minister Koizumi's repeated visits to the Yasukuni Shrine during his tenure, governmental approval of certain Japanese history textbooks downplaying Japan's militaristic past against its neighbours, and Japan's persistent territorial claims over Dokdo all heightened tensions in the region.[15] These cases have been perceived to be the result of Japan's failure to accept its wartime responsibility and have generated cycles of confrontation and cooperation since before the end of the Cold War. It appears that South Korea and China are on the same page when it comes to criticizing what they see as Japan's nostalgia and justification for its aggression in the early twentieth century. The crux of the history dispute in Northeast Asia is that China and South Korea see a discrepancy between Japan's verbal apologies and its actual behaviour.[16]

South Korea and China argue that repeated apologies made by Prime Minister Murayama in 1995, Obuchi in 1998 and Koizumi in 2005, all of which expressed a 'heartfelt apology' and 'deep remorse', seem futile given Japan's educational policy on history textbooks and persistent visits by politicians to the Yasukuni Shrine that honours the 2.5 million Japanese soldiers and class-A war criminals.[17] Moreover, such a gap between words and actions are also indicative of, China and Korea commonly argue, Japan's expansive intentions in today's regional politics, which strengthens the lingering historical animosity and activates popular anti-Japan nationalism in the two countries. Therefore, to China and South Korea, an apology will only be considered to be sincere when their former dominator, Japan, fully acknowledges its wartime history and translates that into visible behaviour and policies. Former President Moo Hyun Roh of South Korea claimed, 'We are not asking that Japan continue to apologize. But Japanese leaders should not behave as if their past apologies are insincere.'[18]

South Korea and China agree that the content of history textbooks is a reflection of how a county represents its own history for the purpose of educating its own future generations. Evidently, both in 2001 and 2005, Japan authorized history textbooks that have unprecedentedly covered up the records of Japan's wartime atrocities, despite China and South Korea's explicit diplomatic warnings.[19] The right-wing history textbook failed to mention that Japan had invaded China in 1932, that the Japanese Army had carried out large-scale civilian massacres in Nanjing in 1937, and that tens of thousands of Asian women were forced into sexual slavery by imperial Japanese forces in the 1930s and 1940s.[20] More specifically, the history textbooks distort the facts of atrocities committed by Japanese troops especially on the Korean Peninsula from 1910 to 1945 and in China during the fourteen years of occupation from 1931. For example, one passage often referred to the 1937 Nanking massacre, in which Chinese historians believe up to 300,000 people perished, as 'an incident'.[21] To both South Korea and China, all these historical issues represented in the forms of historical textbooks and Yasukuni remind them of the unresolved heritage of Japanese colonialism.

The controversies over the differing historical memories will not easily fade away. Formulating any reasonable solutions is beyond the scope of this chapter. But what is clear is that Japan has kept Northeast Asia anxious for too long. This memory politics will remain a formidable hurdle for any Japanese leaders who seek to play an active role in Northeast Asia.[22] The prevailing collective memory of domination and subjugation in each capital has strengthened the nationalist appeal. Irrespective of how future-oriented and functionally integrated Northeast Asia may have become in terms of economic interdependence, the region will remain sensitive to the historical memories. Whether it feels unfair and unjustified or not, Japan suffers a perceptual deficit.

ABDUCTIONS ISSUE AND STRATEGIC DEFICIT IN NORTH KOREA'S NUCLEAR PROBLEM

Abductions Abduct Japan's Strategic Choices

From Japan's national security perspective, its biggest threat may come from North Korea. While a rising China itself poses a set of national security questions for Japan, it is in essence contingent and somewhat futuristic. Therefore, potential threats from China have to be met with future strategic planning. However, North Korea's threat is more direct requiring more real time strategic planning in the security and diplomatic areas. North Korea's testing of nuclear devices and long-range missiles have heightened the sense of vulnerability in Japan.[23] North Korea has also become the centre of the Japanese domestic political debate regarding the abductions issue. The abductions issue functions to add a human face to the North Korean threat within Japanese domestic politics. With this, North Korea has been perceived as a state that poses direct security threats to Japan and kidnaps Japanese citizens. Understandably, no other state than North Korea could be perceived as evil in Japan.

Japan did work laboriously in order to normalize its diplomatic relations with North Korea. It maintained close collaboration with the United States and South Korea in the Six-Party Talks while seeking to establish bilateral talks with Pyongyang in order to enhance its influence on the Korean Peninsula. Koizumi's two visits to Pyongyang in September 2002 and May 2004 at the outset seemed to layout a successful roadmap for resolving the pending issues such as the abductions, the post-war settlements and the bilateral normalization. North Korea responded with conciliatory gestures, and both produced an agreement called the Japan-North Korea Pyongyang Declaration.

According to this declaration, North Korea issued a formal apology for kidnapping thirteen Japanese nationals and dispatching spy ships into Japanese waters. In May 2004, Prime Minister Koizumi achieved the return of five of the recognized abductees. Japan also made clear that North Korea should not miss the chance to gain many benefits from dismantling its nuclear programmes. Until this point of time, Japan was perceived as playing an important and perhaps independent role in mediating between the US and North Korea. This perspective, however, was short-lived.

As five of the thirteen recognized abductees returned to Japan three weeks after the summit in June 2004 their return was expected to bring an end to the most sensitive issue on the road to diplomatic normalization. North Korea also handed over the cremated remains of Yokota Megumi to her family in November 2004. However, DNA testing of the remains showed that they were not Yokota's. Subsequently, Japan accused North Korea of handing over the false cremated remains of Yokota Megumi.[24]

An outraged public demanded the Japanese government adopt unilateral punitive sanctions. While 42% of the Japanese public favoured the imposition of sanctions on the North before Koizumi's second trip to Pyongyang in May 2004, the support for sanctions skyrocketed to 63% among the Japanese public and 83% of Japanese Diet Members by October 2004.[25] The major media outlets in Tokyo also voiced support for stronger actions and pressured the government. The *Mainichi Shimbun* on 4 February commented 'North Korea should understand that there can be no economic cooperation if the abduction and nuclear and missile issues remain unresolved.' The *Asahi Shimbun* also declared 'For Japan, resolving the abduction issue continues to be the top priority. At the same time, however, normalization will only be realized through a comprehensive resolution that deals with the abduction, nuclear and missile dilemmas as well.' The *Sankei Shimbun*, on 5 February, pushed the government by arguing 'Japan should definitely not break the principle that there can be no normalization without resolution of the abduction issue. It's now or never for them.'[26] Therefore, after the return of the abductees, 'a sense of hysteria'[27] in Japan worked against reconciliation with North Korea.

What made the situation worse at the time was North Korea's declaration that it possessed nuclear weapons and would withdraw from the Six Party Talks. Japan's public outrage kept pushing for a narrowing of the range of options for Tokyo to deal with Pyongyang. Subsequently, the Japanese government turned away from its rapprochement policy to North Korea and became hostile. The newly installed Abe Cabinet announced the policy of 'abductions issue-first' on 29 September 2006, by declaring 'there can be no normalization of relations between Japan and North Korea unless the abduction issue is resolved.'[28]

From this moment on, Japan's stance on the abductions issue made it very difficult to consider viable strategic choices towards North Korea and narrowed its range of policy options ultimately to the abductions issue.[29] Against South Korea's and China's opposition,[30] Tokyo pushed to put the issue onto the agenda at the Six Party Talks by claiming 'The nuclear problem, the missile programme and the abductions issue must be solved before the normalization of relations between Japan and North Korea.'[31] This would mean that Japan forced itself into the practice of principled contradiction in dealing with North Korea: without solving the abductions issue, no economic aid as well as no talks. The momentum of reconciliation and possible emergence of Japan as a formidable actor in the region was undermined by the abductions issue.

In Japanese power circles, the hawks emerged and raised their voice in support of hard-line policy positions against North Korea, while the doves such as Ministry of Foreign Affairs (MOFA) became submerged in the policy debate. MOFA negotiators who made the Pyongyang agreement possible were publicly discredited and forced to resign while any intellectuals, journalists and others who supported the agreement were also marginalized.[32] In this vein, Japan carried out its hard-line policy by inspecting some 1,400 North Korean boats in Japanese ports in order to intercept any illegal cargos.[33] It also lifted a tax exemption on Chōsen Sōren (General Association of Korean Residents in Japan), a pro-North Korea civil organization, as a means of restricting the transfer of funds to North Korea. Unilateral economic sanctions were also imposed.

Japan's hard-line policy created coordination problems with the other members of the Six Party Talks. On 13 February 2007, the parties reached an agreement on 'Initial Actions for the Implementation of the Joint Statement.' Under the agreement, North Korea pledged to shut down and seal for the purpose of eventual abandonment the Yongbyon nuclear facilities. In return, the five countries agreed to make an initial shipment of 50,000 tons of heavy oil, totalling 250,000 tons, to the North within sixty days. Japan, however, refused to deliver its portion until the abductions issue was resolved, which meant the four other states had to split the cost of the agreed heavy oil deliveries. Then Japanese Foreign Minister Asō Tarō stated 'Unless there is progress on the abduction issue, we have no intention of paying even one yen.'[34] While Pyongyang claimed that the issue had been already settled, ironically Japan was criticized by other participating states in the agreement that the abductions issue-first policy might jeopardize the Six-Party process. As Pyongyang demanded economic assistance in return for giving up its nuclear programme, Japan's refusal, as well as Pyongyang's failure to meet Japan's demands on the abduction issue, indeed endangered the Six Party Talks.

As a result, the United States was forced to consult with other governments outside of the Six Party framework to replace Japan. South Korea also sought outside donors in the event Japan would not change its position of withholding its share of energy assistance.[35] During this process, the other four states actively looked for ways to keep the aid-for-disarmament accord with the North in order to move forward. Even North Korea claimed that Japan need not remain in the Six Party Talks.[36]

Japan also had to come to terms with a US decision to remove North Korea from a list of terrorism sponsoring states before the resolution of the abductions issue. What was not anticipated from the Japanese perspective was that the United States might shift its North Korea policy towards engagement. The Bush administration removed North Korea from its list of terrorism sponsoring states on 11 October 2008. Japan's firm stance essentially backfired and resulted in a strategic deficit, which was only met with North Korea's malign neglect. At the end of the day, Japan was left with empty hands.

Japan's Strategic Deficit in the North Korean Issue

How did North Korea's abductions of Japanese citizens affect Japan's role in resolving the nuclear issue? The abductions issue ironically improved the image of Japan's reactive diplomacy and helped it establish a tougher and more independent diplomatic posture, even *vis-à-vis* the United States. Japan did not blindly follow the United States. By making normalization and energy assistance conditional upon progress in the abductions issue, Japan succeeded in attracting greater international attention to the issue and gained powerful leverage to punish North Korea for its criminal behaviour. On a deeper level, one can also argue that Japan's firm stance on the abductions issue was a conscious effort to bring it up as the central issue so that it would not be neglected and to reframe the Six Party Talks, which had essentially been framed by North Korea's intrinsic interest in negotiating with the US.

Nevertheless, at the outset, Japan's role in the Six Party Talks was constrained. The Six Party Talks were essentially constructed by China's initiatives for brokering, South Korea's back-up for resolving and the US strategic choice for preventing North Korea's nuclear venture. These three states cooperated very closely while Japan's actual contribution to the process was in essence hijacked by the abductions issue. Thus, at best, Japan's refusal to deliver energy assistance because of the abductions issue did not significantly impact upon trilateral cooperation among these three participants and only marginalized Japan even further.

From a strict national security perspective, Japan's strategic choice was blinded by the abductions issue. The direct and real threat to Japan's national security was then and still is North Korea's nuclear and missile programmes. Any states facing such direct threats would upgrade their military capabilities and seek multilateral cooperation to neutralize such threats. There would be less room for domestic political considerations to affect the strategic calculus. Thus, given the Six-Party process up until 2007, Japan would have had to focus on resolving its direct military threat. However, this was not the case for Japan.

While Pyongyang might have been inadvertently helping the Japanese government to justify enhancing its military capabilities for broader defensive purposes, Japanese politicians and officials could not push for a breakthrough given the emotional and political nature of the abductions issue. Japanese public opinion was not inclined to understand the details of North Korea's nuclear programme and Japan's regional role. Hardliners such as the National Association for the Rescue of Japanese Kidnapped by North Korea became prominent and influenced the agenda pushing for hard-line policies. Thus any strategic consideration for engaging North Korea was effectively killed off. At the height of the issue, Japan's choice for containment essentially limited its strategic choices by preventing any backdoor negotiations. In other words, Japan's government had no choice but to stick to a hardline position of 'no resolution of the issue, no normalization and no engagement'.

Although the participating states in the Six Party Talks sympathetically understood the domestic sentiments that had constrained Japan's range of options, Japan's role in this multilateral setting was diminished in the only multilateral security framework in Northeast Asia designed to address the North Korean nuclear issue. This resulted in the decline in Japan's leverage towards North Korea in the Six Party Talks. Japan's hard-line position forced the other regional actors such as South Korea and China to go ahead without Japan for achieving progress in the talks. Perhaps, no US administration can sacrifice real progress on North Korea's nuclear weapons to the emotional but parochial issue of

Japanese abductees.[37] At the end of the day, Japan learnt that its weight did not impede short-term progress in the Six Party Talks.

IMPLICATIONS OF PERCEPTUAL AND STRATEGIC DEFICITS FOR JAPAN

Throughout the 2000s, Japan has suffered from an apparent decline in its regional influence as a result of its striking perceptual and strategic contrasts in comparison to South Korea and China. Moreover, in relations with North Korea, Japan's traditional leverage used to be economic as it functioned as a chief source of cash flows to the impoverished Stalinist regime. However, as China's and South Korea's trade with North Korea has more than doubled since 2000, primarily due to South Korea's engagement policy towards North Korea, Japan's economic leverage has declined. What then do the aforementioned cases imply for Japan's security role in Northeast Asia?

These two issues are examples of Northeast Asia's unique regional characteristics that have long defined relations in the region. Northeast Asia still suffers from cognitive disputes between Japan and the victims of its imperial aggression. To South Korea and China, the sense of victimhood defines their relational identity with Japan while Japan may feel a lingering sense of unfairness. Yet we have not seen much active Japanese diplomacy aimed at a constructive resolution of the historical disputes. On the other hand, perhaps the abductions issue is the only diplomatic issue that has caused Japan to feel victimized by a foreign country.[38] In this issue, we have witnessed emotional Japanese diplomacy resulting in marginalization from the Six Party Talks.

Whether Japan likes it or not, the historical disputes will linger unless there is a comprehensive resolution initiated by Japan. Unresolved historical issues will constrain Japan's diplomatic attempts to play a constructive role in Northeast Asia. However unfair it may be seen, the popular perception in Beijing and Seoul is that Japan suffers from a form of historical amnesia, which has been partly reinforced by Tokyo.[39] During the Cold War, Northeast Asian states were able to avoid problematizing the issue as strategic concerns were prioritized. However, in addition to the end of the Cold War, which changed the strategic calculus in the region, democratization in Seoul, economic liberalization in Beijing, and increased economic and social interdependence have all served to increase pressure on Japan to resolve the historical problems and to contribute more to the construction of a stable regional order in Northeast Asia.

Moreover, Japan's relationship with its neighbours during the last ten years of LDP rule did create some difficulties over regional cooperation. Perhaps in the eyes of South Korea and China, Japan's becoming a normal state appeared akin to it becoming a right-wing state. On the other hand, it generally took an insensitive, if not ignorant, approach to issues deemed critical to its neighbours. A series of issues relating to Japanese history textbooks, Koizumi's persistent visits to the Yasukuni Shrine, territorial disputes and fishery issues complicated and constrained Japan's relations with China and South Korea.

Regarding the abductions issue, no formal settlement seems possible between North Korea and Japan. Whether North Korea produces any tangible and persuasive evidence or not, given public sentiments, Japan may not trust any new evidence from North Korea unless a team of Japanese investigators conducts a thorough search on North Korean soil. Thus, Japan's demands and uncompromising position seems to be constraining its strategic choices.

For a resolution of the abductions issue, Japan needs to cooperate with China and South Korea. However, as the historical issues between Japan and China are still unresolved, creating negative perceptions in China regarding Japan's behaviour, Japan will be again constrained. While China considers itself as still being a victim of Japanese behaviour on the historical issue, it may not actively seek a resolution to this problem. South Korea will also think similarly since it has its own abductees in North Korea. But South Korea's strategy is focused on denuclearizing North Korea through the Six Party Talks. Thus, the history issue is impeding cooperation between Japan and its neighbours. For Japan to overcome the strategic and perceptual deficits and enhance its influence in the region, it needs to look at its own past and engage its immediate neighbours, South Korea and China.

OVERCOMING THE IMPEDIMENTS: A NEW JAPANESE ENGAGEMENT

Japan is not readily associated with the word 'change'. One royal dynasty has reigned over the Japanese islands since the beginning of its history. A conservative party, the Liberal Democratic Party, ruled for most of the post-war era. Japan's external relations have been closely coordinated with the United States, so much so that some critics have in the past claimed that foreign policy decision making is made in Washington and not Tokyo. However, with the groundbreaking electoral victory of the Democratic Party of Japan led by Hatoyama Yukio, we may have to venture some 'changes' in and about Japan.

Hatoyama's new vision for an East Asian community has stimulated strong interest in Seoul and Beijing, as well as other Asian capitals. While the DPJ's landslide victory in the general election and the fall of the LDP generated excitement, the prospects for a new Japanese policy towards its immediate neighbours requires careful evaluation. This is because Prime Minister Hatoyama's new vision for Asia is different from that of previous LDP administrations. He emphasizes Japan's identity as 'a nation located in Asia' and East Asia as 'Japan's basic sphere of being'.[40] Japan on its route along a new path that is more engaging with its neighbouring states should be put to a series of tests. It remains to be seen if the policies executed by the new administration will be as equally groundbreaking as its landmark victory in the September 2009 Japanese election.

As the differing memories of the past held by each state are still alive, a rapidly growing China, North Korea's nuclear ambitions and South Korea's strive for continued economic development present great challenges to a stable Northeast Asian regional order. In this vein, Japan's search for a mature regional identity as an Asian state is a welcoming sign for the future of Northeast Asia. Japan's attempts to craft such an identity appropriate for its material capabilities require more serious reflection on why Japan has been underappreciated and therefore constrained. Unending cognitive dissonance will only entrap Japan in a circle of distrust and suspicion with its neighbours, which in turn will reduce its strategic manoeuvrability in any issues of importance. To overcome this vicious circle, Japan needs to engage its neighbours in the following key areas.

First, once the Six Party process restarts, Japan must be able to separate the abductions issue from the nuclear issue. North Korea committed unacceptable criminal acts and Japan is justified in being outraged. However, such outrage should not cast a cloud over its strategic contribution to achieving a nuclear-free Korean Peninsula. The new government should adjust its approach and persuade the public that a resolution of the abductions issue can only be achieved as part of a comprehensive settlement between North Korea and the other five states, which includes a complete and verifiable denuclearization of the Korean Peninsula and normalization of North Korea's relations with the US, Japan and South Korea.[41] The Japanese government must also enforce more effectively its strategic leverage including economic incentives. Just imagine a situation in which the Six Party Talks come to a successful conclusion achieving denuclearization of the Korean Peninsula without Japan's contribution. This would be a disaster for Japan and would have important implications for Japan's future role in the region.

Second, Japan must realize that it is not free from the memory of subjugation that informs the national identity of the other two Northeast Asian states. The history dispute in Northeast Asia is essentially a dispute over memory. Such memory conflicts in Northeast Asia have spurred anti-Japanese nationalism in China and South Korea. Therefore, the new Japanese political leadership must be able to make genuine efforts to not problematize historical issues. Cognitive reconciliation requires a sustained expenditure of political energy. A new Japan should be able to exercise political flexibility on the history issue by suspending visits to the Yasukuni Shrine while initiating domestic debate on considering alternative commemorative sites. Renewed political efforts must be made to devise new approaches to the issues of the comfort women and enforced labour during the Japanese colonial period.

Hatoyama Yukio's new Japanese vision for Asia, called the East Asian Community is at least pointing in the right direction. East Asia's regional order should be determined by active participation among the regional actors through a more robust set of institutional arrangements. While realizing that his vision will take a long time to be put in practice, he has so far showcased his strong resolve to push forward with it. If the DPJ government and its foreign policy focus on Asia continues, it will certainly help in establishing a more stable East Asia. However, for it to be able to traverse the bumpy road to establishing an EAC, Japan must be able to engage its immediate neighbors, the two Koreas and China. Without forming stable political relations with the three countries, perhaps, its regional vision for the EAC will merely remain as political rhetoric.

NOTES

1 See A. Friedberg, 'The Future of U.S.-China Relations: Is Conflict Inevitable?' *International Security*, 30(2), Fall 2005, pp. 7–45; D. Roy, 'Hegemony on the Horizon: China's threat to East Asian Security', *International Security*, 19(1), Summer 1994, p. 165. For assessing the future of Asian security in regard to a rising China, see J.S. Nye, 'China's Re-emergence and the Future of the Asia-Pacific', *Survival*, 39(4), 1997, pp. 65–79; G. Segal, 'The Coming Confrontation Between China and Japan', *World Policy Journal*, 10(2) Summer, 1993; Z. Brzezinski and J. Mearsheimer, 'Clash of the Titans', *Foreign Policy*, Jan./Feb. 2005); N. Kristof, 'The Rise of China', *Foreign Affairs*, 72(5) Nov./Dec. 1993, pp. 59–74; G. Segal, 'Does China Matter?' *Foreign Affairs*, 78(5) Sept./Oct. 1999; R. Bernstein and R. Munro, 'The Coming Conflict with America', *Foreign Affairs*, 76(2) March/April 1997, pp. 18–32; B. Roberts and R. Manning, et al. 'China: The Forgotten Nuclear Power', *Foreign Affairs*, July/August 2000, pp. 53–63; P. Saunders and J.D. Yuan, 'China's Strategic Force Modernization: Issues and Implications for the United States', in M. Barletta (ed.) *Proliferation Challenges and Nonproliferation Opportunities for New Administrations, Occasional Paper #4*, October 2000, pp. 40–6; A. Scobell and L. Wortzel (eds) *China's Growing Military Power: Perspectives on Security, Ballistic Missiles and Conventional Capabilities*, Carlisle, PA: Strategic Studies Institute, 2002.

2 C. W. Hughes, *Japan's Remilitarization*, London: Routledge, 2009.

3 P. Katzenstein, 'Introduction: Asian Regionalism in Comparative Perspectives', in P. Katzenstein and T. Shiraishi (eds) *Network Power: Japan and Asia*, Ithaca: Cornell University Press, 1997, p. 7.

4 L. Hagstrom, 'The Dogma of Japanese Insignificance: The Academic Discourse on North Korea Policy Coordination', *Pacific Affairs* 79(3) Fall 2006, pp. 387–410.

5 *Chosun Ilbo*, 24 February 2006.

6 'Roh, Koizumi Fail to Mend History Row', *The Korea Herald*, 21 June 2005, available at http://www.koreahearld.com.

7 'Koizumi Visits War Shrine, as He Pledged', *New York Times*, 17 October 2005, p. A7.

8 'Hu Seeks Action, Not Words, After Koizumi Summit', *South China Morning Post*, 24 April 2005, p. 1.

9 'Koizumi Hints at Visiting Yasukuni Shrine Again This Year', *Kyodo News*, 17 May 2005.

10 K. Ide, Spokesperson of Japanese Embassy to the People's Republic of China, quoted in 'War of Words Over Textbook Escalates', 7 April 2005, *South China Morning Post*, p. 10.

11 *Chosun Ilbo*, 2 March 2005, p. 1 (In Korean).

12 Koizumi's remarks to the Diet quoted in 'Korea and China, Only Two Countries Complaining about Yasukuni', *Dong-A Ilbo*, 25 January 2006, available at http://www.donga.com/english.

13 *Chosun Ilbo*, 27 November 2005, available at http://www.chosun.com/international/news/200511/200511270131.html (In Korean).

14 D. Capie and P. Evans, *The Asia-Pacific Security Lexicon*, Singapore: Institute of Asian Studies, 2002; K. Mahbubani, *Can Asians Think?* Toronto: Key Porter Books, 2001; J. Dosch and M. Mons (eds), *International Relations in the Asia-Pacific: New Patterns of Power, Interest and Cooperation*, New York: St. Martin's Press, 2000; L. Hayes, *Japan and the Security of Asia*, Oxford: Lexington Books, 2001; D. Lampton, *Major Power Relations in Northeast Asia: Win-Win or Zero Sum Game?* Tokyo: Japan Center for International Exchange, 2001.

15 S. Daiki, 'The Yasukuni Shrine Dispute and the Politics of Identity in Japan', *Asian Survey*, 45(2) Summer, 2005, pp.197–215.

16 J. Kingston, *Japan's Transformation, 1952–2000*, Harlow: Pearson, 2001, pp. 45–8, 140–3.

17 See the Yasukuni Shrine website, go to http://www.yasukuni.or.jp/english/

18 'Roh Urges Japan to Respect Conscience of Humanity', *Yonhap News*, 1 March 2005, available at http://english.yna.co.kr.

19 See Tomoko Hamada, 'Contended Memories of the Imperial Sun: History Textbook Controversy in Japan', *American Asian Review*, 20(4) Winter, 2002, pp. 1–38.

20 See H. French, 'Japan's Refusal to Revise Textbooks Angers its Neighbors', *New York Times*, 9 July 2001, p. A3; B. Egelko, 'World War II Reparations: Asian Sex Slaves Hope New Law Will Aid in Fight for Redress', *San Francisco Chronicle*, 1 July 2001, p. A8.

21 'Only Cooler Heads Can Calm Crisis', *South China Morning Post*, 19 April 2005, p. 14.

22 J. Ikenberry, 'Japan has Kept Asia Anxious too Long', *Los Angeles Times*, 16 August 2001.

23 L. Hagstrom and C. Turesson, 'Among Threats and a "Perfect Excuse": Understanding Change in Japanese Foreign Security Policy', *Korean*

Journal of Defense Analysis, 21(3) Fall 2009, pp. 297–314; C. W. Hughes, '"Supersizing" the DPRK Threat: Japan's Evolving Military Posture and North Korea', *Asian Survey,* 49(2) March/April 2009, pp. 291–311.

[24] Controversy over the results of the DNA test still exists. Even the prestigious scientific journal *Nature* reports that the sample of the cremated remains might have been contaminated and therefore incapable of producing accurate results. See D. Cyranoski, 'DNA is Burning Issue as Japan and Korea Clash over Kidnaps', *Nature* Vol. 433 2 February 2005, available at http://www.nature.com/nature/journal/v433/n7025/full/433445a.html.

[25] 'Japanese Public Wants Sanctions on North Korea', *Mainichi Shimbun,* 4 October 2004, http://mdn.mainichi.co.jp/news/archive/200410/04/20041004p2a00m0dm012001c.html.

[26] 'Japan-North Korea Talks Resumes but Abduction Issue Remains Big Stumbling Block', *Media Resources: Japan Brief,* 6 February 2006, available at http://www.fpcj.jp/old/e/mres/japanbrief/jb_605.html.

[27] Hagstrom, 'The Dogma of Japanese Insignificance', p. 406.

[28] *Asahi Shimbun,* 30 September, 2006.

[29] Government of Japan, Ministry of Foreign Affairs, 'Press Conference 29 August 2003', available at http://www.mofa.go.jp/announce/press/2003/8/0829.html.

[30] 'China's Zeng asks Japan Not to Raise Abductions at 6-way Talks', *Jiji Press,* 4 February 2004 quoted on Nuclear Threat Initiative's homepage, http://www.nti.org/e_research/profiles/NK/Nuclear/46_5546.html.

[31] Government of Japan, Ministry of Foreign Affairs, 'Six-Party Talks on North Korean Issues (Overview and Evaluation)', September 2003, available at http://www.mofa.go.jp/region/asia-paci/n_korea/6party0308.html; 'Abduction Issue Better not be Included in Six-party Nuke Talks: S. Korean FM', *Xinhua News Agency,* 4 February 2004, available at http://news.xinhuanet.com/english/2004-02/04/consent_1298631.html.

[32] E. Johnston, 'The North Korea Abduction Issue and Its Effect on Japanese Domestic Politics', *JPRI Working Paper,* no. 101, 2004, available at http://www.jpri.org/publications/workingpapers/wp101.html.

[33] 'Japanese Protesters Meet North Korean Ferry Docking at Niigata Port', *Kyodo News Service,* 20 October 2004.

[34] 'Aso: Unless there is Progress on Abductions, We Will Not Pay Even One Yen', *Yomiuri Shimbun,* 3 March 2007.

[35] 'US Asks Australia to Supply Oil to North Korea', *AFP,* 29 October 2009.

[36] Y.J. Yeh, 'Nuclear Issue Should be Japan's Priority', *JoongAng Ilbo,* 22 February 2007 (In Korean).

[37] J.K. Choi, 'Smart Power or Star Power? Thinking about Clinton's Asian Tour', *Global Asia,* 4(1) Spring 2009, p. 60.

[38] It should also be noted that the Northern Territories dispute and the atomic bomb attacks on Hiroshima and Nagasaki are also believed to have contributed to a feeling of victimization in Japan.

[39] J. Lind, *Sorry States: Apologies in International Politics*, Ithaca: Cornell University Press, 2008, pp. 26–32.

[40] Y. Hatoyama, 'A New Path for Japan', *New York Times* 26 August 2009, available at http://www.nytimes.com/2009/08/27/opinion/27iht-edhatoyama.html.

[41] H. Tanaka, 'A New Leadership Role for Japan', *Global Asia*, 4(1) Spring 2009, p. 12.

PART 3

Social Challenges

9

Japan's Education System: Problems and Prospects in the Post-Industrial Age

BRAD WILLIAMS AND SHOKO YONEYAMA

INTRODUCTION

This chapter examines the two key structural components of Japan's education system: pre-tertiary (school) and tertiary (college/university). In the 1980s, many foreign observers considered Japanese school education to be an important contributor to the nation's economic success, although domestic opinion was less positive. The university system, on the other hand, has not been held in high regard internationally, despite being lauded for its high accessibility resulting in 'massification' at the tertiary level. Today, with mounting problems such as *futōkō* (school non-attendance), *ijime* (bullying), and *hikikomori* (social withdrawal) among youth, the pre-tertiary and tertiary levels of education have converged in their negative reputations. The general perception is that Japan's education system is in decline, and many believe this is closely linked with the nation's socioeconomic malaise.

We argue that central to this decline is the lack of incentive among Japan's youth, which is closely related to weaknesses in other areas such as creativity, individuality, and critical (social) thinking. For a post-industrial, knowledge-based economy, this constitutes a fundamental problem. The Japanese government and industry have accordingly initiated a 'third wave' of education reform at both tertiary and pre-tertiary levels, but there is little indication of its effectiveness. Japanese schools have continued to produce students who have sound basic factual knowledge but lack motivation and critical thinking skills. Universities have continued to reproduce such students, through subordinating learning to operating primarily as hierarchical employment agencies for corporate Japan. Underlying the problem are conformism and hierarchy, at work across both pre-tertiary and tertiary levels. This system may have contributed to the nation's economic success when Japan was industrializing but is inadequate for the needs of a twenty-first century knowledge-based economy.

SCHOOL EDUCATION: WHAT IS IN DECLINE?

Knowledge-based Skills

Few would disagree that school education in Japan faces a mountain of difficult issues. Yet there is almost no agreement about how to interpret and address the issues. Competing discourses present different solutions to particular problems, such as *futōkō*.[1] Yet to ascertain the nature of the challenges school education faces in the post-industrial age, identifying and understanding the core problem are essential. It is also important to contextualize the 'problems' against the backdrop of general student population trends in Japan. Only national scale data with representative samples can show such trends. We therefore use as the main point of reference in our analysis two data sets: 'Trends in International Mathematics and Science Study' (TIMSS) by the International Association for the Evaluation of Educational Achievement and the OECD's 'Programme for International Student Assessment' (PISA). These provide the most comprehensive comparative and longitudinal data on school education.

The first question to address is what exactly is in decline? Some may regard the fact that Japan no longer ranks first in international tests as an indication of national decline. But rankings can be misleading. They are affected by which countries have participated in the test,[2] and there may be no statistically significant differences between the scores of closely ranked countries. On this basis, despite the appearance of slippage, it is fair to conclude there has been no significant decline in Japan's academic standards in the TIMSS mathematics and science results.[3] The first point to establish then is that while Japan's international rankings have fluctuated, Japanese students have demonstrated the highest range of academic standards in knowledge-based skills in mathematics and science since Japan first took part in TIMSS in the 1960s.

'Postmodern Competencies'

The results of PISA, which was begun in 2000, reveal different trends. While Japan ranked first in mathematics in 2000, it declined to sixth place in 2006. Its rank for reading dropped from eighth in 2000 to twelfth in 2003.[4] While TIMSS is mainly designed to measure *knowledge-based basic skills*, i.e. how well students have learned what is on the curriculum, PISA is geared towards measuring students' literacy, i.e. *ability to think* in a given social context by mobilizing relevant mathematical/scientific/reading skills. Typically, questions in TIMSS have 'correct' responses, whereas questions in PISA do not necessarily have clear-cut answers. Questions in PISA require students *to be engaged* in answering the question, i.e. to be motivated to answer, think and reflect, and to explain and express ideas in their own words.

PISA is geared towards measuring what Honda calls 'postmodern competencies', whereas abilities assessed in TIMSS largely correspond to 'modern competencies' (Table 1). Honda believes that *ikiru chikara* (literally, 'power to live'), which has been the catch-phrase of education reform since 1996, typifies postmodern competencies.[5] Here lies the important nexus between PISA and Japan's 'third wave' of pre-tertiary education reform, which was initiated in the mid-1980s.[6] Both envisage 'postmodern competencies' as the key to education in the post-industrial age. Underlying PISA is the OECD's major research project, 'Definition and Selection of Competencies: Theoretical and Conceptual Foundations' (DeSeCo). The notion of key competencies it proposes appears to have legitimized the notion of 'power to live', which was launched before the release of the DeSeCo report, but remained unpopular because of its obscurity.[7] The 'power to live' promoted by the Ministry of Education (MoE)[8] and the 'key competencies' emphasized by the OECD share a 'holistic' conceptualization of learning. The results of PISA can be interpreted as a measure of the success of the 'third wave' of education reform in promoting the postmodern competencies represented by the 'power to live'. The decline in PISA results suggests problems with education reform in cultivating postmodern competencies.

A closer examination of how Japanese students lost marks in PISA reveals a pattern common to both mathematics and reading literacy tests: a large proportion of students simply did not answer questions that required a higher level of engagement involving analytical thinking, explaining and expressing ideas. It is reported that close to 30 per cent of Japanese students left such open-ended questions unanswered in both subjects, which was the highest percentage among all the

Table 1: Comparison of 'modern competencies' and 'postmodern competencies'

'Modern competencies'	'Postmodern competencies'
'Basic skills'	'Power to live' (*ikiru chikara*)
To be standard	To be diverse and innovative
Amount of knowledge	Incentive
Speed of management of knowledge	Creativity
Comparable with a common measure	Individual and specific
Adaptability	To be active
Cooperation and conformity	Networking ability and negotiation skills

Source: Y. Honda, *Tagenka suru 'nōryoku' to Nihon shakai* [Japanese society and diversification of competence], Tokyo: NTT, 2005, p. 22.

participating countries.[9] This suggests that the problem may not be so much with mathematics and reading skills *per se*, but something more fundamental, i.e. the lack of motivation to engage in careful thinking and to express one's ideas.

Analysis of the academic results of TIMSS and PISA suggests that the Japanese education system at the pre-tertiary levels continues to produce students with sound basic skills of the highest standard but with poorly developed thinking skills, especially the motivation to engage in critical thinking. It suggests that Japanese students are strong in 'modern competencies', but their 'postmodern competencies', essential in a post-industrial, knowledge-based society, are underdeveloped.

SUBJECTIVE COSTS OF EDUCATION

Joyless Study

The TIMSS and PISA include questions that assess students' subjective experience of school, which is separate from their academic performance. The data show consistently that students in Japan tend not to enjoy studying, despite their high academic performance. In TIMSS 2007, for instance, Japan was close to the bottom of forty-nine countries regarding students' subjective experience of studying mathematics.[10] The same trend was observed in PISA data on reading. Normally, 'there is a clear positive association between reading for enjoyment and performance'.[11] For Japan, however, despite the high average reading performance, 55 per cent of the students indicated they did not read at all for enjoyment, which was the largest proportion among the thirty-one countries listed.[12] Students' lack of enjoyment in learning has often been justified by their solid examination achievements. This contradiction has been maintained with extraordinary effort and perseverance (*ganbaru*) by students,[13] but with considerable cost: the loss of incentive, dislike of study and alienation from school. This contradiction has not received the attention it deserves.

Alienation from School

The contradiction between 'high performance' and 'low happiness' has also been identified in students' perceptions of school in general. Figure 1 has been adapted from the results of PISA 2000, which *inter alia* investigated student perceptions of school. It shows students' school attendance, on the one hand, and students' sense of belonging to school, on the other. The latter is based on their responses to questions concerning how they feel about school: whether at school they 'feel like an outsider', 'feel awkward and out of place', 'feel lonely', 'do not want to go to school', and 'often feel bored'. Figure 1 shows that Japanese students attend school diligently but with relatively strong sense of alienation from school. It indicates that Japan, South Korea and Hong Kong form a constellation, which suggests analysis of

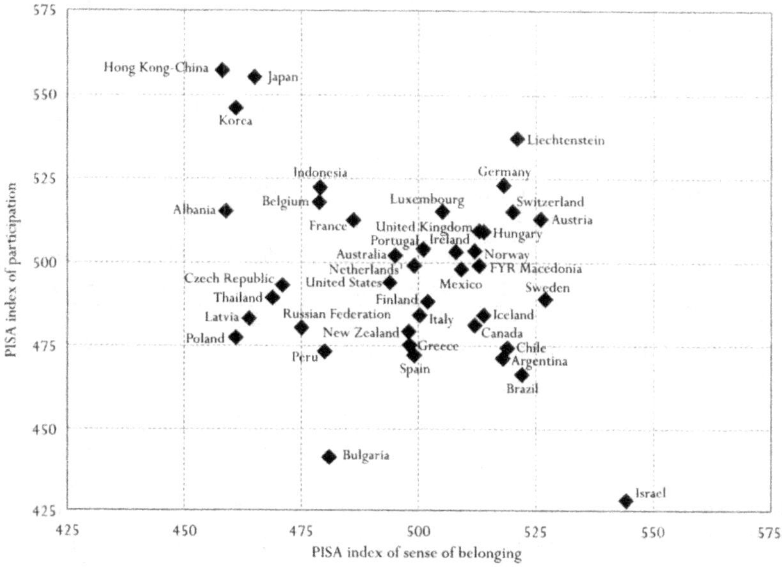

Figure 1: Participation in school and sense of belonging to school Source: OECD (2004), *Education at a Glance 2004: OECD Indicators,* p. 121, OECD Publishing, http://dx.doi.org/10.1787/ eag-2004-en.

Japan's school education would be highly relevant for understanding education in other East Asian countries, especially students' subjective experiences of school.

'The Loneliest Students in the World'

Of the five survey items indicating a 'student's sense of belonging to school', the statement 'my school is a place where I feel lonely' produced the most striking outcome. Almost 30 per cent of some 4,700 fifteen year olds participating in the survey in Japan indicated that they felt lonely at school. The percentage was almost three times higher than the next country on the list (Iceland). Japanese students were labelled 'the loneliest in the world'.[14] Table 2 shows student responses to some questions relevant to understanding student loneliness at school. It also indicates the mean score of the reading/mathematics/science literacy for each group of students.

Table 2 indicates, first, that students' sense of loneliness at school is inversely related to academic performance. Second, slightly more than 30 per cent of the students felt that other students did not seem to like them. Again, there is some negative relationship between this perception and academic performance. In relation to teachers, more than half (54.6 per cent) of Japan's fifteen year olds did not think that teachers were interested in their well-being, including 11.4 per cent

Table 2: Student perceptions on selected aspects of school and the mean value of the group of students in reading, mathematics and science literacy

		Strongly agree	Agree	Disagree	Strongly disagree
My school is a place where I feel lonely	%	9.9	19.7	50.8	19.1
	Reading mean	447	483	509	519
	Math mean	486	520	544	552
	Science mean	498	533	558	566
	OECD mean %	2.3	5.6	33.9	54.9
My school is a place where other students seem to like me	%	5.4	61.9	27.3	3.5
	Reading mean	489	509	487	444
	Math mean	525	544	525	479
	Science mean	534	558	539	500
	OECD mean %	14.9	68.2	11.3	2.4
Teachers are interested in students' well-being	%	5.1	39.4	43.2	11.4
	Reading mean	519	513	494	466
	Math mean	556	547	530	448
	Science mean	581	563	541	512
	OECD mean %	9.7	56.6	26.1	5.5
Most of my teachers really listen to what I have to say	%	4.5	48.8	36.7	9.2
	Reading mean	500	515	490	454
	Math mean	541	550	524	497
	Science mean	563	565	537	501
	OECD mean %	9.3	54.0	28.7	2.3
If I need extra help, I will receive it from my teachers	%	7.4	49.6	33.1	9.0
	Reading mean	502	511	492	458
	Math mean	532	545	530	498
	Science mean	558	561	540	505
	OECD mean %	14.4	60.1	18.9	4.4

Source: Data were obtained using the PISA 2003 interactive database[15]

who 'strongly disagreed' with the statement. This perception was also inversely related to academic performance. Likewise, 42.1 per cent of the students believed their teachers would not provide help when they need it, which is a far higher figure than the OECD average. Again, students who were not doing well academically were most negative about teachers' willingness to help. Although these figures alone do not reveal the causal relationships between these perceptions and loneliness at school, the data suggest that Japanese students' sense of loneliness at school is likely to be associated with some key aspects of school such as the quality of the teacher–student relationship and relationships among students, which both relate closely to their academic performance.

The lack of incentive to think critically, discussed above, may well stem from students' lack of enjoyment in study and sense of alienation from school (e.g. estrangement, loneliness and boredom). In fact, the DeSeCo's final report suggests that for the development of critical thinking, the highest order of thinking, Japan's education system needs to improve both teacher-student relations and the governance of education to allow greater autonomy of learners and schools.[16]

THE PROBLEM OF CRITICAL THINKING

In the West, critical thinking is considered to be an indispensable part of education, as worthwhile as education itself.[17] In Japan, recognition of the significance of critical thinking is recent, and is the concern of very few researchers.[18] At least three reasons account for this curious void in Japan's educational discourse.

The first is the conformist orientation of Japanese schools and society at large. One of the central themes of education has been to train students to become good group members. At the preschool level, children are socialized into developing a group consciousness and perseverance through physical practices and daily activities.[19] In primary schools, the classroom constitutes a community where mutual support, interdependence and self-discipline are emphasized, with the view to developing a collective consciousness. While this approach could produce a caring community of autonomous learners, students' thinking tends to develop within a prescribed framework at the expense of critical, analytical, spontaneous and imaginative thinking.[20]

Pressure to conform becomes obvious in the more regimented environment of secondary schools, where school rules, pressure to perform well academically to pass university entrance examinations, and teachers' confidential reports can silence students.[21] Bullying among Japanese students can be interpreted as their over-adjustment to the pressure to conform, as any form of nonconformity can be used as a reason to victimize a fellow student in highly sensitive group dynamics.[22] This orientation towards conformism in Japanese schools does not provide the best environment for critical thinking. The fundamentally 'emancipatory quality'[23] of critical thinking may very well challenge this conformity, which can jeopardize the social position of the critical thinker. Thus, critical social thinking can be particularly problematic in a highly conformist environment.[24]

The hierarchy of human relations in Japanese schools and society also works against the promotion of critical (social) thinking. Although hierarchy is not unique to Japanese schools, the teacher–student relationship tends to be more hierarchical in Japan than in the West, as is the senior–junior (*senpai–kōhai*) relationship among students. The administrative structure of education, from the MoE to school management through local boards of education, is also very hierarchical. To teach students to think critically means to give students the 'right to question, to challenge, and to demand reasons and justifications for what is being taught'.[25] Critical thinking can challenge the authority of teachers and hierarchical human relations, which are particularly strong in the Japanese school system.

Critical thinking also clashes with the nationalistic agenda that has been one of the consistent undercurrents of Japan's post-war education. Critical thinking itself has been the target of state censorship, as the perennial controversies over history textbooks and the Ienaga trials (1965–97) exemplify.[26] Social studies in post-war education have been increasingly stripped of political and controversial issues. The university entrance examination for social studies (e.g. history) that demands rote-learnt knowledge is complicit with the de-politicized school knowledge. Cultivating critical thinking (or analytical thinking) is very difficult in this environment, because 'critical thinking develops best as it is applied to critical issues'.[27]

Ironically, the 'third wave' of education reform was driven by the hidden agendas of nationalism and neoliberalism[28] and has worked to further suppress students' critical thinking. A widening gap by family background has been observed among students in academic achievement, incentive to learn,[29] and ability to relate with others,[30] all of which constitute key aspects of 'postmodern competencies'. This was the context for decline in postmodern competencies, manifested in the PISA 2000–2006 results.

The challenge facing Japanese schools in the post-industrial age reaches beyond what education reforms alone can address. It likely requires a major shift in some fundamental aspects of school (e.g. the nature of school knowledge, pedagogy, teacher–student relationships); the socio-cultural and political structure of school and society (e.g. conformism and hierarchy); and the socioeconomic climate of nationalism and neoliberalism. The structure that dictates pre-tertiary education most is the university entrance examination, to which we now turn.

HIGHER EDUCATION IN JAPAN: A SYSTEM UNWORTHY OF AN ECONOMIC POWER

In contrast with the intense, regimented learning environment of pre-tertiary education, the general atmosphere in universities, which constitute the core of the tertiary education system in Japan, is markedly relaxed. University life has been described as a 'moratorium' for students,[31] offering a retreat sandwiched between the twin pressures of university entrance exams and the long working hours in corporate Japan.

The perception of indolence and poor standards associated with Japanese universities endures. Students lack the incentive to learn and develop critical thinking skills, and graduate despite apparently spending most of their time doing part-time paid work and club activities rather than in class.[32] The mode of teaching and learning in Japanese universities further diminishes students' incentives to learn and inhibits their development of critical thinking skills. Many university faculty are appointed more on the basis of who rather than what they know, and promotions are based on seniority rather than teaching or research excellence. Many faculty do not hold a doctorate and tend to concentrate on their own research, often to the detriment of their teaching. Poor employment conditions force some to 'moonlight' at other universities to make a reasonable living. Little wonder that Japanese universities have trouble attracting top quality foreign postgraduate students and long-term foreign faculty, despite the call to 'internationalize' since the 1980s. Geography and language are certainly factors but so too is reputation. Foreign students, who are now perceived as both a panacea for university under-enrolments and belatedly as potential contributors to Japan's socioeconomic development,[33] have usually had to face the additional challenges of high living costs, inadequate accommodation and occasional acts of racism. Female participation rates in university teaching, though rising, are the lowest in the OECD.[34] The MoE, which presides over this system, exercises firm control as a bastion of conservatism.

Japanese universities arguably do not compare well internationally. Japan has only a small number of universities ranked in the top 100, despite the multitude of tertiary education institutions (765 as of 2008). Apart from the Tokyo Institute of Technology (*Tōkōdai*), they are all former imperial universities. Two notable absentees from this list are Keio and Waseda universities – the most prestigious private institutions in Japan.[35] Apart from Tokyo and Kyoto universities, the rankings of Japan's universities have, on the whole, declined. According to the *Times Higher Education QS World University Rankings* (THEQS), only Tokyo and Kyoto universities have appeared in the top 100 every year since the first list was published in 2004. Osaka University and the Tokyo Institute of Technology feature in the top 100 in five out of six years while Tohoku and Nagoya universities make an appearance in the most recent list (97th and 92nd respectively).

Caveats

At this point some caveats are in order. The Japanese tertiary education system is diverse – both within and between institutions. It includes universities, junior colleges, technical colleges and professional training colleges. It has pockets of excellence in teaching and research and comprises many diligent and highly capable scholars. The nation's most prestigious institution of higher learning, Tokyo University (*Tōdai*), has provided the core of the nation's bureaucratic elite since the Meiji Era. *Tōdai* was ranked 20th in the Shanghai Jiao Tong University (SJTU) survey, and 22nd in the THEQS rankings in 2009, making it the leading university from the non-English-speaking world. In terms of the highest number of institutions in the SJTU top 100 and the THEQS top 200 for 2009, Japan ranked equal third (with Germany for the former, and Canada and the Netherlands for the latter) behind the US and the UK.

Harsher criticisms of Japanese academia seem to be directed at the humanities and social sciences more than at science and engineering. One study noted that in science departments, over 75 per cent of academics wrote research papers in English compared to most of their colleagues in the humanities and social sciences who wrote only in Japanese.[36] This is not to suggest that papers written in English are automatically of a higher quality than Japanese articles but they are accessible to a broader audience and are probably subject to greater scrutiny, especially if published in internationally refereed journals. It was also noted that the scientific community in Japan is more receptive to change and internationally oriented than its non-science peers, which is reflected in greater research productivity, citations in international journals and a willingness to confer doctorates upon graduate students.[37] Beyond universities, Japan's colleges of technology (*kōtō senmon gakkō* or *kōsen*) have drawn international praise for 'their management, quality and innovation'.[38] Another laudable feature of the Japanese tertiary education system is its accessibility – geographic and as a mass enterprise.

UNIVERSITIES AS HIERARCHICAL EMPLOYMENT AGENCIES FOR CORPORATE JAPAN

Despite the positive indicators in some sectors and fields, Japanese universities are generally not held in high regard internationally and a sense pervades that the university system is in crisis. One may wonder how one of the world's leading economies and a technological powerhouse could get by with a sub-standard tertiary education system. An influential factor lies in the relationship between corporate Japan and the nation's universities. Rather than viewing universities as centres of advanced learning, Japanese companies have traditionally seen them as employment agencies whose prestige, measured by a *hensachi* ranking, is considered a more important indicator of students' academic ability than the actual levels of knowledge students attain there.[39] The university entrance exam period probably represents the academic highpoint for many Japanese students, although the emphasis on rote learning and memorization required to pass impedes substantive learning and creative thinking.

Corporate Japan prefers to provide freshly graduated employees with extensive in-house training to meet the specific skill requirements of a particular firm and places little value on a university education. Large Japanese companies not only prefer malleable recruits but some are also reluctant to hire graduates who display what companies perceive to be too much initiative and creativity.[40] Japanese students understand corporate preferences, and this dampens their pursuit of academic diligence. Universities see that they play an important role in job placement and in a depressed economy many (private institutions in particular) endeavour to follow the motto 'don't graduate freeters and NEETs'.[41]

Japanese companies' generally low expectations of the nation's universities are reflected in research and development (R&D) trends. Rather than seek partnerships with Japanese universities, many companies in Japan have developed their own R&D capabilities or entrust this important task to American academic institutions.[42] However, Japanese companies' inability to shoulder the cost of maintaining R&D facilities in a depressed economic environment, criticisms of over-reliance on the US and increased expectations about the potential role played by Japan's universities have led to a re-evaluation of corporate R&D practices.[43]

SOCIOECONOMIC ACCELERANTS OF UNIVERSITY DECLINE

Japan's demographic and economic woes have compounded the universities' problems. Japan sits atop a demographic time bomb with an ageing population; the number of eighteen year olds (the age at which most enter universities) peaked at just over two million in 1992 and is expected to halve by 2020.[44] A decline in the youth population has left many universities struggling to fill enrolment quotas. Private universities, which receive most of their total income from student tuition and entrance exam fees, have been hit particularly hard, forcing many to devise strategies to attract student applicants. One method diversifies university entrance paths so that as well as through the regime of entrance exams, students can also gain admission through the Admissions Office (AO) scheme that assesses applicants on school records, personal accomplishments, application statement and occasionally an interview. The AO scheme was introduced to encourage applicants with diverse skills and capabilities beyond the capacity to simply memorize and rote learn to pass traditional entrance exams. While on the surface the AO scheme has helped development of critical and lateral thinking skills, some claim it has led to a further decline in academic standards, leading some university departments to abolish it.[45] Other universities have lowered barriers to admission by simply 'dumbing down' entrance exams and allowing students who have failed the option of 'makeups', in order to increase the number of examinees and boost university coffers.[46] These practices have altered the reputation of Japanese universities for being difficult to enter but easy to graduate: in the *zennyū* (all can enter) era, both entrance and graduation are now fairly effortless tasks at many institutions.

Government inability to spur a strong and sustained domestic recovery after the collapse of Japan's bubble economy in the early 1990s has further strained the higher education sector. A prominent feature of Japanese higher education is the size of the private sector. Over 70 per cent of Japan's universities are private institutions that generate most of their revenue from student tuition fees, as mentioned above. Government subsidies constitute just under 10 per cent of their total income and are distributed primarily to national universities.[47] Japanese public expenditure on tertiary education is low by international standards, at 3.5 per cent of GDP, second only to Greece among the OECD members and well below the OECD average of 5.5 per cent.[48] Japanese spending on higher education is sustained primarily by financing from private households, where it is considered a valuable investment in a family member's future. Japan's economic decline has placed strains on the family tertiary education budget and has led some universities to reduce tuition fees – and subsequently revenue – to maintain enrolment levels. Little relief can be expected from a government presiding over a stagnant economy.

REFORMING AN UNCOMPETITIVE SYSTEM

Japan's modern higher education system has not been immune to change; the current series of amendments have been described as a 'third wave' in the history of higher education reform in Japan, following the introduction of a modern education system with the Meiji Restoration and the radical Occupation reforms in the aftermath of wartime defeat.[49] The most recent reforms aim to overhaul radically the current system and some observers see them as a test of the commitment to Koizumi-era neo-liberal reforms to the nation's public institutions.[50]

The current reforms are designed to enhance the efficiency, accountability and, above all, the quality of the nation's higher education institutions. One criticism often levelled at Japan's higher education system is the strict and pervasive control exercised by the MoE. While the MoE has exercised enormous influence over many aspects of academic life in Japan, it has protected universities from external competitive forces.[51] Now state protection has been greatly reduced. To promote greater competition in the sector and more genuinely world-class universities, MoE introduced a 21st Century Centre of Excellence (COE21) Programme in 2002. As COEs, units within universities can apply for grants to conduct research over a five-year period in a diverse range of fields. COE21 research units are selected by an external party, centring on the Japan Society for the Promotion of Science (*Nihon Gakujutsu Shinkōkai*). From 2002 to 2004, 274 COEs had been selected from 1,395 applications.[52] Each project is subject to two evaluations: one conducted after two years and the other after completion, which can result in an increase, decrease or cessation of funding. The anticipated COE21 budget for 2008 was 3.9 billion yen (approximately US$42 million). Funding has been fairly evenly divided among the designated research fields, with the life sciences receiving the most approvals (24.8 per cent) in 2002 and medicine and related fields the most (26.3 per cent) in 2003.[53] National universities have secured the most COEs, averaging over 75 per cent of successful applications, followed by private (about 20 per cent) then public universities (about 3.5 per cent).[54] This is a reflection of national universities' relatively greater strength as research institutions.[55]

The transformation of Japan's national universities into independent administrative corporations (*dokuritsu gyōsei hōjin*) in April 2004 represents another notable reform of the higher education sector.[56] National universities had previously functioned as state administrative organs and operated according to state budgetary and civil service guidelines that restricted aspects of their teaching and research activities. Incorporation has partially removed national universities from the shackles of MoE to increase their autonomy and foster competition. The aim is to encourage institutions to pursue comparative advantages and ultimately attain higher standards in teaching and research. This objective is to be achieved specifically through providing universities authority to manage their own affairs, including granting university presidents the power to appoint faculty, who will no longer be civil servants, allowing outside specialists to participate in university management and introducing a system of *ex post facto* evaluations of six-yearly goals by universities and by the National Institution for Academic Degrees and University Evaluation (NIAD-UE), which will be reflected in subsequent resource distribution.[57] NIAD-UE's involvement in evaluations since 2000 is designed to act as an incentive for improved performance and increase university accountability.[58]

Like the COE21 scheme, incorporation has introduced competition to the moribund higher education sector, which in an environment of economic and demographic decline has inevitably produced 'winners' and 'losers'. This has contributed to a reorganization and consolidation of universities. With MoE's encouragement, the number of national universities has been reduced from 101 in 1997 to 86 in 2008, primarily through mergers of single-purpose higher education institutions with adjacent universities.[59] The small size and specialization of many national and prefectural ('local' national) universities offer further scope 'for continued consolidation within the national university sector, and between it and the prefectural university sector'.[60] Despite Japan's difficult socioeconomic climate, actual university (and student) numbers have evinced a steady increase, reaching 765 in 2008 – up from 507 in 1990.[61] This is largely due to the growth in newly established private universities, in turn the result of MoE's greater flexibility in approving the establishment of new institutions. This flexibility raises concerns about the quality of some of the newly established institutions and will test the quality assurance mechanisms introduced in recent years. One observer claimed that this puzzling decision was driven by a fear of ballooning higher education sector unemployment and a desire to enhance MoE's power by increasing its jurisdiction.[62]

The push for greater research performance has also led universities to expand graduate education. The preference in large firms for recruiting fresh graduates, providing them with in-house training, and paying them according to seniority rather than job performance, probably acted as a disincentive for many undergraduate students considering graduate study. Graduate school was seen generally as an adjunct to what were essentially undergraduate-centred institutions.[63] Japan's economic decline since the 1990s, diminishing confidence in the lifetime employment model and realization within academia of the growing importance of providing future workers with enhanced skills and knowledge to function effectively in a knowledge-based economy have prompted a renewed emphasis on graduate education.[64]

Universities have made significant investments in graduate education through facilities, stipends for teaching and research assistants, and increasing loans and grants for postgraduate students. But according to Asonuma, while national universities have increased enrolments through greater overall emphasis on postgraduate education, private universities have been enticed by the apparent prestige of offering postgraduate degrees, which they hope will help increase undergraduate enrolments.[65] The number of universities that established graduate programmes almost doubled between 1990 and 2008, from 313 to 604.[66] A particularly noteworthy development in the advancement of graduate education is the establishment of professional graduate schools across a broad range of disciplines, with the aim of providing a pool of specialists with theoretical knowledge and vocational capabilities, from which industry and key professions can draw.

Closely linked with this proposal is a plan to select, on a competitive basis, thirty universities in Japan to be earmarked as elite 'Global Universities' with priority in resource allocation. Each will recruit up to 30 per cent of its teaching staff in selected departments from abroad and enrol at least 20 per cent of students from overseas. Thirty per cent of classes at these universities are to be conducted in English and foreign students will be able to graduate by taking courses taught only in English language.[67] This is a creative step in a bid to establish a core of world-class universities. However, it is not without obstacles. First, while students from Asia might see benefit in a partial education in English, those wishing to improve their English-language skills are not likely to flock to Japan for this purpose, especially when education providers offer more rigorous and holistic training in English in Hong Kong and Singapore. Second, given the paucity of competent English speakers in corporate Japan, it is likely that graduates who have taken only courses conducted in English will struggle to find meaningful employment.[68]

FUTURE PROSPECTS

While Japanese education still has numerous problems, there are also signs of change and seeds of hope. At the end of 2009, education is not high on the reform agenda for the new Hatoyama administration. However, this government's stance of critically revising the 'economics-first' mindset is promising. If, as it advocates, introducing the political philosophy of '*yūai*' (fraternal love) increases the safety nets for Japanese society and promotes caring human relations and greater diversity in Japanese society, the cultural climate of school may change and the harmful effects of the modernist characteristics of school such as conformism, regimentation and hierarchical human relationships may diminish. Changing relations between politicians and bureaucrats may alter the power of the MoE and its relationship with local boards of education. The MoE itself could be freed from the influence of the LDP educational clan.

Population shrinkage will further change the market dynamics between universities and applicants. The fall in the number of university-age students paralleling the rise in the number of institutions is probably unsustainable, especially if the government is serious about enhancing the overall quality of the tertiary education system. Increasing the number of foreign students has been offered as a panacea for this problem but unless dominant Japanese attitudes towards study immigrants change, these people will take their skills elsewhere. Proponents of neoliberal reforms will argue that the short-term pain from closing sub-standard universities will be mitigated by the long-term benefits of a more efficient and competitive higher education system. It remains to be seen whether any government is prepared to suffer these costs over the short-to-medium term. One must therefore remain sceptical about the prospects of the tertiary education sector, as a whole, producing reserves of human capital capable of resolving the myriad of economic, political and social problems afflicting post-industrial Japan.

NOTES

1 For instance, on the different discourses of school non-attendance, see S. Yoneyama, 'Student Discourse on *Tōkōkyohi* (School Phobia/ Refusal) in Japan: Burnout or Empowerment?', *British Journal of Sociology of Education*, 21(1), 2000, pp. 77–94.

2 For instance, while Japan was ranked first in the TIMSS mathematics test for Grade 8 in 1981, it slipped to third in 1995 when Singapore and South Korea entered the 'competition', and it dropped again in 1999 when Taiwan took part in the test.

3 See MoE, 'Shiryō 5 TIMSS 2007 kankei shiryō' [Attachment 5, Data relating to TIMSS 2007], distributed at the 74th Kyōiku kenkyū bukai, 2008 [Education research section meeting], Chūō kyōiku shingikai

[The Central Council for Education], http://www.mext.go.jp/b_menu/shingi/chukyo/chukyo3/004/siryo/icsFiles/afieldfile/2009/01/15/12177854.pdf, accessed 26 September 2009.

4 OECD, *PISA 2006 Results*, Chapter 6, Table 6.3b 'Trends in Mathematics Since PISA 2003', http://www.pisa.oecd.org/document/2/0,3343,en32252351322361913971885O1111,00.html, accessed 3 November 2009.

5 Y. Honda, *Tagenka suru 'nōryoku' to nihon shakai* [Japanese society and diversification of 'competence'] Tokyo: NTT, 2005, p. 22 and 54–63.

6 H. Fujita, *Kyōiku kaikaku* [Education reform], Tokyo: Iwanami Shinsho, 1997.

7 MoE, Chūō kyōiku shingikai tōshin 2008 [Deliberations of the Central Council for Education] p. 9, http://www.mext.go.jp/a_menu/shotou/new-cs/news/20080117.pdf, accessed 3 November 2009.

8 The Ministry of Education became the Ministry of Education, Culture, Sports, Science and Technology (or MEXT) following the restructuring of ministries in January 2001. In this paper, MoE is used to refer to the Ministry both before and after the restructuring.

9 S. Fukuta, *Kyōsō yametara gakuryoku sekai ichi - Finland kyōiku no seikō* [Becoming top of the world when it stopped competing: The success of Finnish education] 2006, pp. 30, 36.

10 National Institute for Educational Research Policy, 'TIMSS 2007 Kokusai hikaku kekka no gaiyō' [TIMSS 2007: Summary of International Comparisons], Tables 1.10 & 1.11. http://www.nier.go.jp/timss/2007/index.html (03/11/2009), 2007, accessed 3 November 2009.

11 OECD, 'Knowledge and skills for life, First results from PISA 2000 Executive Summary', http://www.pisa.oecd.org/dataoecd/44/32/33691620.pdf, accessed 3 November 2009.

12 Ibid.

13 See, for instance, Honda, *Tagenka suru 'nōryoku'*, pp. 75–110.

14 Based on the UNICEF 'Child Poverty in Perspective: An Overview of Child Well-being in Rich Countries', dimension 6, 2007, p. 38, available at http://www.unicef-irc.org/publications/pdf/rc7eng.pdf, accessed 3 November 2009.

15 http://pisa2003.acer.edu.au/interactive.php, accessed 3 November 2009.

16 P. Perrenoud, 'The Key to Social Fields: Competencies of an Autonomous Actor', in D.S. Rychen and L.H. Salganik (eds), *Defining and Selecting Key Competencies*, Göttingen, Germany: Hogrefe & Huber, 2001, pp. 121–49.

17 S. Norris, 'Synthesis of Research on Critical Thinking', *Educational Leadership*, May 1985, pp. 40–45.

18 T. Kusumi, 'Kinōteki suiron to hihanteki shikō' [Deductive inference and critical thinking], in S. Ichikawa (ed.), *Ninchi shinrigaku* [Cognitive psychology], Tokyo: Tokyo University Press, 1996, pp. 37–60.

19 E. Ben-Ari, *Body Projects in Japanese Children*, Richmond, Surrey: Curzon, 1997.

[20] P. Cave, *Primary School in Japan,* London and New York: Routledge, 2007, pp. 104, 108, 146.

[21] S. Yoneyama, *The Japanese High School,* London: Routledge, 1999.

[22] S. Yoneyama, and A. Naito, 'Problems with the Paradigm: The School as a Factor in Understanding Bullying (with special reference to Japan)', *British Journal of Sociology of Education,* 24(3), 2003, pp. 315–30.

[23] D. Rear, 'Critical Thinking and Modern Japan', *Electronic Journal of Contemporary Japanese Studies,* 4 March 2008, p. 4.

[24] Ibid.

[25] H. Siegel, 'Critical Thinking as an Educational Ideal', *Educational Forum,* 45(1), 1980, p. 14.

[26] T. Horio, *Educational Thought and Ideology in Modern Japan,* Tokyo: Tokyo University Press, 1986, p. 174; Yoneyama, *Silence and Resistance,* pp. 148–51. Historian Saburo Ienaga mounted a series of law suits against the MoE claiming its textbook screening process violated his constitutional rights of freedom of expression by censoring substantive content.

[27] N. Noddings, 'Foreword', in J. Nelson, S. Palonsky, and M. McCarthy (eds), *Critical Issues in Education,* New York: McGraw-Hill, 2004, p. xiii.

[28] S. Yoneyama, 'Japan's "Education Reform": The Plan for the Twenty-first Century', in J. Maswood, J. Graham and H. Miyajima (eds), *Japan: Change and Continuity,* RoutledgeCurzon, 2002, pp. 192–213; S. Yoneyama, 'The Era of Bullying: Japan under Neoliberalism', *The Asia-Pacific Journal: Japan Focus,* 31 December 2008.

[29] T. Kariya, *Kaisōka shakai to kyōiku kiki* [Japan as a stratified society and the crisis of education], Tokyo: Yushindokobunsha, 2001.

[30] Y. Honda, 'Taijin nōryoku kakusa ga NEET o umu' [Discrepancies in interpersonal skills produce NEETs], *Chūō Kōron,* April 2005, pp. 82–91.

[31] Y. Sugimoto, *An Introduction to Japanese Society,* Cambridge, New York: Cambridge University Press, 1997, p. 129.

[32] At just under 95 per cent, the completion rate for tertiary education in Japan is the highest in the world.

[33] L. Lim, 'Japan's 300, 000 International Student Plan', Asia-Pacific Sub-regional Preparatory Conference for the 2009 World Conference on Higher Education, Bangkok, p. 2.

[34] R. Goodman, 'The Japanese Professoriate', in G. S. Poole and Y. C. Chen (eds), *Higher Education in East Asia: Neoliberalism and the Professoriate,* Rotterdam: Sense Publishers, 2009, p. 28.

[35] D. Askew, 'Nihon no daigaku to kokusai hyōka' [Japanese universities and international rankings], *Ritsumeikan Keizaigaku,* 57(3), 2008, p. 429.

[36] S. Nakayama and M.F. Low, 'The Research Function of Universities in Japan', *Higher Education,* 34, 1997, p. 248. According to the 2009 THEQS World University Rankings, fourteen Japanese universities were ranked in the top 300 in the fields of life sciences and biomedicine, and natural sciences, and fifteen were in the top 300 for technology.

[37] Ibid., pp. 254–6.

38 H. Newby et al., *OECD Reviews of Tertiary Education: Japan*, Paris: OECD Publishing, 2009, p. 16.

39 B. J. McVeigh, *The State Bearing Gifts*, Lanham MD: Lexington Books, 2006, p. 223; Sugimoto, *An Introduction to Japanese Society*, p. 130; A. Yonezawa and R. Kosugi, 'Education, Training and Human Resources: Meeting Skill Requirements', in T. Shibata (ed.) *Japan Moving toward a More Advanced Knowledge Economy: Assessment and Lessons*, Washington, DC: The World Bank, 2006, p. 108. As Sugimoto notes, this is a generalization; students from medicine, science and engineering, as well as those sitting extremely competitive national exams for the legal profession and elite public service jobs, are known to study diligently.

40 Daigaku Kyōju P, Q, R, 'San Kyōju "Gakuryoku": Mondō' [Three University Professors, P, Q and R Discuss 'Academic Achievement'], *Sekai*, May 2000, p. 94.

41 See T. Kobayashi, 'Shūshoku ni Tsuyoi Daigaku no Himitsu o Saguru' [Searching for the secrets of universities that are strong at job placement], *Chūō Kōron*, February 2006, p. 88. 'Freeter' refers to a person who regularly moves from one part-time job to another; NEET is an acronym for someone 'not in employment, education or training'.

42 A. Asonuma, 'Finance Reform in Japanese Higher Education', *Higher Education*, 43, 2002, p. 117; Nakayama and Low, 'The Research Function of Universities in Japan', p. 249.

43 Asonuma, 'Finance Reform in Japanese Higher Education', p. 118.

44 K. Todani, *Country Report: Japan*, Asia-Pacific Sub-regional Preparatory Conference for the 2009 World Conference on Higher Education, Bangkok, p. 2.

45 A. Miura, *Karyū daigaku ga Nihon o horobosu* [Sub-standard universities are ruining Japan], Tokyo: Besuto Shinsho, 2008, p. 24.

46 McVeigh, *The State Bearing Gifts*, pp. 175, 179.

47 Asonuma, 'Finance Reform in Japanese Higher Education', p. 110.

48 OECD, *Education at a Glance 2007*, p. 8.

49 Y. Ogawa, 'Challenging the Traditional Organization of Japanese Universities', *Higher Education*, 43, 2002, p. 85.

50 Newby et al., *OECD Reviews of Tertiary Education*, p. 9.

51 M. Murasawa, 'The Future of Higher Education in Japan: Changing the Legal Status of National Universities', *Higher Education*, 43, 2002, p. 153.

52 Nihon Gakujutsu Shinkōkai, *21 Seiki COE Puroguramu no Gaiyō* [Overview of the 21st Century COE Programme], 2008–2009, p. 4.

53 The selected fields in 2002 were: life sciences (24.8 per cent); chemistry and materials sciences (18.6 per cent); information sciences, electrical and electronic engineering (17.7 per cent); humanities (17.7 per cent) and; interdisciplinary, combined fields, new disciplines (21.2 per cent); 2003: medicine (26.3 per cent); mathematics, physics and earth sciences (18 per cent); machinery, civil, construction and other engineering

(17.3 per cent); social sciences (19.6 per cent) and; interdisciplinary, combinedfields,newdisciplines(18.8percent).Datafor2004isunavailable. Ibid., p. 5.

54 Ibid. The Japan Society for the Promotion of Science also established a Global COE Programme to improve teaching and research quality at the postgraduate level.

55 This research strength in also evident when we consider that the top seven institutions (in terms of number of grants) awarded MoE research grants in 2008 were all (former) national universities. MoE, 'Heisei 20-nendo kagaku kenkyūhi hojokin kikanbetsu saitaku kensū/haibungaku ichiran' [List of institutions receiving scientific research grants and funding allocations], http://www.mext.go.jp/b_menu/houdou/20/04/08 042104/003.pdf, accessed 19 November 2009.

56 The fifty-five national *kōsen* also became independent administrative corporations.

57 MoE, *Kokuritsu daigaku no hōjinka tō* [Incorporation etc. of national universities], 2004, http://www.mext.go.jp/b_menu/hakusho/html/hpab200401/index.html, accessed 21 August 2009.

58 Asonuma, 'Finance Reform in Japanese Higher Education', p. 123.

59 Newby et al., *OECD Reviews of Tertiary Education*, p. 42.

60 Ibid., p. 43.

61 Dokuritsu Gyōsei Hōjin Tōkei Sentā, 'Gakkōsū', *Seifu tōkei no sōgō madoguchi* ['School Numbers, Government Statistics Service], 22 December 2008.

62 McVeigh, *The State Bearing Gifts*, p. 219.

63 Ogawa, 'Challenging the Traditional Organization of Japanese Universities', p. 88.

64 Todani, *Country Report: Japan*, p. 12.

65 Asonuma, 'Finance Reform in Japanese Higher Education', p. 119.

66 MoE, 'Gakkō kyōiku' [School education], *Dēta kara miru Nihon no Kyōiku 2008* [Japanese education based on data], p. 2.

67 MoE, *Kokusaika kyoten seibi jigyō (Gurōbaru 30) Q&A* [Becoming a Centre for Internationalisation (Global 30) Q&A)], April 2009.

68 Lim, 'Japan's 300,000 International Student Plan', p. 9.

10

The Impact of Changing Age Structure on Demographic Dividends and Intergenerational Transfers in Japan

NAOHIRO OGAWA

INTRODUCTION

This chapter examines the impact of unprecedented age compositional shifts in population upon the changing pattern of intergenerational transfers in Japan over the period 1950–2025. To achieve this objective, it draws upon a new methodological approach called National Transfer Accounts (NTA), and makes extensive use of a number of new findings derived from the NTA project for Japan, in which both micro- and macro-level data covering the period 1984–2004 have been applied to the NTA framework.

The chapter is structured as follows. The next section reviews some key features of Japan's demographics and economic dynamics during the post-war period to facilitate later discussion. The ensuing three sections discuss: (1) Japan's first demographic dividend induced by age compositional shifts and its relationship with the nation's long-term economic growth; (2) a rapidly changing pattern of familial transfers between various age groups in Japanese society over the past two decades; and (3) Japan's declining fertility and the rising cost of children's health and education. The final section summarizes the most important findings of this paper, and briefly considers their policy implications.

This chapter emphasizes the economic importance of the first and second demographic dividends. The former is currently depressing economic growth in Japan, while the latter has the potential to boost Japanese economic development, which means that the net effect of the two dividends is likely to determine Japan's future growth potential.

In this context, the government's policies for augmenting the second demographic dividend will play a significant role in determining the economic outlook of Japan in the first quarter of the twenty-first century.

JAPAN'S FALLING FERTILITY AND RAPID POPULATION AGEING

By the end of the Second World War, Japan's productive capacity had been utterly shattered. By 1957, however, Japan's real per capita income had recovered to its pre-war level. During the 1960s, Japan's real GNP grew at a phenomenal rate of about 11 percent per annum. Many such stories about Japan's miraculous economic success have been told repeatedly by a large number of economists.

It should be stressed, however, that Japan's post-war demographic transformations have not been any less phenomenal. Japan's post-war fertility decline was the first to occur in the non-Western world and was the greatest in magnitude among all industrialized countries. Following a short-lived baby boom period (1947–49), Japan's total fertility rate (TFR) declined dramatically. From 1947 to 1957, the TFR halved from 4.54 to 2.04 children per woman, as shown in Figure 1. Subsequent to this rapid fertility decline, there had been only minor fluctuations around the replacement level until the first oil crisis occurred in 1973. Thereafter, the TFR started to fall again, and by the mid-1990s, it had declined below 1.5 children per woman. In 2005, the TFR plummeted to 1.26, the lowest in the post-war period, before it rebounded slightly to 1.37 in 2008. If fertility were to remain constant at the present level, each successive generation would shrink by approximately 35 percent per generation. This post-1973 decline of fertility is often referred to by some demographers as Japan's second demographic transition.[1]

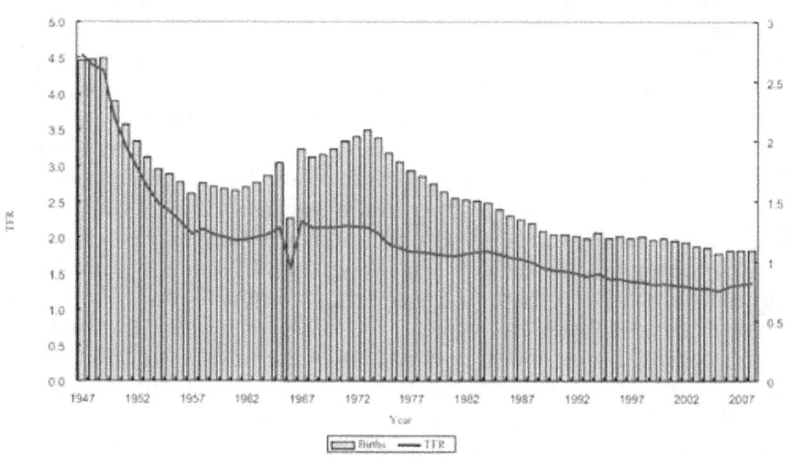

Figure 1. Trends in number of births and TFR: Japan, 1947–2008. Source: Ministry of Health, Labour and Welfare various years.

In parallel with these changes in TFR, the size of successive birth cohorts varied considerably over time, as illustrated in Figure 1. During the baby boom period, there were, on average, approximately 2.7 million births per year, but by 1957, the number of births decreased to 1.6 million. In the early 1970s, however, despite the decline in the fertility rate, a brief surge to more than 2 million births was recorded, as an 'echo' effect of the baby boom cohorts – a generation often called 'second-generation baby boomers'. Since then, births have again declined, marking slightly less than 1.1 million in 2008, which is 60 percent less than the total annual number of births recorded during the baby boom period in the late 1940s.

Japan's recent very low fertility has been attracting a great deal of attention, both domestically and internationally.[2] In contrast, a rather limited amount of attention has been paid to the unprecedented rapidity with which Japan's mortality transition has been under way. Age-specific mortality rates have been declining considerably over the past several decades. During 1947–65, Japan's life expectancy at birth rose from 50.1 to 67.7 years for men and from 54.0 to 72.9 years for women. At the time it joined the OECD in April 1964, Japan's life expectancies for both men and women were the lowest among all the OECD member countries.[3] By the mid-1970s, however, Japanese life expectancy became one of the highest among OECD countries. In 2008, male life expectancy at birth reached 79.3 years to become the third highest in the world, and female life expectancy rose to 86.1 years, the highest in the world. Moreover, between 1950–52 and 2008, life expectancy at age 65 grew to a substantial extent, from 11.4 to 18.6 years for men, and from 13.4 to 23.6 years for women, which implies a marked increase in the retirement period and in the joint survival to older ages for both husbands and wives.[4] Primarily because of such long-term improvements of mortality, the number of centenarians has been increasing at an annual rate of 13 percent over the past four decades, which makes them the fastest growing segment of the entire Japanese population. In addition, the modal age of death changed dramatically. It jumped from 0 to 79 years old in 1958 in the case of women, and from 0 to 75 years old in 1960 in the case of men. In 2007, it was 91 years of age for women and 87 for men, both of which are the highest in the world.

As a consequence of the long-term transformations in both fertility and mortality, the age structure of the Japanese population has been shifting to a marked extent. The proportion of those aged 65 and over increased from 4.9 percent in 1950 to 20.2 percent in 2005, making Japan's population the oldest national population in the world in 2005. (In 2009, the corresponding figure was 22.7 percent.) The proportion of the oldest-old persons (aged 75 and over) in the total population was only 1.3 percent. in 1950, but it exceeded 10.7 percent. in 2009.[5]

In contrast to the rapidly growing number of elderly Japanese, the number of those aged below 15 has been declining for twenty-eight consecutive years, and Japan now has fewer children than at any time since 1908. Furthermore, the overall size of Japan's population began declining from the end of 2005. More importantly, these demographic trends of low fertility and population decline are expected to persist over the period 2005–2025.

CHANGING ECONOMIC DYNAMISM: THE DRAMATIC RISE AND FALL OF THE JAPANESE ECONOMY

The Japanese economy grew very rapidly in both the 1950s and 1960s. Because the economic growth performance particularly in the latter decade was spectacular, the 1960s are often referred to as the 'Golden '60s'. By 1968, Japan's GNP had become the second largest in the world. The rapid economic growth during the 1960s was facilitated by such factors as the use of abundant labour (equivalent to the first demographic dividend to be discussed later), the borrowing of advanced technology from developed countries, and favourable conditions in international trade.[6] However, the oil crisis of 1973 triggered a series of restructuring changes in the Japanese economy, and brought its growth performance to levels significantly less impressive than those in the 1960s.

In the mid-1980s Japan entered the bubble economy phase, but this investment boom abruptly ended in the first half of 1990, causing a number of leading banks and other financial institutions to go into bankruptcy. Tragically, the Japanese government implemented inappropriate macroeconomic policies to rectify the unfavourable economic conditions at the time. Although many of these economic problems were attributable to the influence of globalization, the Japanese government regarded them as part of business cycles, and went about increasing government spending in the hope of boosting the economy but without much success. It took the government several years to realize that more drastic economic restructuring policies were needed to make the Japanese economy more competitive in international markets. As a result, government debts accumulated at an unprecedented rate, reaching US$8.7 trillion in 2009 (at a rate of 100 yen per dollar) or approximately 1.9 times as large as the country's projected GDP for that year.[7] Japan's current debt is, in comparison, by far the worst among all the industrialized nations. Because of such delayed policy responses, some economists call the 1990s 'Japan's Lost Decade'.[8] As a result of a prolonged recession lasting since 1991 and China's spectacular economic growth in recent years, the Japanese economy is likely to slip to third place among the world's largest economies in 2010.

Despite these rapid demographic and economic transformations over the past few decades, Japan's labour market developments have been rather slow. It is important to note that the age-specific labour force participation rates of Japanese women still show an M-shaped pattern, although participation among middle-aged women has been rising in recent years, primarily due to their higher education, shortening of the reproductive span, and a more modern life style.[9] It should be stressed that slightly more than half of married women working as paid employees are part-time workers, and that this proportion grew at a rate faster than that of full-time workers in the 1990s during Japan's 'Lost Decade'.

Also, an increasing proportion of Japanese youths aged 15 to 34 are choosing alternative working life styles. Two terms frequently used to describe young persons who remain outside formal employment are *freeters* and *NEETs*. Persons classified by the government as *NEETs* are completely outside the labour force while *freeters* are youths that are engaged in temporary or part-time employment. The increasing proportion of young people who choose not to seek permanent full time jobs after graduation or who decide to quit their first job is causing considerable concern among policy makers in Japan. Between 1982 and 2002, the proportion of youths aged 15 to 34 who are classified by the government as *freeters* rose from 1.9 to 7.4 per cent. In contrast, the proportion of younger Japanese who are viewed as *NEETs* remained virtually unchanged at 1.6 percent of the population aged 15 to 34. In 2002, this meant that there were 2.5 million *freeters* and 0.5 million *NEETs* among younger Japanese. Thus, 9.0 percent of Japanese aged 15 to 34, or over 3.0 million individuals, were outside of the regular, full-time employment system.[10]

Another interesting labour-related issue in Japan is the employment status of the elderly. Japan's mandatory retirement policies have, to a significant extent, resisted the aforementioned substantial changes in the economy and have remained an extreme case among the practices of industrialized nations. It is important to note that the proportion of firms having mandatory retirement rules increased gradually from 69 percent in 1968 to 91 percent in 1991, and has been oscillating somewhere between 90 to 95 percent since the early 1990s.[11] One of the principal obstacles to changing the mandatory retirement age (generally 60 at present) is related to the practice of the seniority wage system, under which the postponement of the retirement age leads to larger wage bills for companies.[12] It should be emphasized, however, that more changes in national retirement policies are likely. The Japanese government is currently attempting to encourage firms to increase the mandatory retirement age to 65. The Law Concerning Stabilization of Employment of Older Persons, enacted in 2004, requires firms to increase the age of mandatory retirement to 65, but does not stipulate any penalties for noncompliance, which is why to date only few companies have heeded it.[13]

The other deterrent to the extension of the retirement age beyond 60 is related to the provision of lump-sum severance benefits, which are basically determined by the duration of the employee's service. In 2008, an employee with a university education and more than 35 years of service received severance pay equivalent to forty-four months' worth of his/her final monthly salary. Because a substantial proportion of business firms have their own accumulated funds to cover such payments, or have already incorporated such grants into pension benefits provided by employers, these funds can be, in NTA terms, regarded as part of the second demographic dividend, which will be discussed in a later section. More importantly, this lump-sum severance pay programme has recently been drawing much attention from various financial institutions because the baby boom generations are now reaching retirement age.

Another feature of Japan's labour market is a high labour force participation rate among the elderly, many of whom work on part-time bases or engage in agriculture.[14] Japan stands out in terms of labour force participation rates for men and women aged 65 and over. For example, in 2007, the labour force participation rate for elderly Japanese men was close to 30 percent. In sharp contrast, the corresponding figure for several developed countries (France, Germany and Austria) in Europe was well below 10 percent, and slightly higher than 20 percent for the United States.[15]

CHANGING PUBLIC AND FAMILIAL SUPPORT SYSTEMS

Public Support Programmes

As a result of the stunning economic recovery from the devastation of the Second World War, Japan managed to establish its universal pension and medical care schemes in 1961. Since then, Japan's social security system has grown remarkably. Between 1961 and 2007, social security benefits increased from 4.9 to 24.4 percent of national income.[16] Moreover, the proportion of the social security expenditure allotted to the pension schemes increased from 22.7 percent in 1964 to 52.8 percent in 2007, while the corresponding value for the medical schemes fell from 54.4 percent to 31.7 percent over the period in question.[17] Owing to population ageing, coupled with the maturity of the old-age pension schemes, the relative share of pension benefits paid out in national income has been on an upward trend in recent years. Contributions to social security increased somewhat less than did benefits, and the growing difference between benefits and contributions has been covered by general tax revenues.

As regards public pension schemes, a major reform took place in 2004. One of the primary objectives of the 2004 pension reform was to predetermine the level of future contributions to make the programme more transparent for younger workers, thus reducing benefits considerably. The government introduced a mechanism to balance benefit levels automatically according to future changes in the population age structure. The goal was to avoid repeated reforms and to restore the younger generation's trust in government schemes. This may be regarded as a paradigm shift in Japan's social security provisions.[18] Putting it differently, Japan's public pension schemes are now sustainable from a financial point of view, although the adequacy of benefits to be paid out may become a more serious issue in the years ahead. As a consequence of the 2004 reform, the replacement rate for the Japanese public pension declined considerably, and is projected to continuously fall to 50.2 percent by 2023, after which it is assumed to remain unchanged up to 2050.[19]

The second major component of social security benefits is medical. Subject to Japan's economic growth performance, the coverage of medical insurance plans has been revised periodically. Despite these changes in the medical care plans over the past few decades, the absolute amount of financial resources allotted to medical care services has been rising continuously. One of the factors behind the rapid growth of medical costs and what sets Japan apart from other industrialized nations is an extremely long period of hospitalization. In 2005, it was 34.1 days in Japan, which is the longest among the twenty-eight OECD countries, followed by Australia's 17.8 and 13.2 days in France.[20]

It is worth noting that to curb the upward spiral of medical care costs, the Japanese government implemented the Long-term Care Insurance (LTCI) scheme in 2000 with a view to reducing the average duration of hospitalization for in-patient care by facilitating in-home care. The LTCI is expected to alleviate the care-giving burden to be placed upon family members, many of whom are middle-aged women.[21] It should be noted that because the expenditure for the LTCI grew at an alarming rate since its inception, the scope of its services was critically reviewed and downgraded in 2006 with a view to curbing its future costs.

In April 2008, the Japanese government implemented a new medical insurance scheme specifically for senior citizens aged 75 and older as another step towards curbing the nation's ballooning medical costs. Under this new scheme, premiums are automatically deducted from pension payouts. Because premiums have actually become higher under the new scheme for a certain segment of the targeted elderly age group, the revision of this new scheme has already become one of the most urgent political issues at the national level.

Familial Support and Value Shifts

As distinct from developed countries in the West, multigenerational living arrangements are still fairly common in Japan.[22] In the face of the long persistence of three-generational households, the potential for family support for the elderly is expected to steadily deteriorate with the passage of time. The proportion of those aged 65 and over residing with their adult children has been on a downward trend; it declined from 69 percent in 1980 to 44 percent in 2007. In addition, the index called the familial support ratio (expressed as the ratio of women aged 40–59 to elderly persons aged 65–79) is expected to decline substantially over the next twenty years. The value of this index was 1.30 in 1990, and is projected to be 0.65 in 2010, thus indicating that it will decline by 50 percent in twenty years' time.[23] It should also be noted that the present value of this index is the lowest in the entire world and is expected to continue being so for another twenty years.

Apart from these demographic transformations, value shifts among the Japanese people have been dramatic. These changes are well captured in time-series data gathered in the National Survey on Family Planning, undertaken every other year from 1950 to 2004 by Mainichi Daily Newspapers.[24] Since the first round of the survey, except for a few rounds, the question regarding dependence on children for old-age security has been directed to currently married women of reproductive age who have at least one child. (In addition to these time-series data gleaned from Mainichi Daily Newspapers, the time span has been extended, by utilizing data collected in the National Survey on Work and Family, undertaken by the Nihon University Population Research Institute in 2007.)

The precoded responses are as follows: (1) 'expect to depend on children'; (2) 'do not expect to depend on children'; and (3) 'never thought about it'. The proportion of respondents who expect to depend on their own children declined almost continuously over the period 1950–2007. Almost two-thirds of Japanese married women in 1950 expressed the expectation to depend on their children for old-age security, but only 9 percent in 2007 intended to do so.[25] It can be safely hypothesized that these long-term downward trends in parents' expectations for relying on their children in their old age are closely associated with the continuous improvement of old-age pension schemes since the early 1960s.

Also, in the National Survey conducted by Mainichi Daily Newspapers, since 1963, a question about the attitude of these married women towards taking care of aged parents has been asked in successive rounds. The precoded response categories are as follows: (1) 'good custom'; (2) 'natural duty as children'; (3) 'unavoidable due to inadequacy of public support resources'; and (4) 'not a good custom'. (Data gathered by Nihon University supplement these time-series data too.) The proportion of those who chose one of the first two response categories ('good custom' and 'natural duty as children') was, mostly, stable over the period 1963–1986. From 1986 to 1988, however, a sudden decline occurred in this proportion. In the years leading up to 2007, the proportion of married women of reproductive age who chose one of these two response categories has been, by and large, characterized by a downward trend.

Obviously, these demographic and socioeconomic transformations in post-war Japan have been affecting the pattern and mode of intergenerational transfers over time. To analyse these changes in intergenerational transfers, this study draws extensively upon some of the principal findings recently generated from the NTA project for Japan.

A Brief Outline of the National Transfer Accounts

In the recent past, an international collaborative research project has been implemented under the leadership of the East-West Center (Andrew Mason) and the Center for the Economics and Demography of Ageing at the University of California, Berkeley (Ronald Lee). A number of collaborating institutions are involved, and at the time of writing this chapter, a total of thirty countries have participated in this global project. Among the institutions included in the project are: the Nihon University Population Research Institute, University of Toulouse, ECLAC and CELADE, Peking University, the University of the Philippines, Thailand Development Research Institute, the International Institute of Population Studies, Mumbai, and the University of Indonesia.

One of the principal objectives of this international collaborative project is to develop the National Transfer Accounts (NTA), which is a system for measuring economic flows across age groups. These flows arise because in any viable society, dependent members of the population – those who consume more than they produce – are supported by members of the population who produce more than they consume. Societies take different approaches to reallocating resources from surplus to deficit ages, but two methods dominate. One relies on capital markets. Namely, individuals accumulate capital during their working ages. When they are no longer productive, the elderly can support their consumption by relying on capital income (interest, dividends, rental income, profits, etc.) and by liquidating their assets. The other method relies on transfers from those at surplus ages to those at deficit ages. Some of these transfers are mediated by the public sector. Notable examples are public education, publicly financed healthcare, and public pension programmes. Many transfers are private transfers of which familial transfers are most important. The material needs of children are provided mostly by their parents. In Asian societies familial transfers between adult children and the elderly are also very important. Some of these transfers are between households, but intra-household transfers are of much greater importance. In Asia, family members tend to form multigeneration households that involve large intergenerational transfers.

National Transfer Accounts provide a comprehensive framework for estimating consumption, production, and resource reallocations by age. The accounts are constructed so as to be consistent with and complementary to National Income and Product Accounts (NIPA). The accounts are constructed with sufficient historical depth to allow for analysis of key features of the transfer system. Sectoral disaggregation allows the analysis of public and private education and healthcare spending. The accounts can also be projected to analyse the economic and policy implications of future demographic changes.

The NTA system will provide important new information relevant to the following issues:

1. *Intergenerational Equity and Poverty*. How resources are shared across generations is one of the most important determinants of equity and poverty. Children and the elderly are most vulnerable because their responses to economic hardship are so limited. The NTA system measures how consumption varies across generations and will allow for international comparisons currently not possible.
2. *Ageing Policy*. Many Asian countries face the prospect of rapid population ageing. They are developing new programmes and considering reforms of old programmes intended to meet vital needs of the elderly without undue sacrifice on the part of other generations at present and in the future. The NTA system will provide the information base needed to evaluate alternative policies, to assess their effects on intergenerational equity, and their implications for economic growth.
3. *The First Demographic Dividend*. The first demographic dividend arises because changes in population age structure have led to an increase in the working ages relative to the non-working ages. To be more precise, the first demographic dividend arises because of an increase in the share of the population at ages during which production exceeds consumption.
4. *The Second Demographic Dividend*. The second demographic dividend arises in response to the prospect of population ageing. In countries that rely on capital accumulation to meet the retirement needs of the elderly, population ageing provides a powerful incentive to accumulate wealth. This phenomenon has been important to the economic success of East Asia's high-performing economies. In countries that rely on transfers to meet the retirement needs of the elderly, the second demographic dividend may not emerge.
5. *Childbearing Incentives*. Countries vary with respect to the cost of children and the extent to which those costs are borne by parents. The NTA system provides estimates of the cost of children and the extent to which those costs are subsidized by the public sector. This information may be useful for understanding why high fertility persists in some countries and why very low fertility persists in others.

This chapter analyses some of these issues by presenting some of the findings recently produced by the NTA project. It focuses on issues such as first and second demographic dividends, a changing pattern of consumption among generations, and the cost of children and low fertility. The chapter uses the graph in Figure 2 as a base for analysis, which shows estimates of age-specific profiles of per capita consumption, private and public sectors combined, and per capita production (labour income) in five selected years, namely: 1984, 1989, 1994, 1999 and 2004. These profiles have been estimated by drawing upon

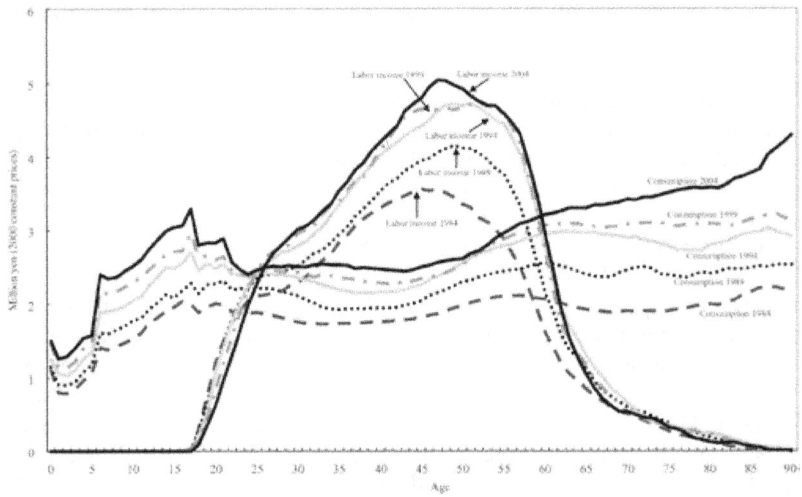

Figure 2. Age-specific profiles of per capita consumption and production in Japan, 1984–2004

private-sector information derived from the five rounds of the *National Survey of Family Income and Expenditure* (NSFIE) conducted during the period 1984–2004 by the Statistics Bureau of Japan, and public-sector information for the corresponding five years, gleaned from various government published data sources. It should be noted that both age-specific profiles have been adjusted, by using data from the National Income Product Account. These estimated results are expressed in terms of 2000 constant prices.

There are two points worth noting in this graphical exposition. First, the age at which an average individual shifts from a net consumer to a net producer gradually rose from 23 in 1984, to 24 in 1989, 25 in 1994, and finally to 26 in 2004. Moreover, at the other end of the lifecycle, the age transition from a net producer to a net consumer was postponed only marginally from 58 in 1984, to 59 in 1989, and to 60 in 2004. The persistency of the crossing age (the age in which one becomes economically dependent, or independent, on others) at the later stage of the lifecycle is attributable to the existence of the mandatory retirement age at 60 in contemporary Japan, as has been discussed earlier.

Second, the age-profiles of per capita consumption rose almost continuously over time, particularly at both younger and older ages. It is worth observing that the amount of per capita consumption rose distinctively among those aged 65 and over in 2004. This seems to be accounted for by the implementation of the LTCI scheme, which came into effect in the year 2000 and presents the largest plan of that kind in the contemporary world. In-home care for the frail elderly, which had until then been informally provided by family members, became formalized as a part of the market economy. As a result, Japan's per capita consumption profiles have been increasingly resembling those for the United States and Sweden, among the NTA member countries.

POPULATION AGEING AND TWO DEMOGRAPHIC DIVIDENDS

As has been recently discussed extensively elsewhere,[26] one of the key linkages between demographic transformations and economic growth is the role of demographic dividends in the process of economic development. When a country's fertility begins to fall, the first demographic dividend arises because changes in population age structure lead to an increase in the working ages relative to non-working ages. To facilitate calculating the effect of such age structural changes on overall economic growth performance in Japan over the period 1984–2004, this study averaged the five sets of per capita consumption and production age-specific profiles observed over the twenty-year period. By applying the computed age-specific results as statistical weights to adjust the entire population over the period 1932–2025, it calculated the effective number of producers, the effective number of consumers, and the economic support ratio, i.e. the effective number of producers divided by the effective number of consumers. The change in the economic support ratio represents the change in output per effective consumer due solely to changes in age structure over the period 1932–2025, as indicated in Figure 3.

As this graph illustrates, from 1948 to 1983, the support ratio grew continuously, thus generating the first demographic dividend. The plotted result in Figure 3 also indicates that the tempo of growth of the support ratio was noticeably fast over the period of the 'Golden '60s'. This substantiates the validity of the view that the unprecedented

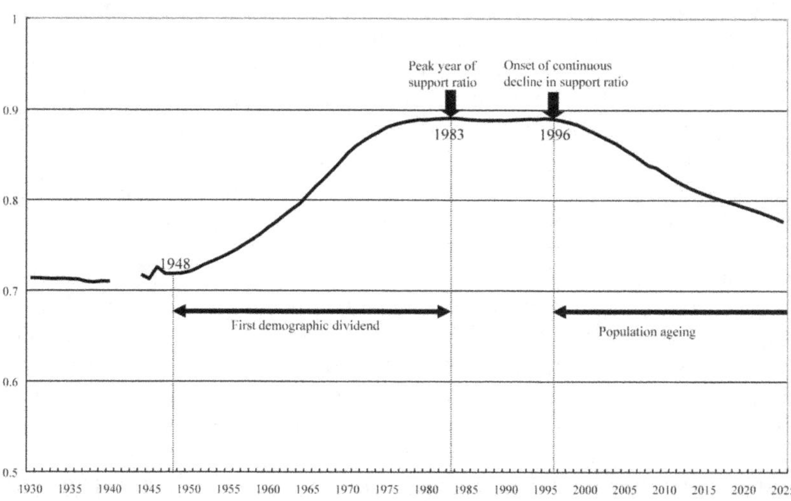

Figure 3. First demographic dividend and population ageing in Japan, 1932–2025

fertility reduction subsequent to the baby boom played a crucial role in boosting the growth of per capita income at a remarkable rate during this high economic growth period.

As has been the case with other developed countries, Japan's first demographic dividend was inherently transitory in nature, and lasted only a few decades. After reaching its peak value in 1983, the support ratio levelled off for slightly more than ten years. Since 1996, the economic support ratio has been on a downward trend, and the first demographic dividend has turned decidedly negative. This change is a direct consequence of population ageing.

In addition to the first demographic dividend, age structural shifts lead to the second demographic dividend, which arises in response to the prospect of population ageing. For instance, in countries that rely on capital accumulation to meet the retirement needs of the elderly, population ageing provides a powerful incentive to accumulate wealth. When life expectancy is increasing, the accumulation of wealth is stimulated, which, in turn, leads to a permanent increase in income. It is important to note, however, that in countries that rely on transfers, both public and familial, to meet the retirement needs of the elderly, the second demographic dividend may not emerge. While the first demographic dividend is purely accounting-oriented, the second demographic dividend consists of both compositional and behavioural effects.[27] In other words, the second demographic dividend is affected not only by the number of the elderly persons relative to younger persons, but also by the extent to which consumers and policy makers are forward-looking and respond effectively to the demographic changes that are anticipated in the years ahead.

Compared with the first dividend, measuring the amount of the second dividend is considerably more difficult, in part because the accumulation of wealth is intrinsically forward-looking. This study, like previous studies,[28] has simplified the computational procedure by making the following two major assumptions. First, it assumes that the growth rates of the capital and lifecycle wealth are equal, and the elasticity of labour income, with respect to capital, is set equal to 0.5. Second, it assumes that the wealth held by those aged 50 and over is closely connected with the effect of demography on lifecycle wealth and the second demographic dividend.

Compared with the computational work pertaining to the first demographic dividend, measuring the amount of the second demographic dividend is far more complicated. Also, since the computational procedure has been described in detail elsewhere,[29] this chapter simply discusses the computed results. The estimates of the second demographic dividend over the period 1975–2035 are shown in Figure 4. Japan's second demographic dividend remained at a considerably high level in the first half of the period under review, particularly over the period 1975–95. In the second half of the time period in question, the growth of the

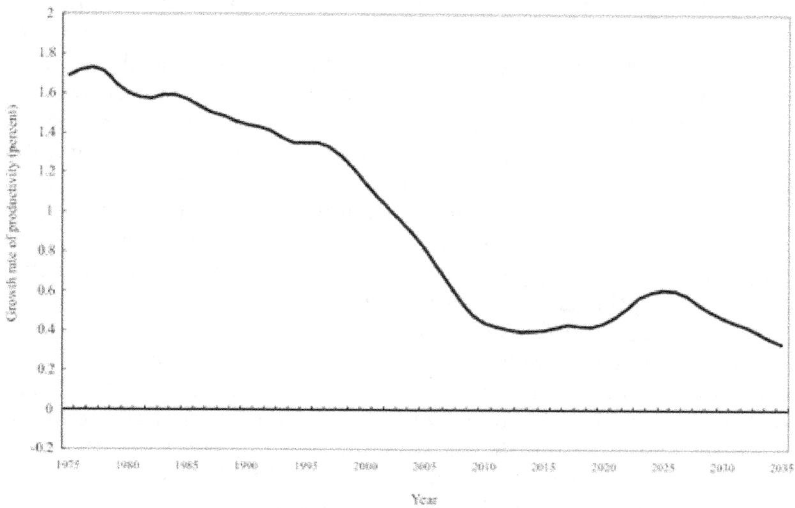

Figure 4. Trend in second demographic dividend in Japan, 1975–2035

second demographic dividend declines to a marked extent, but never plunges below zero. In fact, after reaching a pronounced trough in the 2010s, Japan's future second demographic dividend is expected to show a substantial upsurge in the 2020s and 2030s, boosting saving rates and capital intensification of the economy. More importantly, these fluctuations in the second demographic dividend are substantially attributable to the rapid age compositional shifts in the early part of the twenty-first century, primarily because the second generation of baby boomers enters the age group of 50 years old and over, when they are expected to commence building up financial assets for their retirement life.

THE CHANGING PATTERN OF INTERGENERATIONAL TRANSFERS IN JAPAN

The abovementioned demographic and socioeconomic transformations in post-war Japan have been affecting the pattern and mode of intergenerational transfers over time. To gain further insights into this, this chapter employs the NTA approach. NTA measures intergenerational flows for a certain period of time (usually a calendar or fiscal year), and as explained in detail elsewhere,[30] the following equation holds in the NTA framework:

$$\underbrace{C(x)-Y^{l}(x)}_{\text{Lifecycle deficit}}=\underbrace{\underbrace{\tau^{+}(x)-\tau^{-}(x)}_{\text{Net transfers}}+\underbrace{Y^{A}(x)-S(x)}_{\text{Asset-based reallocations}}}_{\text{Age reallocations}}$$

where Y^l = labour income, Y^A = asset income, τ^+ = transfer received, C = consumption, S = saving, and τ^- = transfer given. It should be noted that this flow identity holds for each age *x* as well as the whole economy. The age reallocations can be further disaggregated into public-sector and private-sector age reallocations, as described elsewhere in detail.[31]

Before proceeding to the discussion of computational results, however, caution should be exercised with regard to the following two points. First, both 'familial transfers' and 'private transfers' are used interchangeably in this chapter; both terms refer to transfers coming from other family members of the same or different households. Second, although net private transfers are comprised of bequests and *inter vivos* transfers, the computation of the bequest component has not been completed at the time of writing this chapter. For this reason, the bequests are excluded from the computational results here.

Figure 5 compares the changing pattern of three components of reallocation of the per capita lifecycle deficits in Japan during 1984–2004. The three components include net reallocations through assets, net public transfers, and net private transfers, measured in terms of 2000 constant prices on a per capita and annual basis. Panels A, B and C illustrate the annual reallocation of the per capita lifecycle deficits observed in 1984, 1994 and 2004, respectively.

A brief comparison of the three panels reveals the following two points of interest. First, the composition of per capita net transfers to the elderly population changed dramatically over the twenty-year period, with the amount of per capita net public transfers to the elderly increasing significantly. Similarly, the amount of per capita net asset-based reallocations grew considerably over time. In contrast, the relative importance of per capita net familial transfers from the young to the elderly declined to

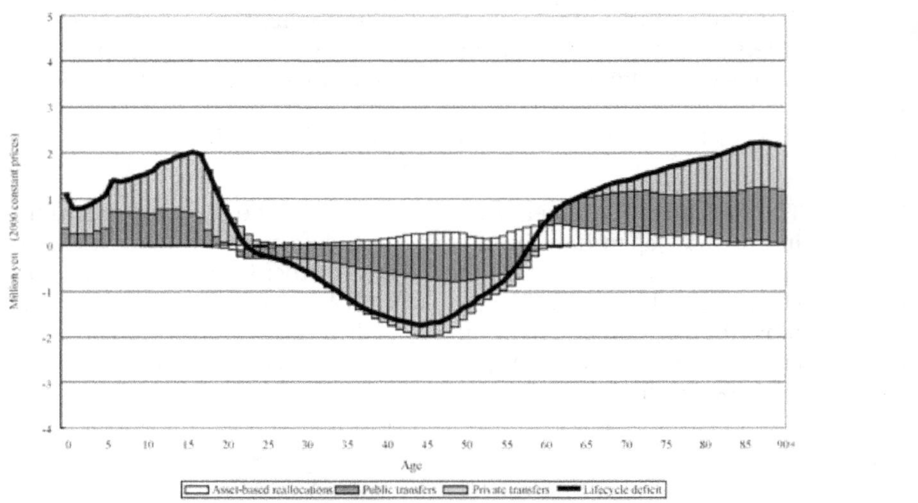

Figure 5. Three components of per capita reallocation of lifecycle deficits: Japan, 1984, 1994 and 2004. Panel A.1984

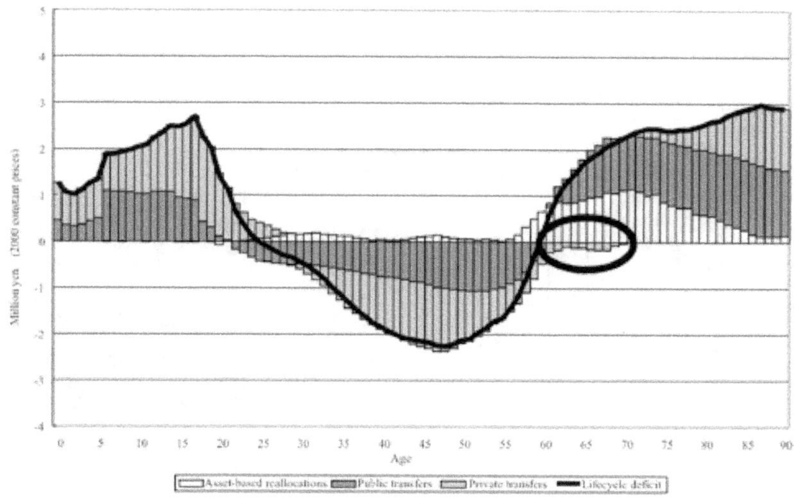

Figure 5 Three components of per capita reallocation of lifecycle deficits: Japan, 1984, 1994 and 2004. Panel B. 1994

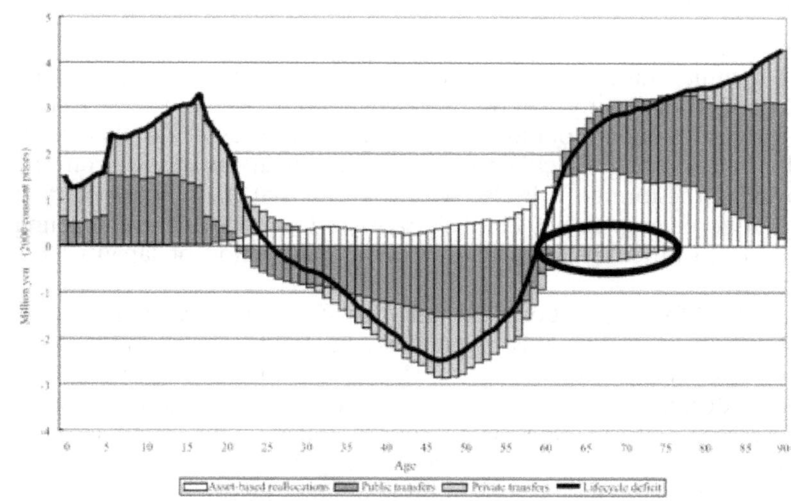

Figure 5 Three components of per capita reallocation of lifecycle deficits: Japan, 1984, 1994 and 2004. Panel C. 2004

an appreciable extent. These results seem to indicate that the Japanese elderly have become increasingly dependent upon public transfers (predominantly old-age pensions and medical care services) and asset-based reallocations in supporting their retirement life.

Second, and more importantly, as marked by two circles in Figure 5 (one in Panel B and the other in Panel C), the amount of per capita

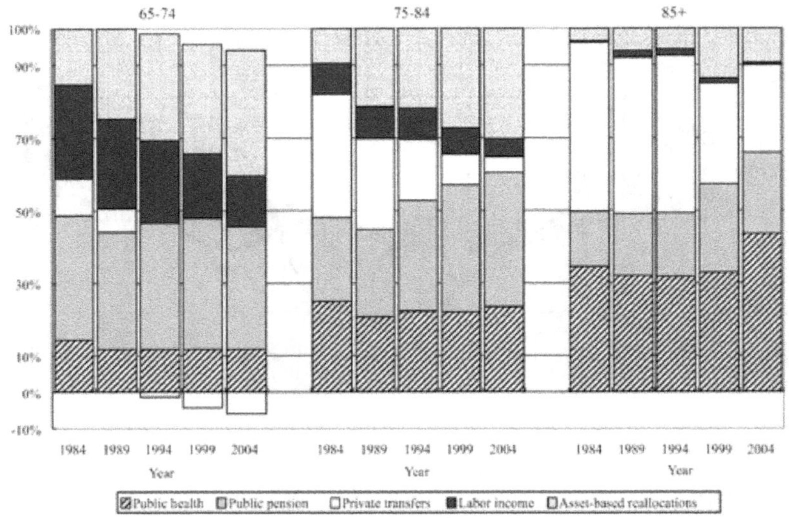

Figure 6. Finance of consumption of elderly aged 65–74, 75–84 and 85 or over in Japan, 1984–2004

net familial transfers to the relatively young elderly persons (roughly in their 60s and early 70s) was negative in both 1994 and 2004, implying that the amount of financial assistance they provided to their adult children and/or grandchildren exceeded monetary assistance from the latter to the former. It is also worth noting that the amount of such negative per capita net familial transfers from the relatively young elderly to other age groups grew during the period of Japan's 'Lost Decade'.

To shed further light on the changing pattern of per capita net familial transfers over time, this chapter has computed a change in the age at which an average individual shifted from a net producer to a net consumer during 1984–2004. The calculated result shows that the crossing age rose from 64 in 1984 to 77 years old in 2004. This can be substantiated by the graphical presentation in Figure 6, where the change in the pattern of financing consumption among the three elderly groups (65–74, 75–84 and 85+) from 1984 to 2004 is plotted. Among those 65–74, the role of public pensions and medical services has become increasingly important. In contrast, familial transfers have become less important over time. Since 1994, the direction of flow of familial transfers has changed from the elderly to the young or working-age population. The amount of the flow has been steadily increasing. It should be emphasized, however, that the inflow of familial transfers from the younger population is still significant among those aged 85 and over. This may be due to the fact that the elderly of this age group receive a relatively limited amount of pension benefits as a result of their shorter contribution period.

CONCLUDING REMARKS

In the first half of this chapter, the rapid demographic changes were linked to a host of socioeconomic developments and familial transformations in post-war Japan. The second half of the chapter examined some of the important impacts of population ageing in Japan, by drawing heavily upon the NTA computed results, ranging from the first and second demographic dividends to the lifecycle reallocations.

Judging from numerous past experiences of many industrialized countries in the West, demographic solutions have been rather unsuccessful in coping with various issues arising from population ageing. For instance, low fertility tends to be resistant to policy, and immigration measures are of limited help. (Particularly, the latter policy option seems to be still a remote possibility in contemporary Japan.) Yet the utilization of the first demographic dividend as well as the accumulated second demographic dividend among the elderly seem to have some promising potential in placing a country's economic growth on a steady growth path. Although Japan's first demographic dividend came to an end in the mid-1980s, its second demographic dividend is expected to increase to a considerable extent from now to the mid-2020s.

In connection with the accumulated second demographic dividend in Japan, one crucial question arises: how do Japanese elderly people make use of their accumulated assets and wealth? Depending upon where they invest their financial resources, Japan's future economic growth performance is prone to considerably differing outcomes. If Japanese elderly people are provided with sufficient knowledge about the dynamics of the financial market, they may have a good potential for investing their accumulated assets possibly outside Japan. Moreover, the timing of the 'first demographic dividend' for selected Asian countries varies considerably. In the case of China, its first dividend lasts for forty-three years from 1973 to 2016. India's first demographic dividend is projected to last even longer: seventy years from 1974 to 2044.[32] In an era of globalization, the wealthier Japanese elderly will be able to invest their assets in fast-growing Chinese and Indian economies, and bring in financial gains back to Japan. Obviously, to facilitate such international transactions, proper institutional and legal arrangements need to be developed to protect the elderly investors.

In contemporary Japan, the elderly are generally considered as 'debts'. However, the above discussion suggests that Japanese elderly persons may become powerful 'assets' to keep the country on a steady growth path in the years to come. In addition, we have also found that the Japanese elderly are still playing a vital role in providing financial support for their offspring when the latter encounter economic difficulties.

ACKNOWLEDGEMENTS

Research for this article was funded by two grants from the National Institute of Health, NIA R01-AG025488 and AG025247. This work was also supported by a grant obtained by the Nihon University Population Research Institute from the 'Academic Frontier Project for Private Universities', a matching fund subsidy from MEXT (Ministry of Education, Culture, Sports, Science and Technology) for the period of 2006–10. Furthermore, the author is grateful to the UNFPA (RAS5P203) and the Japan Medical Association for their financial assistance.

NOTES

1 See R. D. Retherford and N. Ogawa, 'Japan's Baby Bust: Causes, Implications, and Policy Responses', in F. R. Harris (ed.) *The Baby Bust: Who Will Do the Work? Who Will Pay the Taxes?* Lanham: Rowman & Littlefield Publishers, Inc., 2006, pp. 5–47; N. Ogawa, R. D. Retherford, and R. Matsukura, 'Japan's Declining Fertility and Policy Responses', in G. Jones, P. T. Straughan, and A. Chan (eds) *Ultra-Low Fertility in Pacific Asia: Trends, Causes, and Policy Issues*, Abingdon, Oxon: Routledge, 2009, pp. 40–72.

2 Ibid.

3 A. Mason and N. Ogawa, 'Population, Labour Force, Saving and Japan's Future', in M. Blomstrom, B. Gangnes, S. La Croix (eds) *Japan's New Economy: Continuity and Change in the Twenty-First Century*, Oxford: Oxford University Press, 2001, pp. 48–74.

4 National Institute of Population and Social Security Research (NIPSSR), *Latest Demographic Statistics: 2010*, Tokyo: NIPSSR, 2010.

5 Ibid.

6 N. Ogawa, G. Jones, and J. G. Williamson (eds) *Human Resources in Development along the Asia-Pacific Rim*, Singapore: Oxford University Press, 1993.

7 Ministry of Finance Japan, *Central Government Debt as of December 31, 2009*, http://www.mof.go.jp/english/gbb/e2112.htm, Accessed: 10 February 2010.

8 H. Yoshikawa, *Japan's Lost Decade*, Tokyo: International House of Japan, 2001.

9 A. Mason and N. Ogawa, 'Population, Labor Force, Saving and Japan's Future', pp. 48–74; R.D. Retherford and N. Ogawa, 'Japan's Baby Bust', pp. 5–47.

10 R. L. Clark et al., 'Population Decline, Labor Force Stability, and the Future of the Japanese Economy', *European Journal of Population,* 4 March 2009.

11 Japan Productivity Centre (JPC), *Katsuyō Rōdō Tōkei 2010* [Applied Labor Statistics: 2010], Tokyo: JPC, 2010.

12 R. L. Clark and N. Ogawa, 'The Effects of Mandatory Retirement on Earnings Profiles in Japan', *Industrial and Labor Relations Review* 45(2), 1992, pp. 258–266; R. L. Clark, N. Ogawa, and R. Matsukura, 'Population

Ageing, Changing Retirement Policies and Lifetime Earnings Profiles in Japan', in R. L. Clark, N. Ogawa, and A. Mason (eds) *Population Ageing, Intergenerational Transfers and the Macroeconomy*, Cheltenham, UK: Edward Elgar, 2007, pp. 17–37.

13 R. L. Clark et al, 'Population Decline, Labor Force Stability, and the Future of the Japanese Economy'.

14 N. Ogawa, S-H. Lee, and R. Matsukura, 'Health and its Impact on Work and Dependency among the Elderly in Japan', *Asian Population Studies* 1(1), 2005, pp. 121–45.

15 International Labour Organization (ILO), *Yearbook of Labour Statistics 2008*, Geneva: ILO, 2008.

16 National Institute of Population and Social Security Research, *Heisei 19 nendo shakai hoshō kyūfuhi* [The Cost of Social Security in Japan: FY 2007].

17 Ibid..

18 J. Sakamoto, 'Population Challenges and Social Security: The Case of Japan', paper presented at *the Forum on Population and Development in East Asia*, Beijing, 16–17 May 2005.

19 Ministry of Health, Labour and Welfare, *Kōsei nenkin kokumin nenkin heisei 16 nendo zaisei saikeisan kekka (hōkokusho)* [Review of the 2004 Actuarial Valuation of the Public Pension Plans (Report)], http://www.mhlw.go.jp/topics/nenkin/zaisei/zaisei/report/index.html.

20 OECD, *OECD Health Data 2009*, Paris: OECD, 2009.

21 N. Ogawa and R. D. Retherford, 'Shifting Costs of Caring for the Elderly Back to Families in Japan', *Population and Development Review* 23(1), 1997, pp. 59–94.

22 N. Ogawa, and J. F. Ermisch, 'Family Structure, Home Time Demands, and the Employment Patterns of Japanese Married Women', *Journal of Labor Economics* 14(4), 1996, pp. 677–702, and 2) N. Ogawa, R. D. Retherford, and R. Matsukura, 'Japan's Declining Fertility and Policy Responses', pp. 40–72.

23 N. Ogawa and R. D. Retherford, 'Shifting Costs of Caring for the Elderly Back to Families in Japan', *Population and Development Review* 23(1), 1997, pp. 59–94.

24 Population Problems Research Council, *Jinkō, kazoku, sedai yoron chōsa* [National Survey on Population, Families and Generations], Tokyo: The Mainichi Daily Newspapers, 2004.

25 Ibid.

26 See A. Mason (ed.) *Population Change and Economic Development in East Asia: Challenges Met, and Opportunities Seized*, Stanford: Stanford University Press, 2001; A. Mason, and R. Lee, 'Reform and Support Systems for the Elderly in Developing Countries: Capturing the Second Demographic Dividend', *GENUS* LXII, 2, 2006, pp. 11–35.

27 A. Mason, 'Demographic Transition and Demographic Dividends in Developed and Developing Countries', *United Nations Expert Group Meeting on Social and Economic Implications of Changing Population Age Structure*, New York: United Nations, 2007, pp.81–102; N. Ogawa and R.

Matsukura, 'Ageing in Japan: The Health and Wealth of Older Persons', *United Nations Expert Group Meeting on Social and Economic Implications of Changing Population Age Structures*, New York: United Nations, 2007, pp. 199–220.

[28] For example, see A. Mason, 'Demographic Transition and Demographic Dividends in Developed and Developing Countries', pp. 81–102.

[29] Ibid.

[30] N. Ogawa, et al., 'Japan's Unprecedented Ageing and Changing Intergenerational Transfers', in T. Ito and A. Rose (eds) *The Economic Consequences of Demographic Change in East Asia, NBER-EASE Volume 19,* Chicago, London: University of Chicago Press, 2010.

[31] Ibid.

[32] N. Ogawa, A. Chawla, and R. Matsukura, 'Some New Insights into the Demographic Transition and Changing Age Structures in the ESCAP Region', *Asia-Pacific Population Journal*, 24(1), 2009, pp. 87–116.

11

Have Jobs and Hope Gone Forever in Japan? From Family and Firms to a New Social Network

YUJI GENDA*

INTRODUCTION

It is true that the year 1998 was a turning point in Japanese history. 'Japan became a different country after 1998,' a friend who is a prominent lawyer muttered to me at the beginning of the twenty-first century. In 1998, banks, several securities firms and other financial institutions, that no one had thought would go bankrupt before, actually went bankrupt and the Japanese economy went into a long period of recession. Small and medium-sized corporations, the backbone of the Japanese economy, closed one after another due to the reluctance of banks to give out loans. The unemployment rate, which had been significantly lower than other developed countries increased dramatically. After 1998, the number of suicides rapidly increased hitting 30,000 a year and has not declined since.

Undoubtedly, 1998 was an unforgettable year in Japanese history. However, history also tells us that a turning point does not always occur just once. In May 2009, a new book by the famous Japanese novelist Haruki Murakami was published in Japan. The title of the book is *1Q84*, and it has been widely discussed in Japan.[1] Perhaps because *1Q84* was Murakami's first novel in seven years, it sold a million copies soon after publication. Haruki Murakami is popular not only with the Japanese but also with many readers worldwide. His latest novel soon will be translated into several foreign languages and read internationally.

This chapter does not attempt to talk about Haruki Murakami. There are so many books about him and his works. We can however easily imagine that *1Q84* might well have been inspired by George Orwell's famous near future novel *1984*, which was published in 1949. How was the year 1984 then significant for Japanese society? It was 1985 when the Japanese economy, which depended on overseas exports, crashed because of a rapid appreciation in foreign exchange rates. Industry and employment were seriously distressed. It was also in 1985 when *the Equal Employment Opportunity Act between Men and Women* was established. In 1984 then, Japan was on the cusp of broad structural changes.

According to the United Nations, an aged society is one where people aged sixty-five or older make up more than 14 per cent of the population. In 1994, Japan became an aged society. It took just twenty-four years for the aged population to increase from 7 to 14 per cent while many developed countries took more years; for example, seventy-three years in the United States, seventy-one years in Australia, forty-six years in the Great Britain, and forty years in Germany.[2] This means that Japanese society aged extremely rapidly during the 1980s.

Many people believe that serious social themes, such as ageing and globalization, became important issues in Japan after the economic bubble burst in the 1990s. Indeed the Japanese economy faced difficulty in creating jobs in the 1990s and the early 2000s. Looking back from a slightly longer perspective, however, serious problems also occurred much earlier in Japan in the 1980s. If we do not consider long-term changes that have been taking place since the 1980s, we will misunderstand the true nature of the problems in the Japanese society. Therefore, this chapter considers the recent structural changes in the Japanese economy and society since the 1980s, especially focusing on the employment system and labour market. This chapter also examines how Japanese people's hopes might be restored in the context of a rapidly ageing society and a less vibrant economy.

This chapter is organized as follows. The next section describes two symbolic changes that have affected jobs and family since the 1980s in Japan. This is followed by an explanation of the backgrounds of serious declines in employment at firms in the 1990s and 2000s. The next section briefly shows the results of our hope studies (*kibōgaku*) and suggests the importance of creating a new social network beyond family and firms in order to restore hope. The chapter concludes with a summary of the findings and suggests a future direction for Japan.

SYMBOLIC CHANGES SINCE THE 1980s

Self-employment

Readers may be surprised at my first suggestion for a symbolic change since the 1980s: the change in self-employment (*jieigyō*), that is those who own and operate unincorporated enterprises. Not a few self-employed persons operate with unpaid family workers. Among the total employees in Japan, the proportions of self-employed and family workers were 9.5 and 3.2 per cent respectively in 2009, according to the Statistics Bureau's *Labour Force Survey*.

Among developed countries, one unique characteristic of the Japanese economy is its large proportion of workers engaged in small and medium-sized firms. Well-known features of the Japanese employment system such as lifetime employment, seniority-based wage payment and corporation-oriented labour unions have often been noted.[3] These features emerged in large firms during the rapid growth era of the 1950s and 1960s. However, we should not forget that most workplaces in Japan are in small firms, and almost 57 per cent of workers belong to small or medium-sized enterprises with less than 300 workers according to the Statistics Bureau's *Employment Status Survey* 2007.

Why are there so many small firms in Japan? It is simply because there were many entrepreneurs who put their hearts into starting their own businesses after the Second World War. Japanese companies known globally, such as Sony, Honda, Suzuki and Panasonic, began as small factories of self-employed workers. Even though some firms of self-employed workers have remained small businesses, many small high-technology firms are indispensable to large firms all over the world, supplying parts for their products.

However, a significant change has taken place in self-employment in Japan since the 1980s. Figure 1 shows the proportion of self-employed workers to total workers in the non-agricultural and forestry sectors. We can see that a decline in the self-employment rate has occurred since the beginning of the 1980s. The economic bust and deregulation of the 1990s have often been suggested as reasons for the worsening self-employment situation in Japan, but self-employment had already begun to decline in the 1980s.

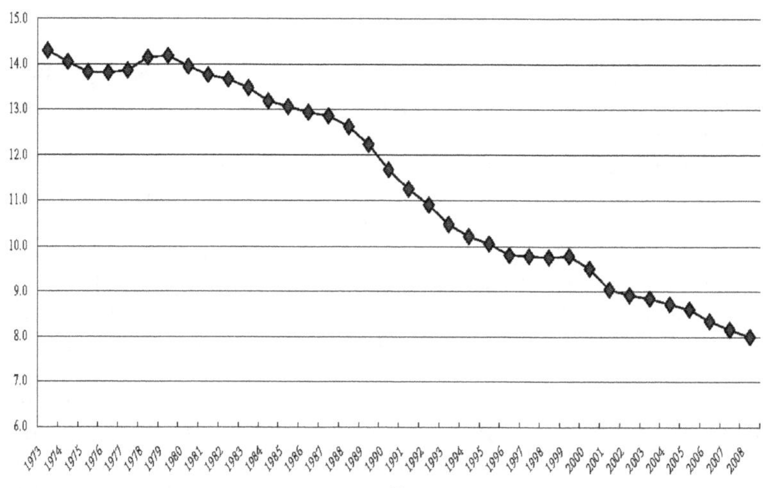

Figure 1. The Proportion of Self-employees among Total Workers in Non-agricultural and Forestry Sectors. Source: Statistics Bureau, *Labour Force Survey*.

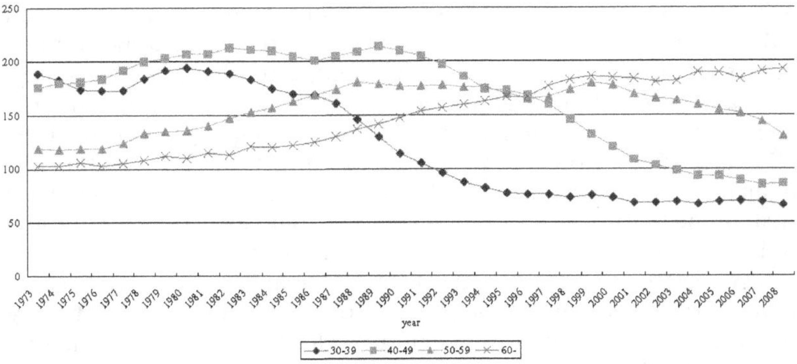

Figure 2. The Number of Self-employees by Age Category (Ten thousands Persons). Source. Statistics Bureau, *Labour Force Survey.*

If we examine statistics from the Organization of Economic Cooperation and Development (OECD), self-employment was more likely to increase in the 1980s and 1990s in most OECD countries.[4] According to this report, it was only in Japan, France and Denmark that self-employment decreased during both of these periods.

The decline in the number of self-employed workers was especially large among younger workers in Japan, as is shown by Figure 2. The proportion of self-employed rose only among those aged sixty and above. Self-employment has largely been decreasing among workers in their thirties, forties and fifties. In general, younger workers in Japan have been less likely to be their own bosses since the 1980s.

Family

Another important change that has taken place since the 1980s involves the family. Since the Second World War in Japan, households in which three generations live together have decreased, but those composed of only a husband and wife have increased. It is also noteworthy that the family unit that symbolized the post-war generations, the so-called 'nuclear family' (composed of only parents and children), had already stopped increasing in the 1980s. Figure 3 represents the structural changes in the proportion of households in Japan according to the *Comprehensive Survey of Living Conditions of the People on Health and Welfare* 2005 by the Ministry of Health, Labour and Welfare.

The phenomenon that best symbolizes the current Japanese family, perhaps, is the rather drastic increase in single-person households. This increase is attributable in part to the many older persons who have lost their spouses, as well as to more than a few young persons who have never been married and are living on their own. Currently, one-quarter of the households in Japan are single-person households.

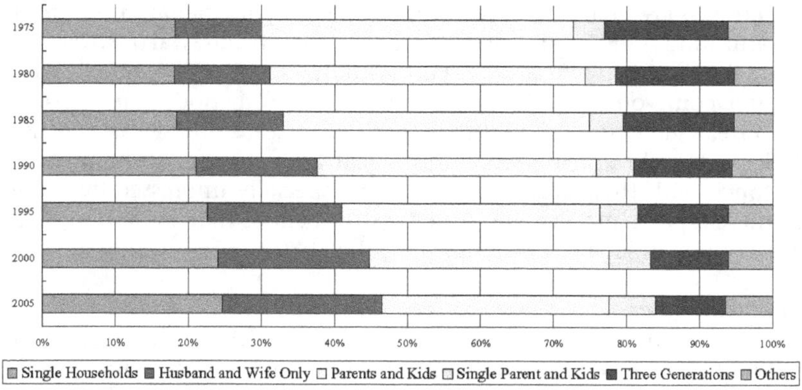

Figure 3. The Composition of Households. Source. Ministry of Health, Labour and Welfare. The *Comprehensive Survey of Living Conditions of the People on Health and Welfare.*

The number of single-person households increased in the 1980s so much that they already constituted 20 per cent of households by the beginning of the 1990s.

However, it may be impossible to capture these serious changes in the Japanese family simply by looking at statistics. In November 1980, an unforgettable murder occurred: a twenty-year-old boy bludgeoned to death his father and mother with a metal baseball bat while they slept. That was the first shocking case of parricide in Japan. The murderer had failed college entrance examinations twice. His father had graduated from the University of Tokyo, and his mother had been born to a distinguished family of traditional Japanese saké brewers. His older brother had graduated from a famous university and worked for a major electronics company. This case was a tragedy that affected what many Japanese would consider an enviable family in the 1980s.

Another unforgettable case exemplifying changes in the Japanese family was the Totsuka Yacht School incident in 1983. The Totsuka Yacht School is a training home for children who cause trouble in family and at school. Hiroshi Totsuka, the owner of the school, tried to rehabilitate children whose families could no longer raise them. In the course of their corrections, the school's staff did not hesitate to use physical violence in teaching children how to sail. When three children died during such training, Hiroshi Totsuka and some of the school's staff were arrested for murder.

At the time, the media criticized the use of violence to rehabilitate children. On the other hand, there were more than a few supporters of Totsuka's Spartan education methods, including politicians, teachers, commentators and parents. They felt that it was no longer possible to raise children properly through formal education and family affection alone.

In the 2000s, I have interviewed many people who manage non-profit organizations (NPOs) to treat children for social withdrawal (*hikikomori*), and school-related refusals.[5] Socially withdrawn children are those who cannot come out of their own room for a long period. Some people who treat such children said that they began seeing these cases in the 1980s. They do not use violence to treat them but try to keep them in touch with their ordinary lives. I am especially impressed by some of these NPO managers who told me they believe that something had gone wrong in Japanese families since the 1980s.

Crumbling Pillars

What do structural changes since the 1980s such as the decline in self-employment and the collapse of the family mean? As many self-employed workers chose their business in order to become their own boss, self-employment symbolizes independence. On the other hand, in the sense that family members mutually guarantee economic dependency and selfless affection, family symbolizes security. I think, therefore, that decreasing self-employment and deteriorating family imply a diminished sense of independence and security in society.

People in Japan have long believed that success in life entails passing the entrance examination of a distinguished university, getting a job in a major firm, and then working continuously until the age of retirement. However, there is actually another important success story in Japan. It involves graduating from a junior high school in an outlying area, boarding a train with former classmates, and moving to a larger city to get a job. These 'successes' worked sincerely in small firms and accumulated skills over many years. They met their lovers in the workplace and got married. Eventually, the president of their small firm might advise them to start their own business, intervening on their behalf with local commercial bankers they have known for years. As a result, even if such workers lacked sufficient education at school and did not work for large firms, they were satisfied with their working lives as self-employees with their family, becoming their own boss. This was another Japanese dream for ordinary people, but it was becoming difficult for this dream to come true by the end of the rapid growth era, and it mostly disappeared in the 1980s, resulting in declining self-employment.[6]

Why did self-employment decrease so much in Japan? One main reason is clearly related to money. Genda and Kambayashi examined the reasons why householders avoid self-employment using the Statistics Bureau's micro data on the *National Survey on Family Income and Expenditure*.[7] In general, accumulating work experiences with age had encouraged householders to be self-employed. However, even those who had much work experiences have been less likely to choose self-employment. We also estimated the earnings functions for self-employed workers and employees. The decline in the real income of self-employed workers relative to employees was more likely to prevent householders from being self-employed.

It has often been argued that lifetime employment and seniority wages for employees have declined in the long recessions following the bursting of the bubble economy in the 1990s and 2000s. Indeed, seniority wages have been falling since the 1990s.[8] However, changing market conditions had a more direct impact on self-employment income, which had fallen much more steeply than salaried incomes.

While working conditions for employees can be difficult, including long working hours and mental health problems, many Japanese would rather work for a company than be self-employed. As a result, in the recession periods of the 1990s and 2000s, the total number of workers in Japan has been falling. However, this is primarily due to the decrease in self-employment, although company employees increased. The number of employees rose from 48.4 million in 1990 to 54.6 in 2009 while the self-employed fell from 8.8 to 5.9 during the same period according to the *Labor Force Survey*.

However, a lack of money may not be the only explanation for declining self-employment. In the 1990s, the Japanese government adopted several policies encourageing venture businesses, such as subsidies for opening businesses. These subsidy policies failed to create new businesses suggesting something important other than money would be required to encourage entrepreneurship.

This is where the family issue becomes important. As discussed above, many self-employed persons emerging in the rapid growth era in Japan came from rural areas, and typically, their parents and brothers who remained in the countryside had farms to make their own livings. Prospective entrepreneurs could always go back to the family farm if they failed at starting a business in the city. They could strive to be independent because they had a sense of security in their family of origin. However, the industrial structure has changed, and agriculture has been steadily declining. The rural family is no longer a source of economic security, and the challenge of achieving independence is becoming more and more difficult.

Independence and security, symbolized by self-employment and family, have been the two big pillars of Japanese life in the rapid growth era. However, these pillars have been crumbling and are almost beyond repair. Japan is currently facing several kinds of difficulties, but losing a sense of independence and safety have been the most fundamental problems since the 1980s.

LOSING JOBS IN THE 1990s AND 2000s

Decline in Jobs for Young Workers

After the so-called bubble economy burst in the 1990s, business performance declined in most Japanese firms. Further, the greying of the workforce, i.e., the increasing numbers of middle-aged and older employees, has raised labour costs, particularly within Japanese firms maintaining seniority-based compensation practices. The ratio of workers aged over forty-five among male full-time employees soared from 27 per cent in 1990 to 34 per cent in 2000, according to the *Employment Trend Survey* by the Ministry of Health, Labour and Welfare.

The creation of such a demographic structure clustered around older workers within firms in the 1990s is the result of both demographic and economic factors. Broad demographic shifts have resulted in an ageing of the population and a shrinking of the birth rate. Further, members of the baby boom generation (*dankai no sedai*) – those born between 1947 and 1949 in Japan, and employed *en masse* during the economic boom years in the 1960s and early 1970s – were aged over fifty by the late 1990s. Finally, the oil crisis curbed employment of the succeeding generations.

An increase in labour costs through ageing within firms would result in a fall in optimal labour demand. Generally, separation costs of existing employees are quite high for firms in Japan because of legal constraints generated by case laws to prohibit dismissals. Consequently, many Japanese firms have tended to concentrate on employment adjustment by reducing the number of young recruits drastically.

The remaining employment adjustment option available to achieve an optimal level of employment during poor business performance is to enhance labour mobility between firms, including transfers and reallocation. At least until the mid-1990s sufficient demand for labour from small and medium-sized firms enabled large firms with excess labour to adjust employment levels by promoting the transfer of workers to smaller firms. However, the severe recession of the late 1990s, unlike those preceding it, had substantially reduced labour demand even from small and medium-sized firms. Consequently, to reduce their employment levels, large firms have no choice but to cease hiring young people.

The situation of declining employment opportunities for Japanese youths can be conceptualized in terms of a job displacement effect; that is, middle-aged and older workers displacing jobs from young workers.[9] By focusing on job openings for recent graduates, which is a direct measure of labour demand, Genda empirically demonstrated that establishments with more middle-aged and older workers tended to depress the hiring of new graduates in the 1990s.[10] As a result, ageing at the company further accelerated the increase in the proportion of older workers by reducing the hiring of young workers. In this sense, ageing has a negative impact on job opportunities through a decline in labour demand, especially demand for young workers, at the establishment level such as the office and the factory, that is *jigyō-sho*, in a company.

In addition, Genda and Kurosawa also found that initial labour market conditions, i.e. when workers first enter the labour market after permanently leaving school, have a significant lasting impact on the employment experiences of workers in their teens and twenties.[11] That is, an increase in the unemployment rate at the time of labour market entry reduces the probability of gaining full-time regular employment, and more importantly, increases the future probability of workers leaving employers in Japan.

Furthermore, Genda, Kondo and Ohta compared effects of entering the labour market during a recession on subsequent employment and earnings for Japanese and American men, using respective labour force surveys.[12] They found persistent negative effects of the unemployment rate at graduation on getting regular jobs in the subsequent period, particularly for less educated Japanese men, in contrast to temporary effects for less educated American men. The school-based hiring system and dismissal regulations prolong the initial loss of employment opportunities for less educated Japanese men.

According to the Employment Security Law written in 1947, when Japan was still in post-war turmoil, the government regulates the recruitment process of graduating seniors from junior high school in order to protect them from illegal and unethical employers. In the 1960s, its coverage expanded to graduating seniors from high school. The law forbids employers from making direct contact with graduating seniors who hope to work or using private employment agencies for their recruiting. Instead, the Japanese law encourages schools and public employment offices to play crucial roles in youth employment decisions.

This unique school-based hiring system can be regarded as a subsidy by firms to hire new graduates as regular workers. This legal treatment enabled newly graduated workers to get secure jobs in the rapid growth period and even in the late 1970s and 1980s. After drastic declines in labour demand for youth resulting from the job displacement effect, however, several newly graduated youths fell behind the hiring system, and as a result, they continued to fail in getting regular jobs for a long time afterwards.

Non-employed and Non-regular Youths

In the first half of the 2000s, the buzzword used to represent dire circumstances in Japan was 'inequality' but this had changed to 'poverty' in the second half of the 2000s. The number of poor families receiving public welfare continues to increase, exceeding 1.2 million households in 2009.

In addition to a sense of security, the motivation for independence sometimes comes from the reality of poverty. It is difficult for the children of poor families to go to college, and thus they have nothing to lose by trying to start their own business, even if they fail; and some of them will succeed in business and escape poverty. Even now in Japan, there are more than a few households in serious poverty.

Recently, however, it has become clear that poverty is not always a driving force behind independence. Young people who are not in employment, education, or training are referred to by the acronym 'NEET'. The term NEET originated in Great Britain at the end of 1990s, but the name is now much more prevalent in Japan.[13]

In Japan, NEET is defined as a non-employed person aged less than thirty-five who has already left school but gave up working. Among the several reports including those by the government, the estimated NEET population in Japan ranges from 600,000 to 900,000 in the 2000s, although the figures differed according to the definition employed. Using the micro data from the *Employment Status Survey*, Genda clarifies that young people whose prospect of expected returns from working would be low, such as females, less-educated and long-term non-employed people, tend to give up working.[14]

Further examining the several characters of the NEET population, the influence of family income stands out. There was a tendency in the past for NEETs to come from rich families. It can be easily explained by standard economic theory that children from rich families prefer leisure to work. In economics, this negative impact of affluence on the desire to work is called the income effect of the labour supply. But this income effect has clearly weakened since the end of the 1990s in Japan; that is, young people who come from poor families are now more likely to be discouraged from working. It may be more and more difficult for them to obtain opportunities for education and training in order to accumulate essential qualifications necessary to find suitable work. This means that serious new poverty issues pertaining to the relationship between jobs and family have occurred in Japan since the 1990s.

It is difficult for NEETs to secure income, so that many of them will depend on government financial assistance in future when their parents can no longer support them. It is the reproduction of poverty that leads children in poor families to give up on work. The reproduction of poverty and its social costs have been a concern in many developed countries. Now the transference of poverty between generations is also a serious issue in Japan.

Similarly, the poor family issue also has a negative effect on non-regular workers. After a sudden worldwide depression in fall 2008, many non-regular employees, including dispatched workers, suddenly lost their jobs. When this happened, there was a problem with housing as well as unemployment for dismissed workers. We learned for the first time that many dispatched temporary workers have neither home nor family to which they can return if they lose jobs and have no way of earning a living.

It is still unclear why many non-regular workers were disconnected from their families when they lost their jobs and needed help. However, complicated family problems in poverty will play a crucial role in the lives of young people who cannot work as regular employees. The difficulties that NEETs and non-regular young workers face cannot be attributed to their personal skills and work ethics but to their circumstances, especially their family background. Such class structure, or social segmentation, evolved during the long recession, and the presence of so many NEETs and non-regular workers in Japan today is one outcome of the changing social structure in Japan in the 1990s and 2000s.

Downsizing of Middle-aged and Older Employees

Serious changes have occurred mainly among youths since the 1990s but some middle-aged and older employees have been also hurt as a consequence. Until the mid-1990s, ageing establishments tended to reduce their hiring of young workers and they attempted to maintain existing employee levels and avoided massive dismissals as much as possible.

One distinct feature of Japanese labour practice is the large proportion of workers who acquire a wide range of problem-solving skills through on-the-job training.[15] While this kind of skill-formation is common among white-collar employees in Japan and other developed countries, Japan is unique in that blue-collar workers in large firms also accumulate a variety of skills similar to white-collar workers. As a result, most middle-aged and older employees have acquired skills along with experience in large firms. Even facing business downturns, this skill accumulation has encouraged employers to maintain experienced employees, in whom human capital investment specific to the firm has already been made.

From 1998 to 2003, however, under the pressure from the serious recession and acceleration of disposing massive bad debt loans, ageing large firms could not avoid reducing the substantial numbers of existing older employees, such as the forty-five–fifty-nine-year-old workers, through the promotion of early retirement payments. In what seemed like a daily occurrence, especially in 1999 and 2002, newspapers ran many stories describing well-known Japanese companies, famous for their lifetime employment practices, being forced to let go not only large numbers of employees but also entire divisions. Some large companies reduced their employees by more than a thousand. Many senior workers who had been hired in the 1970s were obliged to give up their jobs because their salaries were too high to be maintained.

One notable characteristic of such downsizing was that many companies made their plans and implemented them within a very short time, perhaps for the first time.[16] Many companies completed their downsizing plans within half a year of their announcements. Whereas it took substantially more time for Japanese firms to sound out and reach agreement with corporation-based labour unions and, at the same time, to realize personnel reduction in the past, from the historical view of Japanese industrial relations, the downsizing in the end of the 1990s and the beginning of the 2000s appeared to be unique.

REBIRTH OF HOPE

Kibōgaku: Hope Studies

Indeed working conditions have been worse without doubt in Japan, so that it is more difficult for many Japanese people to make a living independently. Families and firms that had provided a sense of security cannot give future prospects any more. Japan seems to be descending from previous prosperity levels.

What can we do to reinvigorate independence and security? It is difficult to imagine the future precisely. Uncertainty deepens throughout the world, and many people have no idea how to behave well in the face of uncertainty. Striving for independence is often overcome by fear of the unknown, producing the desire for something strong that people can depend on. People lose hope when they worry excessively about the future and do not feel secure in any place.

It is often said that many Japanese people, especially the young, are losing hope for the future. It seems that at the beginning of the 2000s, Japanese people had generally lost hope as symbolized by Murakami Ryū's *Kibō no Kuni no Ekusodasu* (Exodus to a Land of Hope) published in 2000 and Yamada Masahiro's *Kibō Kakusa Shakai* (Widening Social Disparities among People With and Without Hope) published in 2004.[17]

Since 2005 the Institute of Social Science at the University of Tokyo has organized a project to research the relationship between hope and society. It is titled the Social Sciences of Hope (hope studies or *kibōgaku*). What exactly is hope? We have discussed the meaning of hope with members from Japan, the United States and Australia. Based on a proposal by Richard Swedberg and Seigo Hirowatari, we settled on one crucial feature of hope as a wish for something to come true by action.[18] Thus, hope consists of four elements: a 'wish', 'something', 'coming-trueness (a way to realize)' and 'action'.

According to an empirical survey in hope studies, we found that one-third of Japanese adults aged from twenty to fifty-nine do not have any hope, or they feel that their most important hope is not attainable. Specifically, nearly 80 per cent of respondents said they had held some hope. Furthermore, 80 per cent of those who reported having hope forecast that it would be attainable. Consequently, about 63 per cent of all respondents had hopes that they thought were attainable.

What kind of hopes do Japanese have? Most Japanese have hopes regarding their work. In response to the multiple choice question on the contents of hopes, the top chosen answer was about 'work' (66 per cent), followed by 'family' (47 per cent), 'health' (38 per cent) and 'leisure' (32 per cent). This result suggests that work and jobs are the most closely related to hopes in the Japanese society.

Hope and Economy

We examined why differences exist between individuals who have or do not have hope. To answer this question, we conducted a quantitative analysis of factors that determine whether a person has hope or not, using the aforementioned mail-in questionnaire (Genda 2010).[19]

The analysis of the relationship between objective attributes and hope concluded that individual factors, such as gender, age and health influenced the possession of hope. Looking at gender, men were less likely than women to have hopes, particularly attainable ones. Focusing on the hope about working, however, women tend to lose hope more than men. In terms of age, in general, younger people were more likely to have hope. Academic attainment also had a strong influence on the possession of hope. Furthermore, those whose health conditions were perceived to be good tended to answer that they had attainable hopes.

Hope is also influenced by income or employment situation. Individuals earning less than three million yen a year were less likely to have attainable hopes and people who had no income at all were very likely to lack hope regarding work. Furthermore, family members with a total annual income exceeding ten million yen tended to answer that they had hope, particularly attainable hopes. In contrast, members of households with annual incomes less than three million yen tended to have unattainable hopes or a negative view of hope itself.

These results indicate that hope is strongly influenced by the possibilities stemming from individual choices and actions. Youth implies the open possibility of time for the future, and the loss of health implies a limitation of the possibility for action. Education, by deepening knowledge, increasing experiences and improving capabilities, also expands the possibilities for choices. The fact that it is still more difficult for women to have hopes regarding work shows that they have more limited employment possibilities than men in Japanese society. Individual or household income directly influences the size of the budget for making purchases in the market. Unemployment means a loss of not only income sources but also of self-fulfilment and sense of self-usefulness gained from employment.

There is sufficient statistical evidence to suggest the possibility that an atmosphere of having no hope for the future pervades Japanese society, as shown by the frequent use of the term, 'sense of stagnation' (*heisoku-kan*) since the 1990s. A stagnation that prevents us from feeling hope has spread with the increase in individuals whose choices have shrunk, as seen in the ageing society, increases in jobless people, and households with low income and deteriorating health situations.

Importance of New Social Networks

While in the hope studies project we have recognized the importance of such economic issues, we have presumed that fundamental social problems are tied to the representation of hope. One problem is the relation between issues concerning interpersonal relationships and hope. Hope studies suggest that we have a chance to revitalize Japanese society again by reorganizing personal relationships or social networks in future.

Our survey also examined the percentage of respondents with attainable hopes according to whether they reported being 'lonely' as their current situation. Among those who answered 'I do not think I am lonely', 70 per cent had attainable hope. On the other hand, only 49 per cent of those who answered 'I feel lonely' had hope, showing statistically a major difference between the two. It is clear from the relation between having hope and the number of friends that hope is influenced by relationships with others. The percentages of people with attainable hopes depending on number of friends was 75 per cent for 'many', 65 per cent for 'quite a few', 59 per cent for 'not so many' and 55 per cent for 'few'. It is obvious that the number of friends has a great deal to do with hope.

The increasing isolation found among Japanese people, as shown by the increasing number of single households in every generation and the emergence of solitary deaths as a social issue along with bullying, truancy, NEETs and social reclusiveness, has become an increasingly serious social problem. The fact that socially isolated individuals are increasing is another facet of a society characterized by the loss of hope.

Human relations, such as those with friends and family members, have a significant influence on the hopes of individuals. An increasing number of people are facing difficulties with interpersonal relations, and the family, which functions as the base for reliability, has become unstable. Furthermore, even people who do not seem to have special problems with their daily personal relationships feel constant pressure to improve their communication skills.

It has been argued, mainly in sociology, that the state of human relations is a crucial issue when thinking about the future in society. Specifically, concepts like 'social network' or 'social capital' have been used as keywords for expressing the social structure of personal relations. Mary C. Brinton proposes the concept of *ba,* or place, as a characteristic of such social networks in Japan.[20] Strong collective ties in families and workplaces with long-term employment practices have provided the bedrock for a sense of security among Japanese people in the past. In contrast to US society, which has been based on 'weak ties' between individuals – a concept proposed by Mark Granovetter[21] – Japanese society instead has valued 'strong ties' within *ba*. According to Brinton, the *ba* has been collapsing within the contexts of globalization and low growth, and this tendency constitutes the basis for change in Japanese society.

Table1. Weak Ties May Generate Hope in Japan: Effects of Personal Relationship except Family Members and Colleagues in Workplaces on Varieties of Hope: Probit Model

Contents of Hope	Marginal Effects	
Job	0.1318	***
Family	0.0253	
Health	0.0161	
Play & Pleasure	0.0782	***
Social Contribution	0.0410	**

Source: Genda (2007b). Note. Significance at 5% (**) and 1% (***) levels.

In Japan, the function of 'weak ties' is also currently more influential in the possession of hope towards work, which most Japanese value highly.[22] Specifically, we analysed the relationship between types of friends and several kinds of hope based on the questionnaires. Consequently, we have found that individuals with friends outside of family members, relatives and colleagues in workplaces, who have 'expectations toward them', 'greatly appreciate their abilities and efforts', and 'listen to their anxieties and problems' are more likely to have attainable hope in a significant manner. It has also been found that the existence of friends outside of work with whom it is possible to speak frankly makes it easier for people to have hope especially towards work, which is the object of highest interest among Japanese, in addition to hopes toward play, pleasure and social contribution, as is shown in Table 1.

Why is this so? Communicating with people outside of our own family and superiors and colleagues in the workplace means talking to people who have lived in a different world from our own and who have accumulated their own values and experiences accordingly, which are different from our own. It can be recognized, from a sociological perspective, that possessing so-called 'third relationships' beyond kin and work and gaining precious information from them, which cannot be obtained in our everyday lives, can help to create hope. Therefore it is becoming more and more important for most Japanese to have a chance at accessing and creating a new social network beyond family and firms such as the weak ties.

In order to build new social networks, for example, it is crucial to support the activities of NPOs by increasing tax deductions for donations to them and to develop new local community businesses and activities by carrying out a significant decentralization of governance.

CONCLUSION: JAPAN TO ASCEND AGAIN

The sense of insecurity many current Japanese have as a result of losing stable jobs is indeed developing due to the structural changes in the economy after the 1990s. However, as is symbolized by the decrease in self-employment and the increase in single households, such a sense of insecurity has been generated by fundamental changes in society since the 1980s. The reasons for such long-term changes are deep rooted, and it will take substantial time and energy to recover. Some may feel that declines in independence and security are irreversible, such is the fate of Japan.

However, we should not pay too much credence to this pessimistic view. A brand new culture awaits us, after continued trial and error and overcoming our current difficulties by organizing new social networks. The new culture will be a substantial driving force for a new economy in Japan, as a matured society. New social networks beyond family and firms, which are more likely to be the 'weak ties', can generate creativity in culture and economy.

Indeed, the shift in social networks from strong to weak ties is not necessarily a smooth one for all individuals. Rather, there is concern that there will be an increase in individuals who lack both security based on strong ties and hope based on weak ties, after being excluded from all networks. However, the possibility of organizing new and original social networks should not be given up because there will be one possibility in an ageing society. The common view about an ageing society is that it is unattractive for youths and is heavily burdened by too many people, high taxes and substantial social costs. However, at the same time, an ageing society is also rich in experiences, with many people who have experiences to overcome obstacles.

The calm communications between different generations in a new social network will play a crucial role in realizing the brand new days of independence and security in Japan. An ageing society with plentiful experience and abundant sympathies can encourage future generations to have new types of hope.

There is another unique tendency for people who take action to realize their hopes according to our hope studies.[23] People with hope are more likely to have experienced serious setbacks in the past and to have discussed their meaning clearly. This means that those who are able to elucidate their previous setbacks are also able to express hope in the future. When individuals understand the meaning of setbacks and can talk about them frankly with appropriate humour, they are able to describe the future more brightly.

Further statistical analyses show that with the background of having overcome obstacles, individuals with attainable hope are less likely to fear that their efforts will be vain. It seems to be difficult for people who are overly concerned about results to have attainable hope. In contrast, it may be true that people who tolerate the possibility of waste and playfulness and have, what John Maynard Keynes dubs the 'animal spirits',[24] are able to find attainable hope.

Those persons who have made every effort to realize their hopes often comment, 'Looking back on my life, there was nothing in vain at all.'

These words can sometimes encourage us and give us hope. If such valuable experiences can be described modestly and with humour by senior generations, younger generations can listen to their voices sympathetically and comfortably. Such dialogue, and the handing down of experience, can ease the tensions between current and future generations. A new social network including different generations encourages younger people to stand up to growing uncertainty and not to care too much about the results of their ventures. They can take risks and actions with a presence of mind gained by learning from their elders' experiences. The new generation will certainly be able to find attainable hopes in the newly ascending Japanese society.

NOTES

* The author is grateful for the many insightful suggestions and advice received at the international symposium 'Japan: Descending Asian Giant?' at the University of Adelaide. He also appreciates the many important comments received during visits to the Clarke Program in East Asian Law and Culture, Cornell University and the Joint East Asian Studies Conference in the University of Sheffield. All errors are my own.

1 H. Murakami. *1Q84*, 2009, Tokyo: Shinchosha.

2 United Nations, *World Population Prospects*, 2006.

3 K. Koike, *Understanding Industrial Relations in Modern Japan*, New York: St Martin's Press, 1988.

4 OECD, *Employment Outlook*, 1992, p. 170.

5 Y. Genda, *Hataraku Kajō* [Too Much Work], Tokyo: NTT Press, 2005.

6 T. Satō, *Fubyōdō Shakai Nippon-Sayonara Sōchūryū* [Japan as an Unequal Society: Farewell to the All-Middle Class], Tokyo: Chūkō Shinsha, 2000.

7 Y. Genda and R. Kambayashi, 'Declining Self-employment in Japan', *Journal of the Japanese and International Economies* 16, 2002, pp. 73–91.

8 Y. Genda, 'Japan: Wage Differentials and Changes since the 1980', in T. Tachibanaki (ed.) *Wage Differentials: An International Comparison*, London: Macmillan Press, 1998, pp. 35–71.

9 Y. Genda, *A Nagging Sense of Job Insecurity: The New Reality Facing Japanese Youth*, LTCB International Library Trust, Tokyo: International House of Japan, 2005, p. 203.

10 Y. Genda, 'Who Really Lost Jobs in Japan? Youth Employment in an Ageing Japanese Society', in S. Ogawa, T. Tachibanaki and D.A. Wise (eds) *Labor Markets and Fringe Benefit Policies in Japan and the United States*, Chicago: The University of Chicago Press, 2003, pp.103–133.

11 Y. Genda and M. Kurosawa, 'Transition from School to Work in Japan', *Journal of the Japanese and International Economies* 15, 2001, pp. 465–88.

12 Y. Genda, A. Kondo and S. Ohta, 'Long-term Effects of a Recession at Labor Market Entry in Japan and the United States', *Journal of Human Resources* 45(1) Winter 2010, pp. 157–96.

13 Y. Genda, and M. Maganuma, *NEET*, Tokyo: Gentosha, 2004.

[14] Y. Genda, 'Jobless Youths and the NEET Problem in Japan', *Social Science Japan Journal*, 10(1), 2007, pp. 23–40.

[15] Koike, *Understanding Industrial Relations in Modern Japan.*

[16] Y. Genda *et al*, 'Ageing and Employment in Japan', in K. Hamada and H. Kato (eds) *Ageing and the Labor Market in Japan*, Cheltenham: Edward Elgar Publishing Limited, 2007, pp. 1–23.

[17] R. Murakami, *Kibō no Kuni no Ekusodasu* [Exodus to a Land of Hope], 2000, Tokyo: Kodansha; M. Yamada, *Kibō Kakusa Shakai* [Widening Social Disparities among People with and without Hope], 2004, Tokyo: Chikuma Shobo.

[18] R. Swedberg, 'The Sociological Study of Hope and the Economy: Introductory Remarks', International Hope Studies Conference in Japan, 2007; S. Hirowatari, *'Kibō to Henkaku'* [Hope and Change], (in Japanese), in Y. Genda, and S. Uno (eds) *Social Sciences of Hope*, Vol.1, Institute of Social Science, Tokyo: University of Tokyo Press, 2009.

[19] Y. Genda, 'Hope and Society in Japan', in R. Swedberg and H. Miyazaki (eds) *Hope and the Economy*, Philadelphia: Pennsylvania University Press, forthcoming.

[20] M. C. Brinton, *Ushinawareta Ba o Sagashite* [Lost in Transition], 2008, Tokyo: NTT Press.

[21] M. Granovetter, *Getting A Job*, second edition, Chicago: University of Chicago Press, 1995.

[22] Y. Genda, 'Kitai to Shinrai ga nakereba Kibō wa Umarenai' [No Reliance, No Hope], *Kokan suru Kagaku,* Institute of Bell System 24, 2007.

[23] Genda, 'Hope and Society in Japan', in R. Swedberg and H. Miyazaki (eds) *Hope and the Economy*, Philadelphia: Pennsylvania University Press, forthcoming.

[24] J. M. Keynes. *The General Theory of Employment, Interest and Money*, London: Macmillan, 1936.

12

The Culture of Migration Politics in Japan

GABRIELE VOGT

1. THE PUZZLE

We find ourselves in the midst of what has come to be known as the 'Age of Migration'.[1] Population movements beyond national borders along with international trade activity 'constitute a key dynamic within globalization'.[2] The International Labour Organization (ILO) claims that 90 per cent of all cross-border movement of people (roughly 200 million persons) occurs in the realm of work.[3] Through a closer look, we observe three major global trends in international (labour) migration. First, the Asia-Pacific region is the world region showing the most pronounced rise in migration flows.[4] Second, the increasing demand for labour migrants in the service sector promotes the feminization of international migration movement.[5] Third, more and more countries that so far have presented themselves as non-immigration countries are gradually opening their borders and granting international migrants access to their domestic labour markets.[6]

This chapter presents a case study that serves as an exemplar to all three major trends: a newly opened avenue for international labour migration with the sending and receiving countries of the predominantly female workforce situated in Asia, and the receiving country being classified as one of the region's new immigration countries in scholarly literature.[7] This chapter addresses Japan's bilateral Economic Partnership Agreements (EPAs) with Indonesia and the Philippines. This latest fundamental shift in Japan's migration policy as of 2008 renders possible the labour migration of caregivers – a predominantly female profession – from these partner countries to Japan.[8] The EPAs thus symbolize a nation-specific and sector-specific new avenue of labour migration to Japan. As shown in more detail in the following sections, this gradual opening of Japan's labour market to 1,000 foreign health caregivers per nation per year is proceeding too hesitantly to have a strong and swift positive effect on the numerical shortages and contentiously restructuring features of the domestic labour market.[9]

Moreover, this policy change does not suffice to secure Japan an attractive position as a receiving country of qualified workers among competitors in East Asia, let alone on a global scale. Taiwan and South Korea in particular have emerged as serious competitors to Japan when it comes to recruiting skilled and unskilled foreign workers alike. Next to traditional countries of immigration such as the United States, Canada and Australia, they have gradually gained attractiveness to potential migrant workers in the Asia-Pacific region.[10] Holding a prominent position as a preferred country of destination, however, will be most crucial for Japan's future economic performance, given its rapidly proceeding demographic change, in particular the ageing of its population and most notably its workforce. Japan's working-age population (fifteen–sixty years old) is predicted to drop from currently (2008) 81.3 million persons to 71.0 million by 2025 and to 49.3 million by 2050.[11] That is, forty years from now, Japan's workforce will amount to a mere 60 per cent of its current size.

A simple question that arises when studying these numbers is 'who will work for Japan in the future?' This question is all the more serious for jobs that are known to come with low pay, low status and long working hours, such as the caregiver profession. Already today we observe a labour shortage in these jobs – a shortage that must be expected to become much more pronounced as a decline in the share of the workforce population proceeds and competition over available workers among different sectors and businesses becomes more severe. Moreover, who will help to buffer the negative impacts that a steep workforce decline will have in the long run on the nation's economic performance, social security systems and consumption rates?[12] Structured international replacement migration of a working age population may serve as one countermeasure – among others such as advancing retirement age and creating family-friendly working conditions – to a demographically-induced shrinking of the national workforce and its negative economic impacts.[13]

However Japan, largely and seemingly willingly, misses out on this option. Once a favorable migration structure is created, Japan will most likely attract skilled and unskilled workers alike. Following standard migration theory, that is, the notion of the regulatory power inherent in the independent variables of demand-pull and supply-push, Japan's population ageing and shrinking is a new strong pull factor of international labour migration within Asia's demographic landscape. Next to already existing labour shortages, in particular in service sector professions, Japan's demographic change exercises a strong demand-pull within the push/pull model of international labour migration. On the supply-push side we observe a steep income difference between sending and receiving countries of inner-Asian labour migration, which serves to make labour emigration attractive to workers. Also, some governments, as for example in the Philippines, are known to 'actively support [...] emigration in order to ease the heavy burden of unemployment at home and encourage the transfer of hard currency remittances'.[14]

The key question here addresses the puzzle of why Japan, a nation in demographic need of labour migrants and obviously economically attractive to labour migrants, refuses to pursue a fundamental revision of its migration policy. Why is it that Japan does not pursue an open-door migration policy? Or, in more scholarly framing, why does the push/pull model not work for Japan, not even in a sector such as health care-giving where push and pull factors, that is, the economic demand and workforce supply, are so clearly in synchronicity?

2. RESEARCH DESIGN

Political scientist James Hollifield draws our attention to states as actors in the realm of international migration when he argues: 'What's missing from these accounts [among others: the economic approach of push/pull logic] is a theory of the state and the way in which it influences population movements.'[15] In other words, we must not neglect the regulatory framework defined by political actors, which sets the playing field for economic demands and supplies. This chapter argues that we can best understand this regulatory framework shaping Japan's migration policy by drawing from the concept of political culture according to Gabriel Almond.[16] Almond explained the essence of political culture as follows: 'Every political system is embedded in a particular pattern of orientations to political action.'[17] Any political system, according to Almond, consists of 'patterned interactions' among political actors.[18] And 'orientations to political action' refer to 'a set of meanings and purposes' in which a political system is embedded; these are, in particular, '"attitudes towards politics", "political values", "ideologies", [...]'.[19]

Based on Almond's theory, in this chapter I conduct qualitative content analyses of primary and secondary sources on Japan's migration policy. I argue that the two concepts inherent in Almond's understanding of political culture, that is, the structure of the political system itself as well as 'orientations to political action',[20] capture the main reasons behind Japan's reluctant stance towards an economically necessary – and therefore would-be pragmatic – open door migration policy.

Two arguments lie at the core of this chapter. First, on the political system: Japan's politics is strongly driven by national-level bureaucrats. For migration politics this translates into a multiplicity of actors aiming at shaping policy trends. Next to the Ministry of Justice (MoJ), in particular since the EPA negotiations were begun, the Ministries of Health, Labour, and Welfare (MHLW), Foreign Affairs (MoFA), and Economy, Trade and Industry (METI) have been gaining weight in these negotiations. They bring to the table diverse opinions. Negotiations between these actors often result in only minimal changes to policies. Supranational level influences (e.g. on the issue of citizenship) as well as subnational level input (e.g. on the issue of integration of migrants into society) translate only slowly into national level policymaking in Japan. By blocking these approaches of multilevel governance, the national government misses out on a huge pool of stimulating policymaking initiatives.

Second, on 'orientations to political action', there is a strong tendency among Japanese politicians and the public to perceive foreigners as a threat to public safety and national security. This tendency has been intensified by the terrorist attacks of 11 September 2001 and the US reaction to the attacks in terms of revisions to immigration procedures. Japan was the first country to follow the US policy and introduce mandatory fingerprinting for foreigners upon arrival in Japan as of November 2007. With the latest revisions to Japan's Immigration Control and Refugee Recognition Act (*shutsunyūkoku kanri oyobi nanmin ninteihō*), which passed Japan's lower house in June 2009 and will gather all information held on foreign residents under the Ministry of Justice's jurisdiction, Japan walks further down the path of closely monitoring the resident status of foreigners. My research on the pros and cons of accepting foreign caregivers in Japanese hospitals and nursing homes for the elderly revealed that this general reluctance towards foreign workers/foreigners in Japan is mirrored in the opinions of potential employers of Indonesian and Filipino caregivers. With these 'orientations to political action' prevalent in the public, it seems almost impossible that political actors will push for an open door migration policy in Japan.

3. JAPAN'S MIGRATION POLICY: OUTPUT AND OUTCOME

By the end of 2008, the number of registered foreign residents in Japan had risen to roughly 2.2 million (2,217,426), which amounts to 1.74 per cent of the total population. Compared to the percentages of foreign residents in other OECD countries (in 2007, e.g. UK 5.8 per cent, Germany 8.2 per cent, Spain 10.3 per cent), the smallness of Japan's figure is striking. The number of registered foreign residents in Japan has, however, been on the rise relatively steadily ever since the post-war years. From the late 1980s and in particular since 1990, the number rose rather speedily.[21]

Two structural reasons are behind this development. First, Japan's period of relatively high economic growth of the late 1980s (the so-called bubble economy) attracted workers from the global labour market. Second, with the 1990 revision of Japan's Immigration Control and Refugee Recognition Act a first, however miniscule and indirect, legal framework for labour migration to Japan was established; the new framework made labour migration to Japan possible to some specific groups. *Nikkeijin*, that is, persons of Japanese descent, are one of the two favored groups. As one result, in particular the Brazilian community of *nikkeijin* in Japan grew rapidly and reached its preliminary peak in 2007 with 316,967 registered Brazilian residents in Japan, a majority of whom stay in Japan on the visa category of 'long-term resident',[22] the category that in the 1990 law revision had been expanded to include *nikkeijin*.[23]

Another ethnic group that profited immensely from the 1990 law revision is Chinese immigrants to Japan. While there is huge diversity in the sociological composition of the Chinese minority in Japan,[24] many Chinese are entering Japan as trainees. In fact, in 2007, Chinese made up three quarters of all trainees residing in Japan – 66,576 of the 88,086 trainees.[25] The trainee system has gained much popularity since the Ministry of Justice decided in 1990 to grant foreign trainees access to Japan's state-regulated internship programme for small firms of less than twenty employees. The numerical rise in trainees was further accelerated when in 1993 a specialized trainee programme (*senmon kenshū*) was added to the existing programme, enabling companies to employ trainees for another year after they had completed a two-year internship. Although initiated as a means of overseas development assistance that would grant some knowledge spillover to developing countries, Japan's trainee system is now recognized as a vehicle for low-wage labour supply to Japanese companies.[26]

A persistent *gap* between policy output (official immigration policies) and policy outcome (on-the-ground result of these policies) in Japan's migration policy becomes clear.[27] While the policy output allows international labour migration to Japan only of the highly skilled and only on a temporary basis – in a nutshell, 'Japan is not an immigration country' – the policy outcome paints a different picture. It is predominantly the lower skilled labourers with the perspective of long-term residence who are employed in Japan as foreign workers. The grounds for this gap between policy output and policy outcome were laid in the 1990 revision of Japan's Immigration Control and Refugee Recognition Act. Japan's latest migration policy reform, the introduction of sector-specific and nation-specific migration channels via EPAs, however, symbolizes a shift towards bridging the gap between policy output and outcome. A perspective for long-term residence is being offered to successful care migrants in a medium-skilled occupational area. All practical problems with implementation of the EPA-administered new migration avenue aside, the system itself is a ground-breaking change to Japan's migration policy framework. The following sections further explain this EPA-administered migration system and link it to Japan's 'culture of migration politics' seen through the political system (section 4) and 'orientations to political action'[28] held by numerous political actors (section 5).

4. POLICYMAKING *À LA JAPON*

Both the Japan–Philippine EPA (implemented in 2009) and the Japan–Indonesia EPA (implemented in 2008) state that 'entry and temporary stay [...] shall be granted to [...] natural persons who engage in supplying services as nurses or certified care workers' (JPEPA Article 110/1/f).[29] The EPAs distinguish between nurses (*kangoshi*) and certified care workers (*kaigo fukushi-shi*). Nurses are to work in hospitals that primarily provide healthcare for the elderly; and certified care workers in nursing homes for the elderly. Candidates for both tracks are chosen in their home countries through a placement test administered by the Japan International Corporation of Welfare Services (JICWELS, *Kokusai kōsei jigyō-dan*), a semi-governmental organization under the Ministry of Health, Labour and Welfare. JICWELS is also in charge of matching suitable migrant candidates with hospitals and nursing homes in Japan before programme participants leave their home country. Mismatching may occur. For example, during the matching process of the first batch of Indonesian caregiver migrants to Japan, in summer 2008, 20 per cent (eighty-six persons) of the potential care migrants could not be matched with Japanese employers. Interestingly, 66 of these 86 unmatchable candidates were male.[30] This indicates that many Japanese employers were concerned about yet another marginalizing factor – next to ethnicity – among their employees in this predominantly female profession, namely gender.

Upon their arrival in Japan, successful candidates take up a six-month programme in Japanese language and culture while receiving some introductory on-the-job training. The Association for Overseas Technical Scholarship (AOTS, *Kaigai gijutsusha kenshū kyōkai*) provides this programme as a part of its general assignment to promote cross-cultural understanding. At the end of this six-month period, the caregivers take up their work as assistant nurses or assistant care workers in their assigned hospitals or nursing homes. During this time they need to be given an opportunity to keep up their Japanese language education while working full-time in their jobs. Developing their language proficiency is crucial not only for ensuring their communication ability with patients and co-workers but also in preparing them for the national caregiver exam that they need to pass after a maximum period of three years (nurses) or four years (care workers) of on-the-job training. In a recent interview with the *Asahi Shimbun*, Ogawa Noriko who works as a Japanese language teacher to Indonesian caregivers talks about how difficult it is to design her teaching towards ensuring the migrants will have a fair chance of passing the caregiver exam while they are not given adequate Japanese language study material by any of the semi-governmental organizations involved in implementing the EPAs. She also mentions that under EPA regulations, the migrant caregivers are given only two afternoons off from work to pursue their Japanese language education – way too little time to achieve solid progress in language studies.[31] Only after passing the national caregiver exam will the care migrants have the prospect of long-term perspective and permission to work in Japan. If they fail the exam, their permits will be revoked.[32]

Several factors make the EPA administered avenue of labour migration unattractive to potential migrants and their potential employers alike.[33] To potential migrants, the system is unattractive for three main reasons. First, their previously acquired skills are not fully acknowledged. No matter what their work status before departing their home country, upon arrival in Japan and until they pass the national caregiver exam, they have to work as assistant nurses or assistant care workers. For many this is a severe downgrading of their status and income. They are no

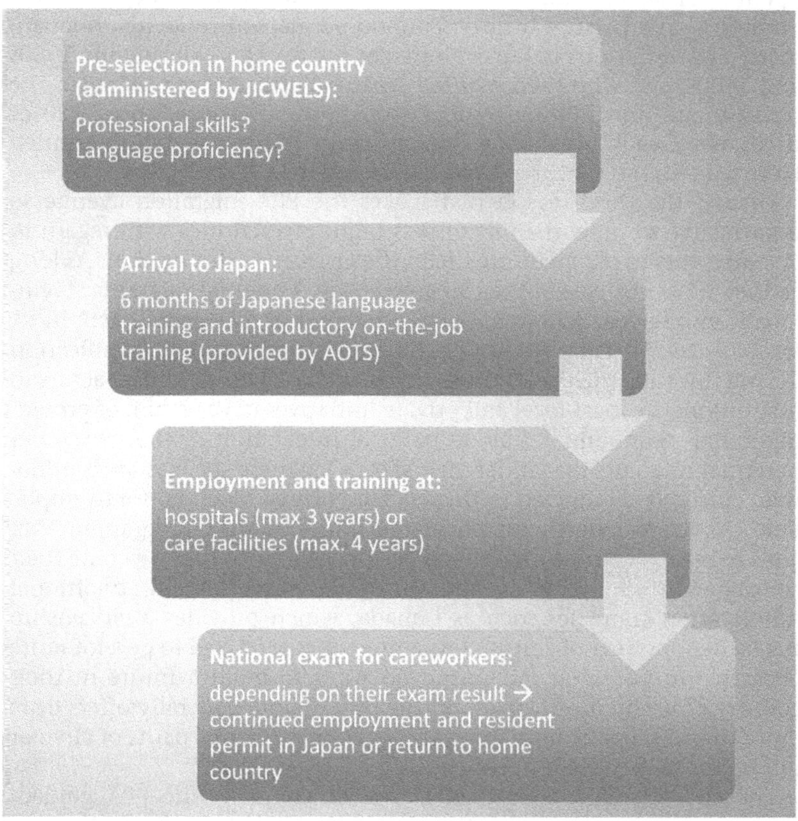

Figure 1: System of caregiver migration to Japan under bilateral Economic Partnership Agreements with Indonesia and the Philippines (author's design).

longer allowed to perform certain tasks that they used to perform in their home countries and are paid not according to their skill level but at the artificially designed employment level.

Second, the programme requires participants to acquire additional skills and knowledge, particularly Japanese language proficiency, before they are allowed to work as certified caregivers in Japan. To many, especially caregivers from the Philippines who often receive their education in English language, migration to an English-speaking country is by far an easier and quicker route to becoming a successful player in the 'big business' that caregiver migration has become.[34] Also, with regard to the first reason why the EPA migration channel is relatively unattractive to potential migrants, easy access to the foreign labour market via a compatibility of educational degrees drives many educated nurses and caregivers from the Philippines to Canada and the US rather than to Japan. It seems, however that one group of caregivers finds this opening of Japan's domestic labour market to foreign caregivers very attractive. In a twist of history, Filipino permanent residents to Japan, many of whom came to Japan – often as sex workers – during the 1980s and 1990s, and who then married Japanese men and stayed on in the country, are now aiming to access the care profession. Some 150 of them are already organizing their interests in an association entitled Licensed Filipino Caregiver Association in Japan (LFCAJ).[35]

Finally, the third reason that makes the EPA migration avenue so unattractive to potential migrants is high uncertainties with regard to any attempts to plan a future life in the country of destination. As long as they have not passed the caregiver exam, potential migrants stay in Japan on one-year renewable visas (category of 'designated activities', *tokutei katsudō*). They are not eligible to claim for family reunification during this time; neither is there any effort by Japan's political actors to institutionalize local-level and private initiatives in the realm of providing social, economic, let alone political integration of the newcomer potential migrants into different walks of Japanese society. Most initiatives currently conducted in this field are private, such as, for example, Keio University's newly established in-house training programme that aims to teach Japanese care-giving personnel how to best welcome their colleagues from Indonesia and the Philippines.[36] Again, traditional immigration countries such as Canada, which provides a citizenship track after one year of continuous employment, proved to be a lot more attractive to potential migrants who want to build a future in their country of destination. Japan, on the other hand, generally offers little more than a transit country or a stopover on migrants' paths of circular migration back to their home countries.[37]

The characteristics identified above which make the EPA guided-migration system so unattractive to prospective migrants largely came about in lengthy negotiations among different Japanese ministries, and predominantly show the handwriting of the Ministry of Health,

Labour and Welfare (MHLW). The Ministry of Justice, head to the Immigration Bureau and as such the leading agency in migration issues, refused any participation in serious discussion on opening Japan's labour market to immigrants,[38] thereby still holding onto Japan's migration policy output as opposed to its outcome. METI, in line with the Japan Business Federation (*Nippon keidanren*), pushed for comprehensive opening of Japan's labour market not only to service sector professions but also in shipbuilding and farming. The Ministry of Foreign Affairs, too, stressed Japan's labour shortages in certain sectors and aimed at utilizing these bilateral treaties as a means of liberalizing the international movement of people without going through legal reforms. MHLW initially was fiercely opposed to the EPA-administered migration system, and agreed to it only after having pushed through certain conditions, which the Japan Nursing Association (*Nihon kaigo kyōkai*) brought into the discourse. The main stumbling blocks for potential migrants – that is, their status as assistants irrespective of previous qualifications, and the significance of Japanese language proficiency that is tightly knit to the national caregiver exam and thereby to their visa status in the long run – are direct results of the Japanese Nursing Association's influence on the negotiations via its lobbying channel, the MHLW.[39]

At first glance the present arrangement seems like an open-door migration system in a particular field of employment, but in practice it has so many pitfalls that are sure to degrade it to, at best, a small-scale testing field for new migration policies. Attempts by interest groups to influence the creation of a migration system have almost exclusively dominated Japan's policymaking process. So far there has been amazingly little supra-state influence on Japan's migration policy. A convergence of international migration norms – for example, on the question of how to acquire citizenship – hardly occurs.[40] We also see relatively little influence on the policymaking process coming from the subnational level. One exception is the diffusion of the concept of 'integration of foreigners', which entered the national-level political discourse as a result of an initiative by numerous local governments in communities with an above-average proportion of foreign nationals, the so-called *Gaikokujin shujū toshi kaigi*.

We may conclude this section with the thesis that Japan's policymaking culture is still very much driven by bureaucracy-led national-level policymaking. Policymakers largely miss out on initiatives through the structures of multilevel governance that would enrich the political culture as well as the contents of many policy fields.

5. PUBLIC OPINION AND POLITICAL ACTION

'Orientations to political action',[41] not only those of policymakers but also those of actors shaping public opinion on Japan's migration policy, are at the core of this section. As outlined in section 4, potential care migrants to Japan perceive the EPA-administered migration channel rather critically. The same holds true for their potential employers, who became voices often heard in the nationwide media coverage linking Japan's ageing and shrinking population with the question of: Who is going to care for the nation's elderly? While one option to solve Japan's labour shortage in the health-care sector is increasing investment in the further development of robot-aids such as the well-known *PARO Therapeutic Robot*,[42] another option is to increase female and youth labour market participation or – as a last resort so to speak – health-care immigrants. Liberal Democratic Party member Kōnō Tarō, then Vice-Minister of Justice, in an interview with the author in 2006 made clear that this was the official line of preferences.[43] Heads of hospitals and nursing homes, on the other hand, are less enthusiastic about robotic care helpers.[44] Their enthusiasm for employing care migrants, however, is equally low, as data conducted in a large-scale survey by the Kyushu University Asia Centre shows.[45]

Researchers at Kyushu University conducted a survey among hospitals in Japan in February 2008, that is, only six months before the first batch of Indonesian EPA care migrants came to Japan. About one third of the responses (37.7 per cent) was positive about accepting migrant workers via this channel, while 61.7 per cent felt negatively about it.[46] Among those who felt negatively about the prospect of employing care migrants, 60.8 per cent had 'concerns about their communication skills with patients', and 45.2 per cent mentioned 'concerns about their [foreign care workers'] communication skills with the Japanese staff'. Also, 55.4 per cent indicated 'the manpower and time required to train them' as a reason for not wanting to employ care migrants.[47] Indeed hospitals and nursing homes need to make sure that in case of an emergency, there is always a Japanese staff member on call during a care migrants' shift. Again, language difference and the uncertainty about whether or not communication can flow adequately is a concern raised. While this is a concern that may fade after several years of good working experiences with care migrant co-workers, structural disadvantages a hospital or nursing home has to face when employing care migrants are prevalent and serious. Is there any incentive at all to employ an Indonesian or Filipino caregiver – and make sure a Japanese colleague is always on call duty, and provide (even if little) spare time for language education – if Japanese workers under the newly emerging strains the economic downturn puts on labour markets worldwide are also increasingly willing to gain employment in care giving? Indeed, the number of facilities offering to employ Indonesian nurses in fiscal 2010 dropped by 60 per cent (from 362 facilities to 141) from the previous year. The matching organization JICWELS attributes this drop to 'the financial burden on the facilities during the recession and an increase in the number of domestic workers applying for jobs'.[48]

The reluctance of potential employers of care migrants is largely based on the fact that the EPAs' employment structure, rather than offering economic benefit to the hospitals and nursing homes – as international labour migration in a low-wage sector usually does – puts additional strains on them in terms of required human resources and time management. Another reason for employers' reluctance to make use of the new migration system should not be underestimated. When asked what kind of special support they thought the foreign caregivers would require, 76 per cent of the respondents indicated 'daily living and working advice'. Also, 63.0 per cent expected an institutionalized 'exchange network between foreign nurses and the Japanese nurses' and 'the provision of Japanese culture (customs and rules) workshops' (60.3 per cent) to be necessary, in order to ensure smooth transitioning of foreign caregivers into their new daily routines. Similarly, 46.6 per cent of employers deem it necessary to prepare 'the Japanese staff concerning the foreign nurses' culture and language'.[49] In other words, employers frame the practical effects of international caregiver migration on the daily working life in their facilities as disturbing rather than helpful. Rather than perceiving the presence of foreign workers as a source of inspiration and new ideas, and a chance for vitalization of the domestic economy via increasing diversification – as suggested by *Nippon keidanren* in a position paper[50] – most potential employers of foreign caregivers perceive them as nothing more than a high-maintenance countermeasure to a national crisis. These perceptions are in line with economist and migration scholar Iguchi Yasushi's arguments on how labour migration is currently being framed in Japan. Iguchi argues that being centred around the issue of demographic change, the current discourse on reforming Japan's migration policy produces a public awareness of Japan being in the midst of *kikikan* (crisis).[51]

The perceived crisis of international labour migration to Japan has yet another dimension. As James Hollifield argues: 'Migration has been redefined [...] as a security threat.'[52] For Japan the process of framing migration as a threat to its national security and public order is closely tied to the terrorist attacks of 11 September 2001.[53] Japan, in November 2007, was the first nation to follow the US model to enforce border control through biometric data collected from foreign nationals upon arrival in Japan.[54] While this measure is directed towards controlling foreigners arriving at national borders, other measures focus more clearly on controlling immigrants once they have settled in the country.

The most prominent example of this is the Ministry of Justice's campaign entitled *fuhō shūrō gaikokujin taisaku kyanpēn* (campaign against illegal employment of foreigners). Since 2004, every June the Tokyo and Osaka Immigration Offices hold a campaign month with police cars increasingly patrolling the cities with a special eye for undocumented foreigners,[55] and large posters presenting the dangers resulting from undocumented migration are placed around major inner-city train stations. Part of this campaign is a MoJ-administered website that calls upon the general public to share information on foreigners who – for whatever reasons of appearance or actions – might be undocumented migrants. Via this website anybody can anonymously insert data on the place of residence, workplace, etc. of anyone who they think looks 'foreign and undocumented'.[56] Yet another piece in this puzzle of tightening the government's control on foreigners in residence is the latest (2009) revision to the Immigration Control and Refugee Recognition Act. This revision aims at combining under MoJ's control all data on foreign residents, data that are currently split among local level and national level administrative bodies.[57]

In survey data provided by the Prime Minister's Office, we see that members of the Japanese public have gradually become more critical towards foreigners living in their society. In 2004, the majority of Japanese (53.1 per cent) followed the issue of foreign workers (*gaikukojin rōdōsha mondai*) with concern. This was up from 49 per cent in 2001, and 48.6 per cent in 1991.[58] Can we conclude that government measures appear to be in line with proceeding changes in public opinion? Or is it the other way round? Is the public opinion, or more generally are 'orientations to political action'[59] in the realm of migration policy as prevalent in the general public, shaped by political actors' framing of international migration as a threat to Japan? Either way, framing the issue of migration as a security threat feeds one main purpose. It draws a clear line between foreigners and Japanese, thereby alienating foreign residents in Japan and presenting them as a non-integral part of the society.

Only a few voices in the current public discourse in Japan offer alternative views on foreign residents. Sakanaka Hidenori, head of the Japan Immigration Policy Institute, is one of them. His credo is that 'immigrants will rescue Japan'.[60] He proposes 'to bring in 10 million immigrants within the next 50 years [...] and to treat immigrants as potential Japanese. [...] In other words, I point out that the Japanese must prepare for a social revolution.'[61] In summer 2008, Sakanaka's migration policy ideas were brought into the public and political discourse as a policy proposal presented by former Liberal Democratic Party Secretary General Nakagawa Hidenao, but these ideas so far remain without any direct impact on the policymaking process. The 'orientations to political action',[62] which are prevalent among actors involved in this discourse on Japan's migration policy reform, show that the economically logical approach of an extended replacement migration politically is not (yet) feasible.

6. CONCLUSION

Japan is currently undergoing a very cautious migration policy reform. With the opening of its domestic labour markets to health care workers from the Philippines and Indonesia, Japan is seeking to bridge its two-decades-old gap between policy outcome (medium/low-skilled workers pursuing long-term settlement) and policy output (exclusively highly-skilled short-term international labour migration). While this move of bridging the gap could be expected to be a major policy change for Japan, a closer look at the contingencies and conditions of this EPA-administered migration system reveals that such groundbreaking change is unlikely. Despite given and predicted economic, particularly demographic, need for international labour migration to Japan, the nation seems to be still pursuing a form of *sakoku* (closed country) policy.

The reason for the miniscule dimension of EPA-administered labour migration to Japan lies in Japan's 'culture of migration politics' as this chapter has argued. Japan's 'culture of migration politics' is characterized by tardy single-level policymaking that suffers from a lack of inspiration, as well as by an image of foreign influences as a threat to Japan's national security and public order, which is strongly prevalent among politicians and public alike. What this gloomy case study on Japan's migration policy can teach us is that Japan currently stands at a crossroads. If Japan cannot overcome its 'culture of migration politics,' it is about to lose its position as an economic global power, that is, it is about to lose touch with the globalization of labour markets, the competition over the best and brightest workforce, as well as the highly sought after service sector workers. Also, it is about to lose its position as a regional powerhouse of ideas and norms, that is, it is to lose touch with innovative and cutting-edge ideas of policymaking and designing a modern society full of cultural diversity and enriching dynamics.

ACKNOWLEDGEMENT

Ruth deserves thanks for manifold practical and moral support and Gerald and Lena, simply for putting up with me.

NOTES

1 S. Castles and M.J. Miller, *The Age of Migration*, New York/London: The Guildford Press, 2003.

2 Ibid., p. 1.

3 Cross-border movement of people specifically for the purpose of work occurs in 40 per cent of the cases; 50 per cent of all cases are work-related migration moves (most often family unification), while the remaining 10 per cent of international migration moves imply refugees, students, etc. (I. Awad, Director of the International Migration Programme at the ILO, Semi-Public Lecture at ILO Office, Tokyo, 1 April 2008.)

4 The United Nations Population Division (UNPD) predicts 214 million migrants worldwide for 2010. In 2010, 61 million are predicted to be on the move in Asia alone; up from 49 million in 1995 and 55 million in 2005 (UNPD, *International Migration Stock: The 2008 Revision,* http://esa.un.org/migration/index.asp?panel=1, accessed 23 February 2010).

5 Oishi provides insights into the proceeding feminization of international labour migration in Asia. See N. Oishi, *Women in Motion: Globalization, State Policies, and Labour Migration in Asia*, Stanford, CA: Stanford University Press, 2005. Kingma sheds light on the nursing profession as a central gateway to international labour migration of women, particularly in Asia. See M. Kingma, *Nurses on the Move: Migration and the Global Health Care Economy*, Ithaca, NY/London: Cornell University Press, 2006.

6 Usually economic demands lead to the opening of domestic labour markets to international labour migration; policy change follows with some delay, creating an (interim) gap between policy output and policy outcome. On the case study of Japan's (persisting) migration policy gap, see for example, T. Tsuda and W.A. Cornelius, 'Japan: Government Policy, Immigrant Reality', in W.A. Cornelius, T. Tsuda, P. Martin and J.F. Hollifield (eds), *Controlling Immigration: A Global Perspective*. Stanford: Stanford University Press, 2004, pp. 439–76.

7 See, for example, T. Tsuda, *Local Citizenship in Recent Countries of Immigration: Japan in Comparative Perspective,* Lanham MD: Lexington Books, 2006.

8 This chapter draws on the definition of 'migrant worker' given in the United Nations 'Convention on the Protection of the Rights of All Migrant Workers and Members of Their Families' (Article 2.1): 'The term "migrant worker" refers to a person who is to be engaged, is engaged or has been engaged in a remunerated activity in a State of which he or she is not a national.' (United Nations General Assembly, *Convention on the Protection of the Rights of All Migrant Workers and Members of Their Families,*A/RES/45/158, 69th plenary meeting, 18 December 1990, http://www.un.org/documents/ga/res/45/a45r158.htm, accessed 19 March 2010).

9 The increase of irregular employment in the health care sector gradually led to lowering wage levels and working conditions for nurses and care giving personnel. The recent economic downturn also pushed inexperienced temporary workers with all kinds of professional backgrounds into the healthcare sector, thereby aggravating the trend outlined above. During the 2008/2009 Lower House election campaign, the Democratic Party of Japan (DPJ) strongly called for an improvement of caregivers' wages and for the implementation of control measures to ensure 'good quality care giving' (DPJ, *DPJ Financial Crisis Action Plan: 'Economic and Financial Crisis Measures': Opening up a Path towards the Future by 'Putting People's Lives First,'* Tokyo: 5 November 2008, http://www.dpj.or.jp/english/financial/f_crisis.html, accessed 23 February 2010).

10 A. Kondo (ed.), *Migration and Globalization: Comparing Immigration Policy in Developed Countries*, Tokyo: Akashi Shoten, 2008. Takeyuki Tsuda (ed.), *Local Citizenship in Recent Countries of Immigration:. Japan in Comparative Perspective*. Lanham MD: Lexington Books, 2006.

11 National Institute of Population and Social Security Research, *'Population Statistics of Japan 2008'*, Tokyo: National Institute of Population and Social Security Research, 2008, p. 15.

12 The economic and social security aspects of Japan's demographic change are addressed in F. Coulmas, H. Conrad, A. Schad-Seifert and G. Vogt (eds), *The Demographic Challenge: A Handbook about Japan,* Boston/Leiden: Brill, pp. 817–1153.

13 I develop this argument further in, for example, G. Vogt, 'Talking Politics: Demographic Variables and Policy Measures in Japan', in F. Kohlbacher and C. Herstatt (eds), *The Silver Market Phenomenon: Business Opportunities in an Era of Demographic Change,* Heidelberg: Springer, 2008, pp. 17–29. Sociologist Chikako Usui, on the other hand, argues that replacement migration will not be needed at all if Japan pursues 'the societal transformation from a Fordist to a post-Fordist economy'. See Chikako Usui 'Japan's Demographic Future and the Challenge of Foreign Workers', in Tsuda (ed.), *Local Citizenship in Recent Countries of Immigration,* p. 58.

14 Kingma, *Nurses on the Move,* pp. 23–4.

15 J.F. Hollifield, 'The Politics of International Migration. How Can We "Bring the State Back In?",' in C. Brettell and J.F. Hollifield (eds), *Migration Theory: Talking Across Disciplines,* New York and London: Routledge, 2000, p. 146.

16 G.A. Almond, 'Comparative Political Systems', *The Journal of Politics,* 18 (3), August 1956, pp. 391–409.

17 Ibid., p. 396.

18 Ibid., p. 395.

19 Ibid., pp. 395–6.

20 For the concept of 'orientations to political action' (Ibid., p. 396), I want to broaden my focus from viewing solely the orientations of traditional political elites to also include orientations of actors influencing public opinion, such as journalists, researchers, and members of the business world.

21 MoJ, *Heisei 21 nen-hatsu shutsunyūkoku kanri* (Immigration Control 2009 edition), http://www.moj.go.jp/NYUKAN/nyukan90.html, accessed 1 March 2010; OECD, Organization for Economic Co-Operation and Development, International Migration Data 2008, http://www.oecd.org/document/52/0,3343,en_2649_33931_42274676_1_1_1_37415,00.html, accessed 1 March 2010.

22 MoJ, *Heisei 21 nen-hatsu shutsunyūkoku kanri.*

23 On the living and working conditions of *nikkeijin* in Japan see, for example, J.H. Roth, *Brokered Homeland: Japanese Brazilian Migrants in Japan,* Ithaca, NY/London: Cornell University Press, 2002; and T. Tsuda, *Strangers in the Ethnic Homeland: Japanese Brazilian Return Migration in Transnational Perspective,* New York: Columbia University Press, 2003.

24 On this diversity and in particular on the transnational community of Chinese in Japan's business world, see G. Liu-Farrer, 'Creating a Transnational Community: Chinese Newcomers in Japan', in M. Weiner (ed.), *Japan's Minorities: The Illusion of Homogeneity,* London/New York: Routledge, 2009, pp. 116–38.

25 MoJ, *Heisei 21 nen-hatsu shutsunyūkoku kanri.*

26 As such, it is harshly criticized, foremost by numerous Japanese non-state actors such as *Ijūren*, an NGO working for migrants' rights, and *Zentōitsu*, a labour union concerned with immigrants' work issues. Head of both organizations is Torii Ippei who speaks of horrible working conditions and below-standard payment that trainees face in Japan. See I. Torii, 'The Controversial Debate on Admitting More Immigrants to Japan', unpublished paper presented at the DIJ (German Institute for Japanese Studies) International Symposium 'Migration and Integration – Japan in Comparative Perspective', Tokyo, 24 October 2007.

27 I draw on the gap hypotheses formulated by Cornelius et al., *Controlling Immigration*.

28 Almond, 'Comparative Political Systems', p. 396.

29 Figure 1 provides a graphic overview of the administrative steps of this migration system.

30 A. Kobayashi and A. Sato, 'Male Indonesian nurses rejected', *Daily Yomiuri*, 1 August 2008, http://www.yomiuri.co.jp/dy/20080801TDY04303.htm, accessed 30 May 2009.

31 *Asahi Shimbun*, 'Kango no puro Nihongo no kabe' [Japanese language blocking nursing professionals], 2 March 2009, pp. 1–2.

32 Apparently from 2012 or 2013 onward, an 'exit strategy' will be added to this system. Care workers who fail in the exam might still be able to stay in Japan and continue working as an assistant caregiver albeit not upgrade their status (and their pay) to that of a certified care worker (K. Inaba, *Doko e iku? Kaigo nanmin* [Where to go? Care refugees], Tokyo: Perikansha, 2008, pp. 38–40). Here we observe a 'loophole' for low-wage labour migration opening up. See also N. Suzuki, 'Carework and Migration: Japanese Perspectives on the Japan–Philippines Economic Partnership Agreement,' *Asian and Pacific Migration Journal*, 16 (3) 2007, pp. 357–80.

33 I address the stance of potential employers of care migrants in section five.

34 Kingma, *Nurses on the Move*, pp. 78–120.

35 See M.R.P. Ballescas, 'Filipino Caregivers in Japan: The State, Agents, and Emerging Issues', *Kyūshū daigaku Ajia sōgō seisaku sentā kiyō* [Bulletin of Kyushu University Asia Center] 3 (March) 2009, 132 - 133. I have written elsewhere on how this 'twist of history' reinforces existing clichés on gender roles that confront Filipina migrants to Japan, and the prevailing image of the 'female nature' of the care giving profession in G. Vogt, 'The Political Economy of Health-Care Migration: A Japanese Perspective', in F. Coulmas and R. Lützeler (eds), *Imploding Populations: Global and Local Challenges of Demographic Change*, Leiden/Boston: Brill (forthcoming).

36 *The Japan Times*, 'Guiding Hand for Indonesian Nurses', 29 January 2010, http://search.japantimes.co.jp/print/nn20100129f1.html, accessed 3 March 2010.

37 Circular migration has become a buzzword recently among European politicians concerned with the question of how to profit from the

workforce of labour migrants while keeping the social costs for integration measures as low as possible. Exemplary in this discourse is a policy proposal by Eva Åkerman Börje, Director at the Department for Migration and Asylum Policy in the Swedish Ministry of Justice: 'Towards a New European Policy on Migration', in Berlin Institut für Bevölkerung und Entwicklung (ed.), *Online-Handbuch Demografie*. http://www.berlin-institut.org/online-handbuchdemografie/bevoelkerungspolitik/towards-a-new-europeanpolicy-on-migration.html, accessed 3 March 2010.

38 Tarō Kōno, Senior Vice Minister of Justice (2005/06), Member of the House of Representatives, Japan: Interview with author in Tokyo, 20 February 2006.

39 G. Vogt, 'Closed Doors, Open Doors, Doors Wide Shut? Migration Politics in Japan', *Japan aktuell. Journal of Current Japanese Affairs*, 5, 2007, pp. 3–30.

40 A. Abe 2006, 'Citizenship, Colonial Past and Immigration Policy. A Comparative Study between Japan and the United Kingdom', *Obirin Review for International Studies*, 18, 2006, pp. 107–30; K. Surak, 'Convergence in Foreigners' Rights and Citizenship Laws? A Look at Japan', *International Migration Review* 42 (3) 2008, pp. 550–75.

41 Almond, 'Comparative Political Systems', p. 396.

42 The seal-type robot was developed by Japan's National Institute of Advanced Industrial Science and Technology (AIST). At the time of writing this chapter, the eighth generation of 'PARO-chan' is being promoted (AIST, National Institute of Advanced Industrial Science and Technology, *Seal-Type Robot "PARO" to Be Marketed with Best Healing Effect in the World*. http://www.aist.go.jp/aist_e/latest_research/2004/20041208_2/20041208_2.html, accessed 3 March 2010.

43 Author's interview with Tarō Kōno, Tokyo, 20 February 2006.

44 Safety guidelines are an issue of concern. See *The Japan Times*, 'Robots Will Have to Comply with Safety Guidelines', 21 May 2006, http://search.japantimes.co.jp/cgi-bin/nn20060521a7.html, accessed 3 March 2010.

45 The Kyushu University research team identified 1,604 large (300 beds or more) hospitals across the country, and sent out its survey to these hospitals. Of them, 541 returned the questionnaire. See Y. Kawaguchi, Y.O. Hirano and S. Ohno, 'Nihon zenkoku no byōin ni okeru gaikokujin kangoshi ukeire ni kansuru chōsa (dai ippō): Kekka no kaiyō' [A Nationwide survey on acceptance of foreign nurses in Japan's hospitals (1): An outline of the results], *Kyūshū daigaku Ajia sōgō seisaku sentā kiyō* [Bulletin of Kyushu University Asia Centre] 3 (March) 2009.

46 In more than half of the cases, the director of the nursing service department responded to the survey. The positive responses can be divided into 'very eager to accept them' (7.0 per cent) and 'would like to accept them if possible' (30.7 per cent); the negative response is made up of 'not very eager to accept them' (52.5 per cent) and 'do

not wish to accept any' (9.2 per cent) (Kawaguchi, Hirano and Ohno, 'Nihon zenkoku no byōin ni okeru gaikokujin kangoshi ukeire ni kansuru chōsa (dai ippō),' p. 55).

47 Ibid.

48 *The Japan Times,* 'Fewer Indonesian Nurses in '10', 18 February 2010, http://search.japantimes.co.jp/cgi-bin/nn20100218f4.html, accessed 3 March 2010.

49 Kawaguchi, Hirano and Ohno, 'Nihon zenkoku no byōin ni okeru gaikokujin kangoshi ukeire ni kansuru chōsa', p. 56.

50 Nippon keidanren, *Japan 2025: Envisioning a Vibrant, Attractive Nation in the Twenty-First Century*. Tokyo: Nippon Keidanren, 2003,www.keidanren.or.jp/english/policy/vision2025.pdf, accessed 3 March 2010.

51 Y. Iguchi, *Gaikokujin rōdōsha shinjidai* [A new era of foreign workers], Tokyo: Chikuma, 2001, p. 44.

52 Hollifield, 'The Politics of International Migration', p. 154.

53 In the public discourse, a connection between these two variables existed long before the 2001 terrorist attacks but had not yet translated into policy measures. Sociologist Ryoko Yamamoto shows how the 'securitization of migration' (Hollifield, 'The Politics of International Migration', p. 155) proceeded in public discourse, enlivened by the National Police Agency's (*Keisatsu-chō*) *White Book* statistics on foreign crime. See Ryoko Yamamoto, 'Alien Attack? The Construction of Foreign Criminality in Contemporary Japan', in A. Germer and A. Moerke (eds), *Grenzgänge – (De-) Konstruktion kollektiver Identitäten in Japan. Japanstudien,* 16, Munich: iudicium, 2004, pp. 27–57).

54 MoJ, *Outline of New Immigration Procedures: Requirements for the Provision of Personal Information*. Tokyo: Immigration Bureau / General Affairs Division, 2007, http://www.moj.go.jp/NYUKAN/nyukan64-2.pdf, accessed 15 August 2008, provides details on the system.

55 According to a statement by Marian Tanizaki, an activist with the Philippine Centre at Maryknoll in Tokyo, there is a strong ethnicity bias in random police checks of foreigners in Japan. Expressed as audience comment during the DIJ (German Institute for Japanese Studies) International Symposium 'Migration and Integration – Japan in Comparative Perspective', Tokyo, 24 October 2007.

56 See MoJ, *Nyūkoku kanrikyoku jōhō uketsuke* [Immigration Office: accepting information], http://www.immi-moj.go.jp/zyouhou/index.html, accessed 3 March 2010. Despite fierce international criticism, for example by Amnesty International, the website is still up and running. In this author's 2006 interview with Kōnō Tarō (20 February 2006), the then Vice-Minister of Justice called the website an unfortunate thing.

57 For a critical assessment of this policy change, see *The Japan Times,* 'Foreigner Registration System to be Revised. May Lead to Better Services, More Control', 26 January 2008, http://search.japantimes.co.jp/cgi-bin/nn20080126a1.html, accessed 3 March 2010.

58 PMO, Prime Minister's Office, *2005 Gaikokujin rōdōsha no ukeire ni kan suru yoronchōsa* [2005 Survey on the acceptance of foreign workers], http://www8.cao.go.jp/survey/h16/h16-foreignerworker/index.html, accessed 3 March 2010.

59 Almond, 'Comparative Political Systems', p. 396.

60 H. Sakanaka, *Towards a Japanese-style Immigration Nation* (translated by Kalu Obuka). Tokyo: Japan Immigration Policy Institute, 2009, p. 24.

61 Ibid., pp. 26–7.

62 Almond, 'Comparative Political Systems', 1956, p. 396.

Index

Abe Shinzō, xvi, 86, 122, 135
ADEOS/Midori series, 101
Administrative Renovation Council, 27
Advanced Satellite with New System Architecture for Observation (ASNARO), 101
age of migration, 205
age-profiles of per capita consumption, 176–7
aged society, definition, 188
ASEAN Regional Forum, 123
Asia-Pacific Economic Cooperation forum, 115
Asia-Pacific Region, definition, 111
Asian Bond Fund, 119–21
Asian Bond Market, 116
Asian Bond Market Initiative, 119
Asian Development Bank, 42, 119
Asian Monetary Fund, 116, 117–19
Asō Tarō, xvi–xvii, 78, 87, 122
Association for Overseas Technical Scholarships, 210

bank failure resolution
    international comparisons, 13–15
banking and financial regulations, advanced, xxii
banking crisis, 'Japan premium', 5
banking system
    bad assets, 8–9
    centralized asset management mechanisms, 9
    clear intervention procedures, 11
    'deleveraging funds', 10
    winding-up process, 12
Basic Space Law of 2008, 92
blue fin tuna, 88
Bridge Bank of Japan, 9
bureaucracy, xv–xvi
    Kasumigaseki district, xvii

centre-periphery differences, xiv
Chiang Mai Initiative, 116, 118–19
China
    concern over growing military power, 124
    economic performance, xiii
    environment cost, 74
    foreign aid policy, 45–7
    influencing interaction within region, 122
    recognition of Japan's post-war pacific behaviour, 131, 132
    relations with, xix
    trade networks, 114
Chōsen Sōren, 135
civil society growth, xxii
climate change, 78–80
    leadership role, 82–8
    politics, 80
    public views, 85
    support by environmental non-government organizations, 84
closed country approach, xx
COMETS/Kakehashi, 100
Communication Satellite/Sakura (CS/Sakura), 99
company staff downsizing, 197
'compensated dating' (*enjo kōsai*), xiv–xv
Cool Biz campaign, 85
Cooperative Credit Purchase Company, 9
Copenhagen Accord, 79
corporate bankruptcies, xiii
corporate Japan, universities as employment agencies, 156–7
cultural, industry, xx

death penalty, 30
Declaration on Security Cooperation with Australia, 123
Declaration on Security Cooperation with India, 123
Defence Intelligence Headquarters, 100
Democratic Party, 19

Democratic Party of Japan, xvii
demographic decline, 30
Deposit Insurance Corporation of Japan, 5, 11
Dokdo Island, 130
dolphin hunting, 75, 88
Domestic social problems, xiv

'Earth Summit', 77–8
East Asia and Pacific Central Banks, 116
East Asian Common Currency, 119–21
East Asian Community, 120–1, 139–41
Economic Partnership Agreement with Indonesia, 205
Economic Partnership Agreement with Philippines, 205, 207
economic policy, regional, role of networks, 115–20
Eda Satsuki, 32
education
 alienation from school, 150–1
 critical thinking, 153–4
 'high performance' vs 'low happiness', 150
 joyless study, 150
 lonely students, 151–2
 'modern competencies', 149
 'postmodern competences', 148–50
 school knowledge-based skills, 148
 school troubles, xiv
 subjective costs, 150–3
 university critical thinking, 153–6
 university international comparisons, 155
EETX-VIII'Kiku-8, 100
electoral system reform, 25
 single member districts, xv
Employment Security Law of 1947, 195
entertainment industry, xx
environmental policy
 citizen activists interested in issues beyond immediate neighbourhood, 76–7
 grassroots movements against industrial pollution, 75–6
ETS-VII/Kiku-7, 102
Experimental Communication Satellite /Ayame (ECS/Ayame), 99

familial support ratio, 172–3
family changes, 190
fertility, falling, 167–9
Financial Reconstruction Commission, 8
Financial Revitalization Act of 1998, 8
Financial Supervisory Agency, 6, 7
first demographic dividend, 177–8
Foreign Affairs Establishment Law, 60
foreign policy, xvii–xviii
 China, xviii, 29
 foreign Japan no longer the key regional power but still a key player, 110
 'International Contribution', 56, 57–8
 North Korea, xviii
 Russia and the Kurile Islands, 29–30
 security relations with USA, 29
 South Korea, xviii
 'UN centred diplomacy', 59
 uncompromising stance, xviii
 Yasukuni shrine, xviii
freeters, 170
Fukuda Takeo, 26
Fukuda Yasuo, xvi, 86–7

'Global Universities', 160
graduates, employment, 194
Great Hanshin-Awaji Earthquake, xix
Great Kantō Earthquake, 18
Green Party, lack of, 87
greenhouse gas emissions, xvii
'Gross National Cool', xx

habatsu, 23–4, 26
hallyu, xx
Haruki Murakami, 187
Hata Tsutomu, xv
Hatoyama Yukio, xix, 78, 88, 116, 121–2, 139

bureaucratic influence, 23
reform in decision making, 21
hikikomori, xiv, 21, 192
history textbook issues, 131, 132–3
Hokkaido, effectively bankrupt, xiv
hope
definition, 198
economy, 199
influence of choices and actions, 199
new types, 201–203
relationships with others, 200
sense of stagnation, 199
social science of, 198
'third relationships', 201
work and jobs, 198–9
Hosokawa Morihiro, xv
Housing Loan Administration Corporation, 9

IGS satellites, 100–101
immigration
lack of support, xx
policy, 30
Immigration Control and Refugee Recognition Act, 208–209, 216
India, role in region, 112
Industrial Revitalization Corporation of Japan, 10–11
Institute for Unmanned Space Experiment Free Flyer, 101
Institute of Space and Astronautical Science, 93
intergenerational transfers, 179–82
International Cooperative Initiative of 1985, 60
International Disaster Relief Law of 1987, 65
international humanitarian relief operations, xx
international peacekeeping operations, 58–9
international terrorism, 67–70
International Year of Biodiversity 2010, 88–9
IQ84, 187

Japan
banking crisis, 4–5
'convoy system', 4–5
economic ascent, xii
economic deterioration, xii
economic expansion, 3–4
economy rebound, xiii
'Lost Decade', xii–xiii, xviii–xxiii, 3–4
perceived decline, xii
'quiet transformation', xxii
regional institutions, xxii
role in Asia, xxi
role in Northeast Asia, 129–30
world's second largest economy, xxi
Japan Aerospace Exploration Agency, 97
Japan as Number One, xiii
Japan Bank of International Cooperation, 41
Japan Disaster Relief Teams, 65
Japan Immigration Policy Initiative, 216
Japan International Cooperation Agency, 40–1, 65
Japan International Corporation of Welfare Services, 210
Japan Nursing Association, 213
Japan Socialist Party, xv, 22
Japan Society for the promotion of Science, 158–9
Japan-North Korea Pyongyang Declaration, 134
Japanese aid
characteristics of Japan's ODA programme, 41–2
China, 45–7
environmental issues, 51–2
historical context, 39–40
Indonesia, 41
overview, 49–51
reliance on loan aid, 50–1
South Korea's experience as recipient and donor, 42–5
structural arrangement, 40–1
Thailand, 47–9
Japanese Experimental Module (JEM/Kibō), 97
jieigyō, 188
job displacement effect, 194

Kan Naoto, xix
Kasumigaseki district, xvii

Keiō, University, 155
Kibō Kakusa Shakai, 198
Kibō, Kuni no Ekusodasu, 198
kibōgaku, 198
Kishi Nobusuke, 58
Kobe Earthquake 1995, xix, 77
kōenkai, 24
Koizumi Junichirō, xvi, xviii, 19, 27, 67, 132, 134
Kōmeitō, 19
Korean Wave phenomenon, xx
Kyoto Protocol, 78, 79
  rhetoric and reality, 83
  targets, 81–2

Law Concerning Stabilization of Employment of Older Persons of 2004, 170
LDP, responsible opposition, xix
Liberal Democratic Party, xv, 19–20
Licensed Filipino Caregiver Association in Japan, 212
Long-Term Care Insurance scheme, 172
Long-Term Credit Bank, 8
'Lost Decade', 169
low carbon society, 80–2

Malaysia, trade agreements, 116
'Manila Framework, 117
Maritime Self Defence Forces, xviii
medical system, 172
memory politics, 130–1, 133, 138, 140
Mexico, trade agreements, 116
Micro-LabSat, 101
migration
  absence of open-door policy, 207, 208
  age of, 205
  Brazilian community, 209
  bureaucracy-led national-level policies, 213
  caregivers, 210–12
  caregiving profession, 204, 205, 208
  Chinese community, 209
  closed country policy, 217
  competition from East Asia, 205
  feminization, 205
  foreigners seen as threats, 208
  output and outcome, 208–10
  public concerns, 214
  recent changes, 209–10
  security threats, 215–16
  unattractive avenue, 212–13
military space power, xxii
Millennium Development Goals, 42
Miyazawa Initiative, 117
moral standards, xv
Mori Yoshirō, xvi, 26
mortality transition, 168
Murakami Ryū, 198
Murayama Tomiichi, xv, 19, 62, 132

National Institution for Academic Degrees and University Evaluation, 159
national security, 122–4
National Strategy Bureau, 27
National Survey on Family Planning, 173
National Transfer accounts, 166
  outline, 174–7
NEETs, 170
  definition, 196
network diplomacy, 124–5
'network diplomacy'
  definition, 110–11
  regional engagement, 111–15
networks
  concept and context, 113–15
  politico-security, 120–4
  regional financial cooperation, 116–17
  role of diplomatic networking, 120
New Progress Party, 23
Nikeijiin, 209
Nippon Credit Bank, 8
Non-Profit Organization Law of 1998, xix
North Korea
  abductions issue, 133–8, 140
  nuclear facilities and weapons, 134–6
  strategic defeat for Japan, 135–8
nuclear power, 82
Nye, Joseph, 37, 38, 52

Obuchi, xvi, 132
official development assistance, xxii, 37–40

Ohira Masayoshi, 39
Okinawa, USA base, xix
Outer Space Treaty 1967, 96

Pacific Basin Economic Council, 115
Pacific Economic Cooperation Council, 115
Peacekeeping Law of 1992, 56, 60–2
Pencil rocket, 96
People's New Party, 27
Persian Gulf War, 56
political changes, xvii–xviii
political sclerosis, xv–xvii
politics
  dynastic families, 24
  'electoral super-earthquake' 30 August 2009, 18–21
  evolution 1900s–2009, 25–7
  international comparisons, 20
  'iron triangles', 25, 27
  social issues, 30
  stability prospects, 31
  twisted Diet, 20
  Westminster model, similarities and differences, 21–5
population ageing, 167–9
  summary, 183
Post Office system, xvi
postal service reform, 28
poverty transfer between generations, 196
Prime Ministerial apologies, 132–3
Programme for Financial Revival, 7
Programme for International Student Assessment, 148–9
Promotion, of Outer Space Development and Utilization, 103
Prompt Recapitalization Act of 1998, 5, 8
public welfare, 195

Quasi Zenith Satellite System (QZSS), 100

reallocation of lifecycle deficits, 180–2
regional networks, xxi
renewable energy, 81–2
Resolution and Collection Corporation, 9
Resolution Collection Bank, 9
Resona Bank, 11
rural socioeconomic malaise, xiv

Sakanaka Hidenori, alternative approach to migrants, 216
sakoku, xx
science strengths, xxii
second demographic dividend, 178–9
'second-generation baby boomers', 168
Seikatsu Club Consumer Cooperatives, 76–7
Selenological and Engineering Explorer (SELENE.Kaguya), 97
Self-Defence Forces
  collaboration with non-military organizations, 65–7
  disaster relief operations, 63–5
  examples of peacekeeping, 62–3
  human contributions, 57–8
  peacekeeping missions, 55, 56
self-employment, 188–90
  by age category, 190
  decline, 192–3
  in non-agricultural and forestry sectors, 189
  rural family no longer a source of economic security, 193
  seniority wage system, 170
Singapore, trade agreements, 116
single-person households, 190–1
Six Party Talks, 134–8, 140–1
SmartSat programme, 101
Social Democratic Party, 22, 27, 55
social science of hope, 198
social security system, 171
social welfare policies, xvii
social withdrawal, 191
'soft power', xx
  concepts, 38–9
  definition, 37
solar energy, 81
South Korea
  as recipient and donor of aid, 42–5
  recognition of Japan's post-war pacific behaviour, 131, 132
  relations with, xix

Space Communication Corporation, 99
space programme
civilian developments emphasis, 96–8
communication and navigation satellite systems infrastructure, 99–100
dual use, 94, 95
future directions, 102–103
military angle, 92–3, 94–6
reconnaissance satellites infrastructure, 100–101
small satellites and ASAT systems, 101–102
spacecraft technologies and the players, 98–9
spysats, 100–101
Space Situational Awareness, 102
Special Yen Loan Facility, 117
Status of Non-Performing Loans, 6
strategic deficits, for Japan in Northeast Asia, 138–9
Strategic Headquarters for Industrial Revival and Employment, 10
Strengthening Financial Functions Act of 2004, 6
'success literature', xii

Taepodong incident, 100
Taiwan Straits, 70
Takenaka Plan, 4, 6, 7
Takeshima Day, 130–1
Takeshita Noboro, 60
Tanigaki Sadakazu, 31
technology strengths, xxii
Thailand
economic crisis, 117
foreign aid policy, 47–9
'The Cove', 88
three-generation households, 172
Tōhō Sōgo, 5
Tōkōdai, 155
Tokyo University, 155
Totsuka Yacht School incident, 191
Toyota, xxi
financial difficulties, xiii
operating loss, xiii
Trends in International Mathematics and Science Study, 148–9
twisted Diet (*nejire kokkai*), 20

United Nations Conference on Environment and Development, 77–8
United States of America, hub of Japan's security ties, 123
universities
decline, 157–8
employment agencies for corporate Japan, 156–7
future prospects, 161
'Global Universities', 160
graduate education, 160
independent administrative corporations, 159
National Institution for Academic Degrees and University Evaluation, 159
reforming an uncompetitive system, 158–60
21st century Centre of Excellence, 158–60
USA, Japan and Australia Trilateral Security Dialogue, 122

Vogel, Ezra, xii
volunteerism, xix

wartime memories, 55–6
Waseda University, 155
whale hunting, 75
WINDS/Kizuna, 100
working life styles, 170

Yamada Masahiro, 198
Yanagisawa Hakuo, 8
Yasukuni Shrine, 131, 132, 140
young people, decline in jobs for, 193–5